FOREIGN FIRMS, INVESTMENT, AND ENVIRONMENTAL REGULATION IN THE PEOPLE'S REPUBLIC OF CHINA

FOREIGN FIRMS, INVESTMENT, AND ENVIRONMENTAL REGULATION IN THE PEOPLE'S REPUBLIC OF CHINA

Phillip Stalley

Stanford University Press
Stanford, California

Stanford University Press
Stanford, California

Printed in the United States of America on acid-free, archival-quality paper

Library of Congress Cataloging-in-Publication Data

Stalley, Phillip.
    Foreign firms, investment, and environmental regulation in the People's Republic of China / Phillip Stalley.
        p.   cm.
    Includes bibliographical references and index.
    ISBN 978-0-8047-7153-5 (cloth : alk. paper)
    1. Environmental policy—China.   2. Business enterprises, Foreign—Environmental aspects—China.   3. Investments, Foreign—Environmental aspects—China.   4. Environmental law—China.   I. Title.
GE190.C6S73 2010
333.70951—dc22

                                                            2010013024

Typeset by Motto Publishing Services in 10/14 Minion

For Evance

Contents

Illustrations

Figures

Tables

Acknowledgments

Throughout the course of completing this book I have relied on the advice and support of more people than I have space to acknowledge. Numerous individuals have aided this project through conversations that they have probably forgotten but that I found extremely useful. This includes Elizabeth Economy, Craig Allen, Hussein Anwar, Ma Jun, Kelly Sims Gallagher, Wang Hua, Petra Christmann, and a great number of environmental, health, and safety specialists in China. None of these people had any incentive to talk to me, yet each took time out to share his or her experience and knowledge. I would also like to thank those in the George Washington University and Washington DC community who have provided advice and/or encouragement including but not limited to Bruce Dickson, Forrest Maltzman, Lee Sigelman, Jennifer Turner, Miranda Schreurs, and John Donaldson. Like many books, this one is built on the foundation of a dissertation, and I owe a special thanks to my original dissertation committee—David Shambaugh, Susan Sell, and Martha Finnemore. Whether reading a draft chapter or guiding me through fieldwork, they always provided me with frank, perceptive comments and often went beyond the call of duty in offering assistance. They asked the tough questions—the ones that a student may not want to hear but that serve to identify weaknesses, clarify arguments, and in general improve the overall product. Finally, I am forever indebted to Sidney Rittenberg, who sparked my initial interest in Chinese politics and inspired my first trip to China.

There are also many institutions to which I owe a significant debt of gratitude. The Sigur Center for Asian Studies at The George Washington University provided me with a Numata fellowship, which allowed for an extended research trip in China a year prior to the official commencement of field research. It is difficult to overestimate the importance of that initial experience in China in facilitating subsequent research. The Blakemore Foundation offered a very generous fellowship that allowed for language study at the Berkeley/Qinghua Inter-University Program (IUP). With the aid of the Blakemore fellowship and the dedicated teachers of IUP, I was able to utilize a number of Chinese sources that I hope have enriched the book's analysis. The Chiang-Ching kuo Foundation provided a fellowship for my field research and the Environmental Economics Center (EEC) at Fudan University served as my host unit while I was in Shanghai. I am thankful to Li Zhiqing of the EEC for not only his practical advice but his friendship during my stay in China. Xu Jianwei and Zhou Yihong also provided me with important research assistance. I am especially indebted to the Woodrow Wilson School at Princeton University and to Iain Johnston and Tom Christensen for allowing me the opportunity to spend a year working on the book as a visiting research fellow in the Princeton-Harvard China and the World Program. My interactions at Princeton with other visiting fellows, faculty, and graduate students proved invaluable in helping me develop and refine the arguments presented in this book. Finally, DePaul University's University Research Council provided funding that allowed me to revise and complete the manuscript.

I also owe a word of thanks to Stacy Wagner at Stanford University Press both for her insightful comments on the original manuscript and for patiently guiding me through the review process. Thanks as well to the anonymous reviewers for the considerable amount of time and care they put into reading my work. The external reviews offered many useful ideas for improvement that ultimately contributed to a cleaner and stronger manuscript, but of course all remaining errors are my own.

Finally, I would like to thank my family. My parents certainly never imagined their son would take off for China upon graduation from college and likely marvel at my ability to study so much and earn so little, yet they always offered their unconditional support. I would also like to thank my wife, Evance. She has spent more time than I imagine she cared to listening to my ideas and complaints and has steadfastly offered much-needed love and encouragement through the long process of writing and publishing this book. More than anything else it is the happiness Evance has provided in my personal life that has helped me complete this project.

Abbreviations

ADB	Asian Development Bank
AICM	Association of International Chemical Manufacturers
CASS	Chinese Academy of Social Sciences
CICETE	China International Center for Economic and Technical Exchanges
CLAPV	Center for Legal Assistance to Pollution Victims
CPCIA	China Petrochemical and Chemical Industry Association
CTE	Committee on Trade and Environment (of the World Trade Organization)
EDTZ	Economic Development and Technology Zone
EHS	Environment, Health, and Safety
EIA	Environmental Impact Assessment
EMS	Environmental Management System
EPB	Environmental Protection Bureau
EPL	Environmental Protection Law of the People's Republic of China, 1979/1989
EPZ	Export Processing Zone
ERM	Environmental Resources Management
ERS	Environmental Responsibility System
ESIA	Environment and Social Impact Assessment
FDI	Foreign Direct Investment
FIE	Foreign-invested Enterprise
FSR	Feasibility Study Report

FYP	Five-year Plan
GRI	Global Reporting Initiative
INGO	International Non-governmental Organization
ISO	International Standards Organization
MEA	Multilateral Environmental Agreement
MEP	Ministry of Environmental Protection (SEPA prior to 2008)
MNC	Multinational Corporation
MOC	Ministry of Commerce
MOFTEC	Ministry of Foreign Trade and Economic Cooperation
MSDS	Material Safety Data Sheet
NDRC	National Development and Reform Commission
NEPA	National Environmental Protection Administration (SEPA after 1998)
NIC	Newly Industrializing Country
PIP	Project Impacted Persons
POGWG	Petrochemical, Oil, and Gas Working Group (of the European Chamber of Commerce)
POP	Persistent Organic Pollutant
PPE	Personal Protection Equipment
SEPA	State Environmental Protection Administration (MEP after 2008)
TRI	Toxic Releases Inventory
UNDP	United Nations Development Programme
UNEP	United Nations Environment Programme
WEP	West-East Pipeline Project

Note on Translations and Legal Sources

The translations from Chinese legal sources, periodicals, and interviews are my own. Many of the main Chinese laws (e.g., 1989 Environmental Protection Law, 1997 Criminal Law) are readily available in English. When utilizing these documents, I drew on both the English and Chinese versions. However, I relied only on the Chinese version for the numerous other types of government regulations (e.g., administrative measures, opinions, notices, implementation guidelines). In the references, I offer both the English and Chinese name for each legal document. I discuss use of Chinese legal sources more extensively in Chapter 3 (see in particular Note 1).

FOREIGN FIRMS, INVESTMENT, AND ENVIRONMENTAL REGULATION IN THE PEOPLE'S REPUBLIC OF CHINA

1 To Go Green Is Glorious? China, Foreign Investment, and Environmental Regulation

To get rich is glorious. This motto, of uncertain origin but often attributed to the late Deng Xiaoping, succinctly captures the feverish desire for economic development that has gripped China since the launch of the reform and opening era in 1978. No country has moved up the economic ladder as quickly as China. Over the last three decades, China's 9 percent per annum growth is faster than that of any country in history. This growth has lifted 250 million people out of poverty and made China a major producer and consumer of goods that just a generation ago were beyond imagination for most Chinese. From 2002 to 2006, for instance, the number of air conditioners in China tripled (Fergusson 2009). As late as 1990, only 42,000 cars were produced in China (Kelly Gallagher 2006). By 2007, the figure was 8.8 million (Associated Press 2008).

As the name "reform and opening" indicates, a major pillar of Beijing's get-rich strategy has involved opening China to foreign direct investment (FDI). Initially viewed with suspicion, especially by China's more conservative cadres, Beijing began setting up special economic zones to attract FDI in the late 1970s. Although investment was modest through the 1980s, after Deng's southern journey in 1992 FDI skyrocketed. Today China leads all developing countries in attracting foreign investment, and in recent years China has annually attracted more FDI than all of Central and South America combined. Between the years 2000 and 2003, foreign firms built 60,000 manufacturing plants in China (Palmisano 2006). By 2007 China was receiving almost $75 billion in FDI per year, which translates into just under 38,000 individual foreign-investment projects.[1] The result of this investment inflow is that today foreign firms account for a considerable portion of economic activity in China. In 1990, foreign-invested enterprises produced 2.3 percent of industrial output. By 2002, the figure had increased to a whopping 33.4 percent. One-third of China's industrial production comes from foreign-invested enterprises (National Bureau of Statistics 1994–2004).

To go green is glorious? To my knowledge no Chinese policymaker has ever uttered these words, but one would hardly be surprised to see this phrase on a billboard in China. The language of environmentalism has unmistakably entered the Chinese vocabulary. In 2008, when the State Environmental Protection Administration (SEPA) was promoted to the Ministry of Environmental Protection (MEP), the announcement indicated that China's central leadership was on a "green drive" to address environmental deterioration (Sun 2008e). Over the last few years Beijing has experimented with a "green GDP" that would employ environmental criteria in assessments of government officials' performance. In 2007, SEPA announced the launching of a "green credit policy" to prevent bank loans to industries in energy- and pollution-intensive sectors. A year later this was followed up with a "green insurance" program intended to compel companies to purchase insurance for industrial accidents and a "green securities" scheme that requires companies raising funds in Chinese capital markets to disclose environmental data.

Driven by concerns over product safety and "green trade barriers" that limit the access of Chinese companies to overseas markets, Beijing has also actively been promoting "green label" and "green food" programs to help domestic companies demonstrate their environmental credentials. In 2006, Beijing announced a "green procurement policy" that obliges government agencies at all jurisdictional levels to select products from a "green purchasing list." Since 2000, Shanghai has maintained a "Green 110" telephone hotline to collect complaints about environmental issues. And perhaps most famously, to deliver on its promise of a "green Olympics" Beijing spent $15 billion and took drastic steps such as restricting heavy industry in five neighboring provinces, banning construction, limiting driving privileges, and closing factories in the immediate Beijing area. One county government in southern China, in a highly unusual attempt to heed Beijing's calls for greater emphasis on environmental protection, spent $56,000 to paint the side of a mountain green (Associated Press 2007). Few things, it seems, hold more cachet in "red China" than the color green.

This green push from Beijing is in large part a reaction to the severe environmental strain produced by China's breakneck economic growth. Over the last three decades China has emerged as one of the most polluted nations on earth. It is difficult to overstate the seriousness of China's environmental challenge. Sixteen of the twenty most polluted cities in the world are in China (Economy 2004, 72). China has the world's highest rate of chronic respiratory disease, with a mortality rate five times that of the United States (Dexter Roberts 2003). Air pollution is estimated to contribute to somewhere on the order of 750,000 premature deaths every year (World Bank 2007). Half the population drinks water that is at least partially polluted and more than half of China's cities are affected by acid rain (Shi 2005b). Already environmental degradation is estimated to cost China somewhere between 8 and 12 percent of its GDP each year (Economy 2004, 88).[2]

Much of China's ample pollution is the result of industrial production. In 2000, SEPA estimated that 40 percent of water pollution and 80 percent of air pollution stemmed from industry (Wang Hua et al. 2004). In 2003, it was estimated that industry accounts for 83 percent of China's sulfur dioxide (SO_2) emissions and more than 80 percent of total particulate emissions (Shi and Zhang 2006, 271). Industry also contributes to pollution problems through environmental accidents, which are all too common in Chinese factories. In December 2005, a chemical company made headlines when it spilled thousands of tons of benzene into the Songhua River, which created an international incident, as it not only affected the drinking supply of millions of Chinese, but also threatened downstream cities in Russia. In the ten months following the benzene incident, China experienced another 130 spills into water supplies, which is the equivalent of one every two to three days (Associated Press 2006; Reuters 2006b).

The strain on the environment contributes to a host of social challenges including increasing internal migration, rising public health costs, and environmental protests, which although scattered are common in China's rural areas (Jing 2000). In 2005, the number of environmental protests increased by 30 percent to more than 50,000, including one in Zhejiang Province that involved more than 30,000 demonstrators protesting against thirteen chemical plants. Two months later residents of another Zhejiang village marched on a foreign-invested battery factory and locked over one thousand workers inside the facility. Again, the issue was pollution, as villagers claimed the factory was contributing to abnormally high levels of lead poisoning (Savadove 2005). In 2007, thousands of citizens protested the construction of a chemical factory in Xiamen, eventually forcing the suspension of the project (Tatlow and Kwok 2005). Incidents like these led Zhou Shengxian, currently head of the MEP, to refer to China's pollution problem as the "blasting fuse of social instability" (Beck 2006). As Zhou's comment implies, China's current rate of environmental damage is not sustainable and threatens to reverse many of the achievements of the reform period. In that respect it is hardly surprising that China's leaders have attempted to green China and strengthen industrial environmental regulation.[3]

Just as has been the case with China's attempt to "get rich," attracting foreign capital has also been an integral part of China's push to "go green." The National Eleventh Five-year Plan for the Environment (FYP), which lays out environmental targets and broad policy guidelines, declares that in the 2006–2010 period China "will expand the channels for using foreign capital." Part of this "foreign capital" strategy involves sustaining a high level of FDI into the Chinese manufacturing sector, which Chinese leaders have long argued has an environmental protection dividend. For much of the reform and opening period, for example, it has been common to hear Chinese leaders declare that, aside from providing the income growth necessary to strengthen environmental protection, trade and investment liberalization also facilitates access to advanced clean production technology and compels China to adopt more stringent environmental standards as foreign investors demand better environmental protection (*Asian Economic News* 1999; Jahiel 2006, 315). In 1992, for instance, Qu Geping, the former director of China's National Environmental Protection Administration (NEPA)—a forerunner to the current MEP—stated that economic development demands pollution prevention: "Foreign investors would be hesitant to invest in a heavily polluted area because the cost of cleaning up would be much higher than the cost of prevention" (Kent Chen 1992).

This argument was echoed in the period around China's entrance into the World Trade Organization (WTO) in 2002, when government officials and analysts asserted that the increased openness of China's economy would compel stricter environmental regulation to avoid an influx of pollution-intensive products and encourage the adoption of stringent international standards for corporate environmental management. This view that foreign investment brings with it an environmental benefit is often echoed by foreign companies operating in China. According to the Business Roundtable, an association of CEOs of leading U.S. companies that collectively represents $4.5 trillion in annual revenues and more than 10 million employees: "China's liberalization of its trade and investment controls has opened the door for American companies to invest in China. U.S. companies operating in China typically bring environmental 'best practices' and habits of good corporate citizenship with them. This sets a good example for Chinese companies to emulate" (2009). The assumption underlying the assertions of both Chinese leaders and the international business community is that foreign investment and environmental protection are positively correlated. Attracting foreign investment leads to better environmental regulation.

This assertion is not without scholarly support. Numerous studies have shown that foreign investors, particularly multinational corporations (MNCs), often use a common set of environmental management standards in their developing-country operations. Because multinational firms have facilities in a large number of countries, they value predictability and stability and prefer to use a single set of environmental standards. This reduces the transaction costs associated with adapting environmental policy to different regulatory settings (Glen et al. 2000; Wheeler 2001). These standards have been developed in the MNC's home country and so typically surpass the requirements of the developing host country. Along the same lines, several scholars point out that MNCs tend to use the latest technology, which is typically cleaner (Bhagwati 2004). This increases the likelihood that MNCs' own operations meet environmental regulatory requirements.[4] Several empirical studies have found a positive correlation between foreign ownership and environmental performance standards (Christmann and Taylor 2001; Glen et al. 2000; UNCTAD Secretariat 2002; Wang and Jin 2002). Christmann and Taylor (2001), for example, show that foreign-invested enterprises in China report that they are more likely than domestic companies to comply with environmental regulation and even to go beyond compliance.[5]

Many have presented cases in which MNCs, and foreign investment more broadly, contribute to environmental regulation via an influence on government officials and domestic firms.[6] Already equipped to comply with strict standards, MNCs may have an incentive to press local governments in less stringent nations for tougher regulations in order to achieve reputation gains and possibly disadvantage domestic competitors that are less equipped to meet higher standards. In this case, "desire for a level playing field in time produces a higher-quality field" (Braithwaite and Drahos 2000, 281). Foreign firms may also exert a salutary influence on the environmental policies of domestic partners. For instance, to the extent that foreign investors transfer clean technology to domestic firms in their host country, they contribute to local environmental regulation (Andonova 2003). Indeed, facilitating local firms' access to advanced foreign technology, which is typically less pollution-intensive, is one of the more common justifications for promoting investment liberalization in developing countries (Drezner 2000, 66). In China the opportunity to acquire new, clean production technology was a highly anticipated and frequently cited benefit of WTO membership prior to China's admission in 2002 (Jahiel 2006, 314; Zhao Yuhong 2007, 81).

Just as important as the transfer of technology is the diffusion of corporate environmentalism norms facilitated by foreign investment. Since the 1980s there has been a marked enhancement in the approach to environmental protection within the business community in the developed world (Hoffman 2000, 2001; Prakash 2000). The result is that leading companies routinely publish environmental data in annual reports, conduct environmental audits of overseas facilities, seek third-party certification of their environmental management systems, and often seek to go "beyond compliance" with regulation. Some have argued that MNCs promote these environmental norms in their operations abroad and "export environmentalism" to developing-country governments and firms (Bailey 1993, 142; Christmann and Taylor 2001; Florida 1996; Garcia-Johnson 2000; Hutson 2004; Rosen 1999, 152). The reasons for exporting environmentalism include: a desire to lessen the cost advantage domestic competitors gain by shirking pollution abatement, an attempt to enhance the company's reputation and minimize legal liability, and a genuine belief in the importance of corporate environmental stewardship. Efforts to promote corporate environmentalism are often part of a multinational's "green supply chain" policy, through which it screens a potential domestic supplier's environmental record and management system prior to the signing of commercial contracts (Christmann and Taylor 2006).

But not everyone agrees that foreign investors help a country go green. A highly contested strand of academic theory argues that the quest for foreign investment can create a downward pressure on environmental regulation. Those arguing in this vein are united by a shared concern that a fundamental characteristic of globalization is a transfer of power from governments to corporations. The logic of this position is straightforward. In today's world of international production, corporations can pick and choose among a number of locations in which to set up operations. IBM, the quintessential American company, has over 40,000 of its approximately 320,000 employees in India. A typical Dell computer sold in the United States will have each of its critical components—microprocessor, memory, hard drive, battery, keyboard—produced in a different country, and altogether the manufacturing process can involve four hundred companies in North America, Europe, and Asia (Friedman 2006, 515–20). As companies have more choices about where to produce and supply, the fear is that they are becoming footloose and less subject to government control. The diminishment of government authority is not just a result of capital mobility, but also stems from developing countries' increasing reliance on foreign investment. In 1990, inward FDI was approximately 10 percent of the GDP for developing countries. By 2003, that number had increased almost threefold to 28 percent. For countries particularly open to foreign investment, such as Chile, the figure approached 70 percent (UNCTAD 2006). Capital is thus both more desired and more mobile, a situation that logically increases the weight of industry at the expense of government.

In this context of enhanced corporate authority, the fear is that foreign-investor environmental strategy is more often characterized as "exploitative" rather than "responsible." Child and Tsai provide a useful definition of these ideal types: "A socially responsible strategy would devote substantial resources towards ensuring environmental protection, possibly on the expectation that superior long-term revenues will compensate for the additional costs. An exploitative strategy would be manifest in a policy of short-term profit maximization that minimized environmental protection measures on the grounds of their costs" (2005, 101). There are many examples of foreign investors adopting environmental strategies that tend toward the "exploitative" end of the continuum. Rosenberg and Mischenko (2002) argue that oil MNCs in Russia often ignored local environmental laws. Clapp and Dauvergne describe the poor record of transnational corporations in developing countries, especially those in extractive industries (2005, 169–74). Focusing on the logging industry in the Asia-Pacific region, Dauvergne argues that "both domestic and foreign firms continue to rely on networks of state and local allies to skirt regulations—such as forging export documents or smuggling logs overseas" (2005, 191). Kelly Gallagher provides an overview of foreign investment in China's automobile sectors and finds there has been minimal transfer of environmental technology from foreign to Chinese companies. The net result of China's dependence on foreign direct investment is that China has been "'locked in' to outdated, inefficient, and polluting vehicle technologies for many years"

(2006, 125). Several other studies focusing on China have found examples of foreign investors in pollution-intensive industries either shifting production to China in order to take advantage of lax environmental laws or entering into joint ventures with local township and village enterprises, which tend to be beyond the reach of environmental officials (Richardson 2004a). In a similar vein, some have argued that in order to escape the costs of pollution abatement, foreign firms operating in the developing world simply contract out pollution-intensive products to domestic suppliers and then turn a blind eye (Leonard 1988; Mabey et al. 2003).

Not only are there questions about the environmental performance of foreign-invested enterprises (FIEs); a related concern is that the contest to attract foreign investors leads developing-country governments to weaken, avoid tightening, or disregard transgressions of environmental standards. Eager for investment, developing-country governments accede to investors' demands or take unilateral initiatives to lower the cost of business by relaxing the regulatory setting. This phenomenon, in which a combination of pressure from firms and government concerns about investment competitiveness results in weaker environmental regulation, goes by a variety of labels. When fear of capital loss or a desire to enhance attractiveness to mobile capital results in a jurisdiction failing to enhance standards, it is often referred to as a "political drag effect" that results in a "regulatory chill" (Esty 1994, 162–63; Neumayer 2001a). When more than one jurisdiction engages in a competitive weakening of standards in order to enhance their attractiveness to outside investors, it is typically referred to as a "race to the bottom."[7] In the extreme, a global race to the bottom can cause standards to converge at the level of the jurisdiction with the least stringent regulation; in a weaker form, it compels high-standard areas to loosen regulation or keeps low-standard jurisdictions "stuck at the bottom."[8] Whether one uses the term "chill" or "race," the essence of the assertion is that environmental regulation would be stronger if governments were not seeking to enhance their attractiveness to mobile capital.[9]

When competition concerns induce a developing country to keep its environmental standards low *and* it experiences an inward flow of investment from companies seeking to enjoy lower pollution-abatement costs, the country can become a "pollution haven." As Clapp and Dauvergne point out (2005, 162), a pollution haven is not simply a country with low environmental standards and/or a large amount of pollution. Otherwise, virtually any industrializing country might be deemed a pollution haven. For a pollution

Industrial flight: Impact of regulation on firms' investment decisions

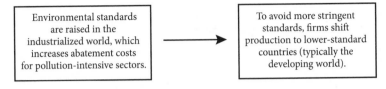

Race to the bottom / regulatory chill: Impact of competition for capital on regulation

Environmental exploitation: Impact of foreign firms on environmental regulation

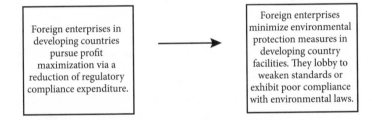

FIGURE 1.1 Three ways foreign investment can challenge environmental regulation.

haven to exist, one must also see "industrial flight," which refers to the migration of pollution-intensive industries from strict-standard countries to weak-standard jurisdictions where they enjoy lower pollution-abatement costs. In other words, a pollution haven is conceptualized as the result of a combination of government strategy (captured by the notion of race to the bottom or regulatory chill) and firm strategy (conceptualized strictly as industrial flight).[10] These three concepts—industrial flight, race to the bottom or regulatory chill, and environmental exploitation—are illustrated in Figure 1.1.

In recent years, as China's pollution problem has become increasingly severe and foreign multinationals more prominent in the Chinese economy,

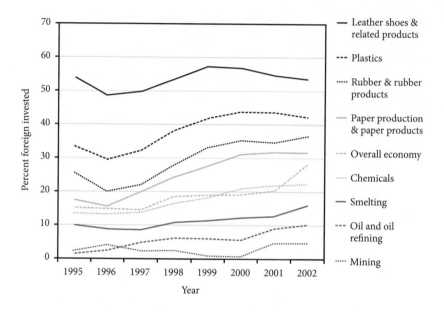

FIGURE 1.2 Foreign investment in pollution-intensive sectors.
SOURCE: Peng and Zhang 2004.

Chinese analysts have started to buy into the pollution-haven argument. For example, a *China Daily* editorial states:

> The key reason for the entry of polluting foreign enterprises into China is that local governments are so eager to attract foreign investment, they usually neglect environmental standards. Many multinational companies cherish their reputations as environmental protectors, but in China, this is not the case. These companies consume a great amount of resources and reap huge profits, leaving severe pollution behind. The fundamental reason for China's overheated economy and excessive liquidity is that these multinationals have focused on China's cheap labor force and loose environmental regulations. (*China Daily* 2008)

Accusations and incidents of foreign-firm malfeasance have also become common in China. Articles in the Chinese press in which developed countries' firms are accused of "transferring pollution" (*wuran zhuanyi*) are almost too numerous to count.[11] The "pollution transfer" articles make much of the fact that foreign firms invest in pollution-intensive industries.[12] As seen in Figure 1.2, there is significant foreign involvement in China's heaviest-polluting sectors. The percent of foreign investment in the chemical sector, for instance, has increased steadily from around 13 percent in 1995 to over 20 percent in 2002 (Peng and Zhang 2004). In Chinese academic work, a commonly cited statistic offered as evidence of pollution transfer is the fact that in 1991 there were approximately 11,000 FIEs in China, of which 29 percent were categorized as pollution-intensive (e.g., Wang Hengjin 2003; Xu and Zhao 2004).[13]

Accompanying these concerns over investment in pollution-intensive sectors are charges that foreign firms are all too willing to breach China's environmental regulation and take advantage of China's thirst for foreign capital. A 2007 editorial in the *China Daily* asserted that MNCs are "taking advantage of China's low environmental standards by doing things they would not dare do in their home countries" (Chen Weihua 2007). In late 2006, the Chinese NGO (non-governmental organization) Institute of Public and Environmental Affairs (IPEA), established by Ma Jun, one of China's most well-known environmentalists, accused thirty-three multinationals of violating China's environmental protection laws. A year later the list of polluting MNCs was up to almost one hundred (of four thousand total companies listed), and by early 2008 Ma claimed that over three hundred MNCs had a record of polluting air or water. This list included well-known companies such as Pepsi, 3M, Nescafé, Yamaha, Samsung, KFC, and Pizza Hut.

It is not only NGOs but also the Chinese government that has accused MNCs of poor environmental practices. Particularly since the start of the Hu-Wen era, Chinese government officials and analysts have frequently urged local governments to avoid a one-sided focus on the quantity of investment and give greater weight to the quality of foreign investment by enhancing supervision of FIEs (e.g., Chen and Zhu 2003; Liu Yuqi 1997). A Carlsberg Brewery was temporarily closed in 2007 for dumping untreated wastewater into a local river in Gansu Province. The company reportedly preferred paying a twice annual fine of roughly $650 to constructing a wastewater treatment plant. In the same year, two foreign companies, Unilever and Hitachi, were randomly selected for inspection and found to be violating wastewater discharge standards. This led a SEPA official to state: "Environmental pollution caused by foreign-funded companies has come to the attention of SEPA, and we will strengthen our supervision" (Sun 2007). Also in 2007, SEPA blacklisted 130 multinationals for excessive pollution stemming from activities dating back to 2004. Although by early 2008 all but 3 of the 130 companies on

SEPA's list were found to have rectified their environmental practices, a SEPA spokesman still indicated that "a series of environmental degradation incidents involving MNCs in recent years shows a lack of fulfillment of corporate social responsibility on their part" (Sun 2008d; *People's Daily* 2006). Charges have also been leveled against local governments deemed to be colluding with foreign investors. A 2008 *China Daily* editorial lamented, "In their hunger for economic growth, many local governments have tried to absorb as much foreign investment as possible, regardless of the energy and environmental costs" (*China Daily* 2007).[14] Clearly, the current Chinese leadership itself is concerned that the ceaseless quest for foreign investment is undermining its attempt to balance getting rich with going green.

To summarize, China is both heavily foreign-invested and polluted. The combination of foreign investors' prominence in the Chinese economy and China's considerable pollution problem makes it critical that we better understand the relationship between FDI and environmental regulation. Because the pollution-haven debate explores the links between the competition for foreign investment and environmental regulation, it can help shed light on environmental protection challenges in China. In this book I use the concepts generated in the pollution-haven debate to provide scholars with a better understanding of the nature of China's environmental challenge. In particular, I offer insight about the extent to which foreign investment contributes to and undermines China's environmental regulation.

In the following chapters, I examine the development of Chinese law that regulates firm activity and controls the environmental impact of FDI (Chapters 2 and 3), describe the manner in which subnational competition for investment has influenced the implementation of environmental standards (Chapter 4), and analyze the environmental practices of both foreign-invested enterprises and Chinese companies with connections to foreign-invested enterprises (Chapters 5 and 6). In developing the book's argument, I employ a variety of original data, gathered during a year of in-country research. I present the results of a quantitative survey of 228 firms and several case studies, including a controversy between Royal Dutch Shell and a major Chinese oil company over the environmental policies for a natural gas pipeline. In addition to the firm survey, I base my analysis on interviews with representatives from sixteen foreign and twenty domestic firms, as well as various local experts, including industry-association representatives, environmental consultants, lawyers, NGO workers, scholars, journalists, and just over a dozen environmental officials. I also draw heavily on articles in industry journals and the Chinese media and the burgeoning Chinese-language academic literature on the topic of trade and the environment, published principally in university journals and books printed by the China Environmental Sciences Press.

An Overview of the Argument

The previous section provided a brief overview of the competing assertions about the impact of foreign-firm investment on the process of environmental regulation. To what extent do these claims accurately describe the situation in China? And how can China, which is arguably the most economically and environmentally important of developing countries, inform the academic debate about the empirical saliency of the pollution havens? As elaborated in the subsequent chapters, in the case of China, the influx of foreign firms and capital has not triggered a widespread race to the bottom nor a systemic regulatory chill. There is little evidence that China's integration with the global economy has transformed China into a pollution haven. As China has liberalized its domestic market and allowed entry to a greater number of foreign firms, it has also strengthened its environmental protection regime (Chapter 2). Just as important, Beijing has steadily tightened oversight of the environmental policies of foreign firms. The government's approach toward the environmental aspects of foreign investment has evolved from a tacit acknowledgment that the inflow of FDI brings new challenges in pollution management to a more active attempt to rein in the pollution caused by foreign investors (Chapter 3). Moreover, in several important ways foreign firms have contributed to China's environmental governance. Multinational companies in the chemical and energy industries, for instance, have created upward pressure on environmental regulation both through their own behavior and via the imposition of environmental, health, and safety demands on their domestic commercial partners (Chapter 5). In this sense, multinationals have exerted a private authority that fills in gaps left by the weak capacity of China's environmental protection bureaucracy. In certain instances domestic firms possessing or seeking commercial relations with foreign firms have been driven to implement stronger environmental management systems, although this phenomenon is not particularly widespread (Chapter 6).

But while China's opening to foreign investment has generally contributed constructively to environmental protection, the story is not entirely positive.

Foreign firms (and the competition to lure them) have posed important new challenges in controlling industrial pollution. China's reliance on foreign investment has indeed exerted a negative influence on China's environmental regulation, but only under a particular set of circumstances. The first is related to the stage of the regulatory process. China has experienced a regulatory chill in enforcement, as there are numerous examples of government desire to attract external capital leading to weak environmental regulation. However, regulatory chill has typically manifested as a lack of enforcement of existing laws rather than a relaxation of standards. Simply put, the issue is one of implementation rather than legislation.

This is an important finding because, when scholars have expressed concern about the possibility of a global race to the bottom or regulatory chill, the worry has typically been that the competition for investment leads to the weakening of environmental law, conceptualized as a lowering of standards. Frankel and Rose (2005, 85), for example, define the race-to-the-bottom argument by stating that "open countries in general adopt looser *standards* of environmental regulation, out of fear of a loss in international competitiveness. Alternatively, poor open countries may act as pollution havens, adopting lax environmental *standards* to attract multinational corporations and export pollution-intensive goods" (emphasis added). Prakash and Potoski (2006) use evidence about ISO 14000 adoption across national settings to make a case against critics of globalization who they say "argue that international trade spurs a race to the bottom among national *environmental standards*" (emphasis added).[15] Far less attention has been given to the impact on implementation and enforcement, which rarely make it into definitions of the race to the bottom. A brief appendix to this chapter demonstrates in greater detail how scholars have traditionally limited their definition of "race to the bottom" to a lowering of standards.[16]

Widening the focus beyond trends in standards is important because looking only at the development of China's formal environmental law, one would conclude there is no sign of regulatory chill in China. As discussed in Chapters 2 and 3, Beijing has steadily ratcheted up national environmental law, including policies designed to control the environmental behavior of foreign firms. In addition, there is no evidence that local governments have taken advantage of China's political decentralization to legally weaken subnational standards. But when attention turns to enforcement and implementation (Chapter 4), there is evidence that local governments have neglected to implement environmental law and, critically, done so to gain an advantage in the race to attract external capital. The broader implication is that a focus on standard-setting may have caused scholars to underestimate the extent to which the quest for foreign capital can work against the development of environmental protection. In the developing world, where government capacity and societal pressure are weaker, a lack of government enforcement and a failure of firms to comply with environmental standards are equally likely manifestations of a race to the bottom or regulatory chill that leads to pollution havens.[17]

The second condition under which foreign investment has greater potential to weaken environmental regulation is related to the institutional context of the jurisdiction. Not all areas are equally attractive to outside investors, and in the case of China it is the poorer regions lacking comparative advantage in the contest to secure foreign capital in which environmental standards have often been neglected or disregarded entirely (Chapter 4). The strongest version of the race-to-the-bottom argument would say that the competition for foreign capital has triggered a competitive race between jurisdictions, which results in a convergence of standards at the lowest common denominator. However, it is more accurate to think that in many of China's poor regions, the attempt to woo foreign capital is another item on an already sizable list of factors contributing to the poor implementation of industrial environmental regulation. The fact that China displays a considerable implementation gap between environmental law as it exists on paper and enforcement on the ground is hardly news—it is among the problems most frequently cited by those writing about the Chinese environment. What is less discussed is the role the quest for foreign investment plays in sustaining or even widening the gap.

Finally, the potential for foreign investment to have a negative impact on environmental regulation is influenced by firm type, as there are clear differences across firms in terms of environmental strategy. As the industrial-flight hypothesis might expect, China has seen heavy investment in pollution-intensive sectors (Chapter 4). As important as investment patterns, however, is the difference across foreign firms' environmental practices once in China. The environmental performance of foreign firms in China appears to in large part reflect the stringency of the firms' home country. Firms from developing countries lacking a long history of stringent environmental governance have exhibited environmental behavior that fails to comply with Chinese regulation and that largely resembles the "exploitative" environmental strategy described in the previous section. In some cases, their environmental performance has been worse than that of domestic firms (Chapter 6). As discussed in Chapter 6, the fact that investment between southern countries is rising rapidly makes this finding particularly worrying for those concerned about environmental protection in the developing world.

The bottom line is that, while China has not turned into a pollution haven or engaged in a race to the bottom in environmental standards, the decision to rely on foreign investment as a means of development has had important negative repercussions for environmental regulation. It has led some local governments to neglect environmental law and has opened China to a host of investors willing to take advantage of the lax regulatory setting. If any of China's leaders genuinely see glory in going green, enhancing oversight of foreign investment should continue to be a major pillar of China's development strategy.

The case of China shows that the impact of foreign-firm investment on environmental regulation is conditional—a great deal depends on where the investment comes from and where it goes. This straightforward proposition is relevant for how scholars move forward in the pollution-haven debate. For most of its history, the empirical debate over investment and the environment has been driven by an attempt to prove or disprove the existence of pollution havens and races to the bottom. Indeed, as one textbook on global environmental politics points out, scholars have been arguing whether pollution havens are real since the 1970s (Clapp and Dauvergne 2005, 162). The result is that the pollution-haven debate has often been framed in a simple yes-or-no dichotomy. The titles of journal articles, which often put a question mark after the term "race to the bottom" or "pollution haven," help illustrate this fact (e.g., see the titles of Birdsall and Wheeler 1993; Konisky 2006, 2007; Mani and Wheeler 1997; Prakash and Potoski 2006).

A great deal of empirical evidence has been mustered on both sides of the pollution-haven debate, and in the end scholars have compellingly demonstrated that foreign investors, and the competition to attract them, have both undermined and contributed to environmental regulation. In that sense, what previous research has proven is that pollution havens and races to the bottom are "indeterminate affairs" and much depends on the underlying conditions (Spar and Yoffie 2000, 31).[18] Given that the impact of foreign investors is itself indeterminate, the challenge for scholars, to paraphrase Spar and Yoffie, is to identify the underlying conditions that give rise to the particular outcomes.

In other words, scholars might be better served by shifting attention from the question, Do pollution havens exist? and toward the question, Under what conditions and through what mechanisms do foreign firms and the quest to lure them weaken (or strengthen) environmental regulation?[19] Toward that end, I have outlined three scope conditions under which foreign investment potentially weakens environmental regulation. I recognize that one can generalize only so far based on a study of a single country and so I do not consider these conditions as hard findings or the final word on the pollution-haven debate. Rather, I offer them as a set of hypotheses for scholars to apply to other regions of the world.

At first glance, China may seem like a poor choice of location for generating hypotheses about the impact of foreign investment on environmental regulation. After all, China is not Guatemala or the Gambia and the desire of foreign business to access the colossal Chinese market increases the leverage of Beijing over foreign investors.[20] But like other developing countries, China and jurisdictions within China exhibit a strong desire for foreign capital, which is a fundamental factor that is expected to strengthen the bargaining power of business and ultimately weaken environmental regulation. Despite the large amount of FDI flowing into China, investment has not been even across jurisdictions. Provinces—and localities within provinces—compete intensely for both foreign and domestic investment. China's eastern provinces typically prevail in this competition, as they account for 64 percent of GDP but attracted almost 88 percent of FDI from 1983 to 1998. China's west attracted only 3.3 percent (Tseng and Zebreg 2003, 70–71). Moreover, the amount of FDI flowing into China is large, but it is not sufficient to meet every locality's needs. By one estimate, in the mid-1990s there was only enough foreign investment to meet 20 percent of the capacity of development zones set up for the express purpose of attracting foreign investment. Zweig describes China as characterized by a "feverish demand for global linkages" (2002, 44), with localities driven by a "fear of being left behind" (95). In short, although awash in foreign direct investment, China is not immune from competitive pressures, and therefore the China case can shed light on the larger theoretical debate in the globalization literature.[21]

A Caveat

The theoretical concepts upon which I draw in this book (e.g., race to the bottom) are part of a larger academic and policy debate about whether trade and investment liberalization help or harm the environment in developing countries.[22] This book says a great deal about the relationship between foreign companies and environmental protection in China, but it does not seek to answer the larger question of whether free trade, foreign investment, or globalization writ large is good for the overall quality of China's natural environment. There are simply too many factors at play to make strong claims about the larger "trade versus the environment" debate given this book's highly restricted focus on firms' role in the process of environmental regulation. Trade liberalization, for example, is typically conceptualized as having three separate effects on the environment: scale, composition, and technique (SCT). The scale effect refers to the increase in industrial production, while the composition and technique effects refer, respectively, to changes in the range of goods produced and the technology used in industrial production. The hope is that countries liberalizing their trade will over time shift production to less pollution-intensive industries and adopt cleaner production manufacturing processes (Chai 2002). In other words, the SCT theory holds hope that the positive impact of the composition and technique effects will overwhelm the negative scale effect. This process of enhancing environmental protection is potentially facilitated by the income growth spurred by increased trade and investment (Wheeler 2002). Many argue that, although initially leading to more pollution, higher incomes eventually benefit the environment, a phenomenon typically illustrated by the environmental Kuznets curve (EKC). Income growth results in a cleaner environment because it enhances government capacity and leads to stronger societal demand for environmental protection.[23]

As one might expect, both the SCT theory and the EKC are hotly debated topics that have generated scores of articles in academic journals. While these debates are highly relevant to China, they ultimately are beyond the scope of this book. Rather than exploring the macro-effects such as the impact of foreign investment on income, or the influence of income on pollution outputs, I have instead chosen to maintain a narrow focus on one of the single micro-processes through which investment liberalization exerts an influence on environmental protection (i.e., the influence of foreign business on environmental regulation).[24] The point is that in examining the role of foreign corporations in the process of environmental regulation, this book looks at a critical, but by no means the only, influence on the quality of China's natural environment.

Appendix: Defining "Race to the Bottom"
Based Solely on Standards

What follows is a brief summary of how several scholars have defined the "race to the bottom" concept. As evident from the italicized portions of the quotations, each definition refers to standards, rather than implementation or enforcement. Collectively, they provide a sense of the extent to which scholars have neglected the issue of implementation and enforcement in their attempt to understand whether regulatory competition undermines environmental protection.

Klevorick gives perhaps the most complete definition of the race to the bottom, stating:

> The concern that motivates the "race to the bottom" literature and discussion of trade policy is that to attract mobile resources, especially firms, governments will choose policies—for example, environmental *standards*, occupational health and safety *standards*, competition policies. . . . The idea is that to render its country a hospitable location for business, a government would establish lax *standards* to be imposed upon those it wishes to draw. The result, it is argued, is that all countries will impose *standards* that are much more lax than those they would set if they did not have to compete with one another for the mobile resources. (1996, 178)

Revesz (1997, 538), one of the most articulate opponents of the race-to-the-bottom hypothesis, offers a similar definition: "The race-to-the-bottom rationale posits that states will try to induce geographically mobile firms to locate within their jurisdictions, in order to benefit from additional jobs and tax revenues, by offering them sub-optimally lax environmental *standards*." Among scholars that focus solely on the environment, Zarsky (1999) gives a standard summary of the environmentalists' argument, stating: "The drive to remain or become competitive in a high globalised economy will drag down *standards* in OECD [Organization for Economic Cooperation and Development] countries, creating a global 'race to the bottom.'" Harrison summarizes environmentalists' views in similar fashion: "Pessimists fear that international trade at best will chill any inclination to strengthen environmental standards and at worst will provoke a 'race to the bottom' as individual jurisdictions compete for foot-loose investment by *relaxing their environmental standards*" (2002, 4). Like Harrison, Boyce also mentions the "chill" and "race" variants of the argument and defines the race to the bottom as a situation in which "competition for private investment undermines environmental regulation. In its weaker variant, this argument holds that global competition impedes new regulation so that southern countries remain 'stuck at the bottom' . . . and northern countries are 'stuck in the mud.' . . . In its stronger variant, globalization spurs the competitive lowering of *standards* in the North, ultimately leading to convergence on the lowest common denominator" (2004, 109–10). This definition is comparable to Panayotou, who indicates that the race-to-the-bottom hypothesis asserts that "capital mobility results in lower environmental *standards* as governments compete with each other to attract scarce investment by lowering environmental standards below efficient levels" (2000, 23). Zeng and Easton, although arguing that FDI leads to more stringent compliance and enforcement, nonetheless define the race-to-the-bottom argument with reference to standards, stating: "In order to attract and retain FDI, developing countries often have incentives to compete to lower production costs by engaging in lax environmental regulation, thus creating a 'race to the bottom,' or a downward convergence in environmental, labor, and other social *standards*" (2007, 974). Wheeler presents a multilayered conceptualization of the race to the bottom, stating:

> In the race-to-the-bottom world, decent environmental standards impose high costs on polluters in high-income economies. To remain competitive, these firms relocate to low-income countries whose people are desperate for jobs and income. Local governments ignore regulation to promote investment and economic growth, allowing businesses to minimize costs by polluting with impunity. Driven by shareholders to maximize profits, international firms follow suit. Rising capital outflows force governments in high-income countries to begin relaxing environmental *standards*, but this proves fruitless because the poorest countries have no environmental standards at all. As the ensuing "race to the bottom" accelerates, all countries converge to the hellish pollution levels that afflict the poorest." (2001, 1–2)

Thus, in Wheeler's conceptualization, in order for a race to the bottom to occur, one must witness a relaxation of standards, the neglect of existing standards, and industrial relocation, all of which must result in a rising level of pollution. Wheeler sets the bar for proving the existence of a race toward the bottom quite high.

There are exceptions, as some scholars of American politics have focused on enforcement (e.g., Konisky 2007). Woods, for instance, points out that enforcement may "be subject to a different type of political dynamic than setting of standards," implying that empirical findings may differ depending on whether the explained variable is standard-setting or enforcement of existing standards (2006, 186). Neumayer is also an exception, as he states: "A country provides a pollution haven if it sets its environmental standards below the socially efficient level or fails to enforce its standards in order to attract foreign investment from countries with higher standards or countries that better enforce their standards" (2001b, 148). Post (2004), although not focusing on races to the bottom or regulatory chill, provides a good example of how, for developing countries, implementation of environmental standards is as relevant an issue as legislation.

2 The Politics of Industrial Pollution in China: Laws, Institutions, and Challenges

This chapter introduces China's environmental protection system and the main challenges China faces in controlling industrial pollution. It provides context for subsequent empirical chapters and offers a background for readers unfamiliar with Chinese environmental politics. In the process, it highlights a feature of the Chinese regime that is critical for a study of the relationship between foreign firms and environmental regulation—a lax regulatory setting characterized by the absence of a strong enforcement presence. China has an admirable set of environmental laws. However, the combination of local autonomy, weak courts, elites bent on economic growth, and a tightly controlled media and non-governmental organization (NGO) sector creates a setting in which there is ample opportunity for both industry and government to violate or ignore environmental law. This underscores the importance of the question posed in the previous chapter, which is whether foreign firms take advantage of, or help foster, a lenient regulatory environment. That question is the subject of subsequent chapters; for now, the goal is to illustrate the regulatory situation that foreign companies face when they invest in China. Most of the material presented in this chapter is based on secondary sources; readers already conversant in the intricacies of China's environmental politics may prefer to skip to Chapter 3.

China's Environmental Protection Laws and Regulations

In the three decades since the initiation of the reform era, China has established an impressive set of environmental laws and regulations. Although there are some environmental law precedents predating the Cultural Revolution, prior to the late 1970s environmental degradation was generally considered a problem of capitalist countries and therefore not an issue for China. Despite the enormous damage done to the environment during the Mao era (Shapiro 2001), it was only at the insistence of Zhou Enlai that China sent a delegation to the 1972 Stockholm conference, the first major global environmental conference. Shortly after Stockholm, China held its first national environmental conference, and then in 1979 China passed its first environmental law—the Environmental Protection Law for Trial Implementation (EPL) (NPC 1979b).

Over the last thirty years, China has made impressive strides in establishing an environmental legal infrastructure. China's environmental protection regime has gradually expanded, so that today it is comprised of approximately twenty laws, forty regulations, five hundred standards, and six hundred other legal norm-creating documents related to environmental protection and pollution control. In addition, there are roughly one thousand local environmental regulations (Ferris and Zhang 2005; Ross 1994).[1] China is also party to more than fifty environmental treaties (SEPA 2006). According to Ferris and Zhang (2003, 585–86), "most subjects or activities generally considered to be within the purview of environmental law have been covered to some extent in China by one or more legal norm-creating documents."

China's environmental legal regime is multifaceted and encompasses a myriad of laws, regulations, standards, and other forms of policy measures. By one count, there are at least ten sources of Chinese environmental law running from basic laws (*jiben fa*) to State Council administrative regulations (*xingzheng fagui*), standards (*guojia biaozhun*), and rules issued by national ministries (*bumen guizhang*).[2] Some of the principal laws are listed in Table 2.1. Typically a basic law, such as the Law on the Prevention and Control of Water Pollution, provides a broad outline of government policies (e.g., enterprises that pollute beyond national standards will be fined). Following the release of the law, the State Council issues regulations or guidelines that provide details about procedures for implementation (e.g., the method for calculating fines for each pollutant).

One of the defining features of China's environmental protection law is that local governments are afforded a great deal of authority and responsibility. The 1989 Environmental Protection Law (a revised version of the 1979 EPL), the foundation of China's environmental protection regime, stipulates that local governments can set standards for environmental quality and the

TABLE 2.1 Examples of China's environmental protection laws

Law	Year
Environmental Protection Law for Trial Implementation	1979
Marine Environmental Protection Law	1982 (revised 1999)
Forestry Law	1984 (revised 1998)
Water Pollution Prevention and Control Law	1984 (revised 1996, 2008)
Grasslands Law	1985
Mineral Resources Law	1986
Fisheries Law	1986
Air Pollution Prevention and Control Law	1987 (revised 1995, 2000, 2002)
Land Management Law	1988 (revised 1998)
Water Law	1988 (revised 2002)
Wildlife Conservation Law	1988
Environmental Protection Law	1989 (revised 2001)
Water and Soil Conservation Law	1991/1992
Agricultural Law	1993
Solid Waste Law	1995
Energy Conservation Law	1997 (revised 2008)
Environmental Impact Assessment Law	2002
Clean Production Law	2002
Measures on Open Environmental Information (for Trial Implementation)	2007
Circular Economy Law	2008

Data from Ross 1994 and the Ministry of Environmental Protection website (www.zhb.gov.cn).

discharge of pollutants that either are not specified in the national standards or that are more stringent than national standards (NPC 1989, Articles 9, 10). Article 16 places responsibility for environmental quality squarely on the shoulders of local governments, stating: "The local people's governments at various levels shall be responsible for the environment quality of areas under their jurisdiction and take measures to improve the environment quality" (NPC 1989). This stress on the role of local government is repeated throughout China's major environmental laws related to water, air, and solid waste pollution control.

The emphasis on the responsibility of local governments running through China's environmental laws, along with the organization of the environmental protection system and the Chinese state as a whole, means that most of the routine execution of China's environmental protection laws occurs under the administration of local governments. Typically, when a new law is issued by the central government, local governments issue their own version of the national law. Although local governments are expected to treat national regulations as minimum standards and are free to make local regulations that are more stringent than national regulations, the vagueness of national law affords local governments a great deal of influence. As one study states, "Because China's environmental laws are general and often intentionally ambiguous, they allow the State Council, national agencies, and local governments to add details that influence implementation" (Ma and Ortolano 2000, 15).

In addition to describing the broad division of authority between central and local governments, China's basic environmental laws outline behaviors that are encouraged, required, or prohibited. Running throughout these laws are eleven main programs. Though referred to as systems (*zhi du*) in Chinese texts, these "systems" are really more fundamental principles or programs that can be applied across numerous aspects of pollution control and prevention. The programs form the basis of China's environmental regime and are referred to in all of China's main environmental laws. For the purpose of providing a broad overview of China's regulatory system, these programs are described in Table 2.2. Of these programs, the "three simultaneous," the pollution levy system, and the environmental impact assessment (EIA) system are most relevant to the environmental regulation of industry. The EIA program is central to the governance of foreign firms and has evolved considerably in recent years. It is dealt with extensively in the subsequent chapter.

The Organization of Environmental Protection

All these laws and regulations are designed and implemented by a network of organizations that collectively comprise China's environmental protection regime. China's environmental protection administration shares two features with the larger Chinese state. First, authority is fragmented and a large degree of power and autonomy resides at the local level. Second, it is a system in which rule of law has yet to take hold and individuals possess a patent ability

TABLE 2.2 China's environmental protection programs

Program	Description
Three Simultaneous (*San Tong Shi*)	This policy requires all new investment projects, as well as any enterprise that is renovating or expanding its facility, to implement pollution control measures at the same time as it plans, constructs, and operates the main project.
Environmental Responsibility System (ERS)	Along with the Centralized Pollution Control System, the Environmental Responsibility System places responsibility for a jurisdiction's environmental quality on the local government. Governments at all levels are required to establish and try to reach environmental targets. According to the ERS, success in reaching environmental goals is part of the criteria for assessing a government's administrative proficiency.
Centralized Pollution Control System	Though referred to as a system in Chinese publications, this is more a principle that makes local governments responsible for pollution levels in their jurisdictions. In the early reform period, pollution control efforts focused on individual enterprises. In the 1980s, this approach was changed and local governments were given responsibility for pollution control efforts.
Urban Environmental Quality Assessment	The Ministry of Environmental Protection is required to conduct annual assessments of China's cities' environment. Items that are inspected include air and water quality, noise pollution, solid waste handling and control, and the "greening" of urban areas. Local governments are responsible for making any required adjustments, and results are supposed to be made available to the general public.
Pollution Levy System	Under the pollution levy system, enterprises are fined for pollution discharged beyond a certain preset standard. The system began in 1982 and was gradually extended, so that by 2000 it was operating in all Chinese cities and counties (Wang and Jin 2002). By 2000, almost a half million factories had been fined. Charges are imposed for air, water, solid waste, and noise pollution, but water fines comprise almost two-thirds of the collected fines (Wang and Wheeler 2000). For both air and water pollution, the fine is levied only for the pollutant that most violates the standard. Originally, the penalty was based on the concentration and not the volume of pollutant discharged, but in most areas this is being amended because determining the fine on concentration alone induced enterprises simply to dilute their discharges rather than lower pollutant volume (Panayotou 1998, 434). A large portion of the fine, typically 80 percent, is made available to the enterprise as a grant or loan for investments in pollution control. The remainder of the collected fee is used by the local environmental protection bureau (EPB). The levy system has been criticized because it does not provide an incentive for firms to reduce all pollutants, but only the pollutant that most violates standards. In addition, many have noted that the fees have failed to keep up with inflation and are often too low.

TABLE 2.2 *(continued)*

Program	Description
Pollution Discharge Assessment System	Also called the pollution discharge permit system, this program was initiated in the late 1980s largely as a means of rectifying weaknesses in the pollution levy system. The system is designed to lessen both the concentration and the magnitude of pollution discharges. Under the permit system, EPBs issue permits to enterprises specifying the limits on pollution discharges based on targets for air and water quality in their jurisdiction. By 2002, over 80,000 enterprises had been issued permits for water discharges. There is also a permit system for air emissions, but it is less extensive and developed than the water discharge permits system. The discharge permit scheme, unlike other programs such as the Environmental Impact Assessment System, is not based on its own law or set of regulations. Rather, its origins lie scattered in sundry clauses in a variety of environmental laws (e.g., Environmental Protection Law and Water Pollution Prevention and Control Law) and local directives (Li Zhiping 2005; Wang 2008).
Pollution Control Within Deadlines	This arrangement is designed to allow older enterprises that are facing financial difficulties a certain period of time to implement pollution control measures.
Environmental Impact Assessment (EIA) System	The EIA system dates back to the late 1970s, but was cemented in the 2002 EIA Law and its 2006 implementation guidelines. It requires that economic development projects carried out by enterprises or government agencies submit an EIA statement for approval to environmental authorities prior to the commencement of construction. The administrative level of the approving agency and specific requirements for the EIA statement differ depending on the size of the investment and the nature of its environmental impact.
Control and Elimination of Outdated Equipment and Technologies	This policy prohibits the use of facilities that are deemed excessively pollution- or energy-intensive. The State Council often publishes lists of proscribed technologies and standards for energy/pollution per unit of output. Most of China's main environmental laws specifically state that the importation and use of outdated technologies is forbidden.
Administrative System for the Handling and Transfer of Hazardous Waste	This system is set up in recognition of the fact that numerous units that produce hazardous waste lack the facilities to handle it. Because hazardous waste is produced in small quantities, rather than requiring each enterprise to establish handling facilities, administrative centers have been established to accept waste.
Pollution Discharge Quantity Control System	This is closely related to the discharge assessment system and its stated goal is to enable China to reach its environmental protection goals. It is designed to control the total quantity of pollution discharges, rather than just the concentration of discharges, which was the target of early reform policies.

to affect and even evade official policy. Writing about the Chinese political system, Tony Saich states, "Despite the stress in the post-Mao period on the need to move to a rule of law and away from personal dictate, it is still a system where individuals hold immense capacity to circumvent formal regulations. This is true not just at the center but also at the local levels" (2001, 107). Saich's description of the Chinese political system can apply just as easily to the environmental protection system.

Before discussing the organization of China's environmental protection regime, it is first necessary to provide background information about the Chinese state. The Chinese state is organized hierarchically into several territorial levels: center (or national), province, prefecture, county, and township and village. All governments below the center can be referred to as "local." In addition to territorial units, the state is composed of numerous government functional units (such as ministries and bureaus), which oversee various efforts such as education, foreign affairs, and environmental protection. At the center, these functional ministries and commissions comprise the State Council, which is officially the executive organ of the National People's Congress (NPC). The functional units at the center are replicated down through each of the lower territorial units. Therefore, a lower-level government, such as a county government, resembles a miniature central government in terms of structure and functions. It has a chief executive (county magistrate), a county people's congress, and a county government with functional agencies similar to those comprising the State Council. Distant from the provincial government or prefectural administration that oversees them, counties tend to possess a great deal of autonomy (Zhong 2003, 69).

With regard to environmental protection, the central government agency that oversees the implementation and administration of China's environmental laws is the Ministry of Environmental Protection (MEP). Akin to the Environmental Protection Agency (EPA) in the United States, MEP is among the twenty-seven government agencies that comprise the State Council. MEP performs a number of duties, including formulating national plans for pollution control. Traditionally, MEP has sought to achieve pollution control targets through the establishment of national environmental standards. These include ambient environmental quality standards for geographic jurisdictions, pollution discharge standards for industrial sectors, and technological standards for industrial production (Lin Shuwen 2004).

MEP only achieved full ministerial status in 2008. Prior to its promotion,

MEP, then known as the State Environmental Protection Administration (SEPA), had been a part of the State Council for ten years, but was in essence a second-tier agency because the director of SEPA was not a full member of the State Council and could only vote on issues related to environmental protection.[3] Shortly after its promotion, it was announced that MEP would increase its staff by fifty (to roughly three hundred) in order to establish two new supervision and monitoring departments. Although MEP is still severely lacking in personnel, the expansion is important because it took place in the context of government reorganizations designed to shrink the size of China's overall state bureaucracy. In addition to MEP, in 2006 Beijing also created five regional environmental protection offices to promote coordination. These developments are generally considered an indication of the broader trend toward stronger environmental governance (Li Jing 2008b).

Aside from MEP, there are several other national organizations that play a role in environmental protection. Since 1993, the Environmental Protection and Resource Conservation Committee (EPRCC), which is within the Standing Committee of the National People's Congress, has played an active role in both facilitating the environmental legislative process and supervising implementation. The National Development and Reform Commission (NDRC) has taken the lead in many initiatives designed to green Chinese industry, including most recently the promulgation of the Circular Economy Law in 2008. The NDRC has also been active in the Clean Production Law since 2002 and in overseeing China's participation in climate-change negotiations (Shi and Zhang 2006, 282–83). With the elevation of MEP to full ministerial status, it is possible that the NDRC will play a decreased role in environmental protection and focus more on its primary mission of guiding the economy and promoting balanced development. It is expected that MEP, for instance, will be the primary agency in charge of addressing the challenge of water pollution and that the National Energy Administration, which is a new department that began operating in 2008, will assume the NDRC's portfolio for energy conservation. However, whether MEP's gain equals the NDRC's loss remains to be seen.

Below MEP, replicated at each level of the administrative hierarchy, are environmental protection bureaus (EPBs) (see Figure 2.1). Thus, there are provincial, municipal, and county EPBs. The principal responsibility of EPBs is to implement regulations passed down from parent units and to aid the process of adapting national regulations to local conditions. The county-level

EPB is where the brunt of implementation occurs. County-level EPBs, and their affiliated organizations such as monitoring stations, are in charge of various activities such as conducting inspections, assessing fines, monitoring environmental quality, approving environmental aspects of construction projects, and investigating environmental accidents. EPBs, in theory, have a variety of tools available to control industry. They can issue warnings, impose fines, revoke permits, and initiate court cases against an enterprise or its management if it fails to comply with national discharge standards and other environmental programs. However, the reality on the ground is significantly more complex, and environmental regulation is rarely, if ever, a process of a local-level EPB simply implementing directives passed down from above.

A principal factor complicating the work of local-level EPBs is the fragmented nature of the Chinese state and the fact that EPBs are deeply embedded in local goverments. In the Chinese system, a government organ below the center, such as a county-level EPB, has both *tiao* (line) and *kuai* (area) relationships and "the dominance of one over the other will affect how central policy is implemented and how authority is exerted" (Saich 2001, 109). *Tiao* relationships are vertical links between bureaucracies. For instance, a county-level EPB has *tiao-tiao* relationship with the township environmental monitoring office to whom it gives orders as well as with the municipal-level EPB whose directives it implements. The *kuai-kuai* relationship refers to horizontal coordinating bodies within a geographical area that have equal levels of authority (Lieberthal 1995, 169–70). So, for example, the county-level EPB has the same amount of formal authority as a county-level construction bureau, which may also play a role in environmental regulation for a new investment project via its ability to issue permits. The key element to the *tiao* and *kuai* organization is the fact that there may be several functional units that play a role in environmental regulation, each of which may have competing bureaucratic interests. In addition to industrial bureaus, these functional units include local units of the Ministry of Land and Natural Resources, Ministry of Construction, and Ministry of Water Resources, as well as the National Development and Reform Commission.

Complicating matters further is the fact that the county-level EPB is subordinate to and dependent on the county-level government. The county-level government itself answers to both the county-level CCP (Chinese Communist Party) committee and the provincial-level government (see Figure 2.1). The county-level EPB is dependent on the local government because the lion's share of its budget comes *not* from the higher levels of the environmental pro-

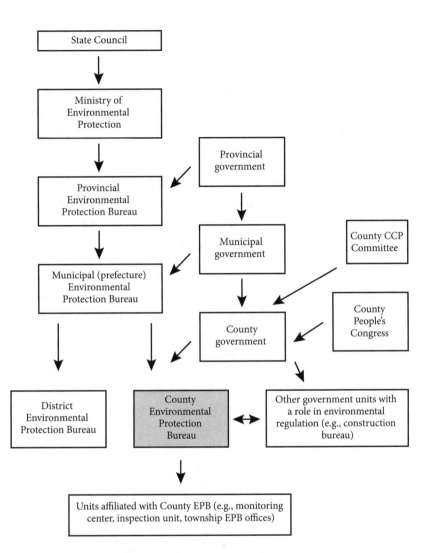

FIGURE 2.1 Organization of the Chinese environmental protection system. Note: This table is a drastic simplification and for the sake of simplicity several units are not included. Data from Jahiel 1998; Lieberthal 1995; Ma and Ortolano 2000.

tection administration, but from the local county government. Local governments also control promotions and appointments of cadres as well as the allocation of personnel and resources. In recent years, Beijing has experimented with the organization of environmental protection to attempt to increase the influence and autonomy of EPBs. For example, in Shaanxi the provincial environmental protection administration has required municipal and county EPBs to report directly to the provincial administration rather than to the local government. Similar experiments have been conducted in Dalian, Ningbo, and Xiamen (Xinhua 2005). It is also hoped that SEPA's promotion to MEP will improve the authority of EPBs at the local level. But the fact remains that the vast majority of China's approximately 2,500 EPBs remain reliant on local governments for funding and support. This dependent relationship makes it relatively easy for high-level local officials in the county government, such as mayors, to influence the work of environmental regulators. EPB officials are understandably hesitant to halt projects that have received the local mayors' seal of approval. As Ma and Ortolano state (2000, 128), "EPBs have little hope of taking enforcement steps opposed by local leaders or powerful agencies."

In sum, a director of an EPB is influenced from above by upper-level EPBs and the local government and at the same time may compete with other functional ministries within the jurisdiction. Referring to the Chinese political system as a whole, Kenneth Lieberthal characterizes this arrangement as one of fragmented authoritarianism and states that one of the principal features is that "the officials of any given office have a number of bosses in different places" (1995, 169). The key question at the local level is whether the horizontal serves the vertical or the vertical serves the horizontal (Lieberthal 1995). In the case of environmental protection, because of EPB dependence on local governments, it is often the horizontal that serves the vertical, as local EPBs are subject to the dictates of local county governments. Abigail Jahiel notes that China's "complex arrangement of diffuse agencies" has many implications for China's environmental protection, one of which is that "environmental work is not always strongly inclined toward environmental interests" and among agencies there is a "competition for scarce environmental funds" (1998, 764). The bottom line is that China's system of ambiguous, overlapping authority has created a situation in which there is no single set of environmental regulators, but multiple bureaucratic agents with overlapping authority and divergent interests.

The Missing Link: Enforcement

In 2008, as SEPA was being upgraded to MEP, Zhou Shengxian promised to build a law enforcement system of "iron and steel," and in recent years government authorities have taken a number of steps to compel Chinese firms to pay greater attention to environmental protection, especially with regard to air and water pollution (Sun 2008a).[4] Chinese leaders have shown an increased willingness to threaten pollution-intensive firms with closure and to publicly censure negligent enterprises. In the course of its "EIA storms," the first of which was launched in 2005, SEPA ordered several high-profile companies to cease operation and even denied some cities permits for new construction, pending compliance with environmental regulation (Liu Jiangqing 2007). In 2007, SEPA singled out over 3,700 firms (of 80,000 investigated) as environmental polluters (Mitamura 2008, 114). In 2008, Guangdong identified 50 companies as poor environmental performers and indicated they would be blocked from government approval for an initial public offering (Song 2008).

Despite the steady drumbeat of headlines in the Chinese media about the shuttering of factories and enhanced implementation of environmental laws, the single biggest weakness in China's environmental law is the lack of enforcement. This is hardly surprising given the organizational deficiencies and the fact that most developing countries suffer from an "enforcement gap." It is difficult to determine precisely how large China's enforcement gap is, but it appears considerable. In May 2007, Wen Jiabao noted that despite the government's efforts to slow the growth of pollution- and energy-intensive sectors, they still grew by 21 percent in the first quarter of that year (Mitamura 2008, 74). A study by the World Bank found that China missed ten of the thirteen targets for air and water pollution control outlined in the Tenth Five-year Plan (2001–2005). Among those missed, the emission of industrial SO_2 was most off the mark, increasing by more than five million tons and overshooting its target by 50 percent (World Bank 2007).

A major reason Beijing has been unable to meet its various emission targets is that the absence of strong government enforcement creates a situation in which industrial compliance is minimal. A detailed study of Shanghai Municipality found that in one district in 2001, among the enterprises targeted by local environmental officials for enforcement, only about half complied with discharge standards. If one includes the large number of firms that are not targeted for enforcement, only 10 percent of firms are known to be in compliance with discharge standards (Warwick 2003, 284–85). Elizabeth Economy (2007b) cites a 2005 survey of 509 cities that demonstrated only 23 percent of factories properly treat sewage before disposing of it. The same survey indicated that fully one-third of industrial wastewater is released without being treated at all. Wang Canfa, head of the Center for Legal Assistance for Pollution Victims, estimated that "the rate of China's environmental laws and regulations that are actually enforced is 10 percent" (Lin Gu, 2005). A joint investigation by SEPA and the Ministry of Land and Natural Resources in 2004 showed that approximately 40 percent of mining construction projects completed the environmental impact assessment procedure as required. In some areas the figure was as low as 6 percent (Lin Gu, 2005). Even when there is enforcement, it may be of dubious quality. In 2006, environmental consultants from a firm based in Hong Kong discovered that local authorities who had deemed a local factory compliant with air pollution requirements were taking regular readings of soot concentrations, but doing so outside the gates of the factory rather than inside the chimney as required (Kirk 2007).

There are several reasons China suffers from weak enforcement and minimal industrial compliance. Four of the more commonly cited include: regulatory agents' modest capacity, the limitations of China's legal system, a "pollute first, pay later" mentality among government officials, and the absence of a public sector to serve as a corporate watchdog. Each is briefly described in the following sections.

Low Capacity of China's Regulators

A lack of capacity often undermines the ability of local environmental officials to implement pollution control policies (Morton 2005; Schwartz 2003). For example, a 2002 U.S. Embassy study of Anhui Province notes that, despite adopting a progressive "total emissions" approach to governing industrial pollution, "Anhui environmental officials readily admit . . . that they lack the manpower and expertise to effectively enforce 'total emissions' guidelines. Compounding the shortage of personnel, the Anhui EPB is relatively inexperienced. The provincial EPB was established only in 1995, with most counties and municipalities setting up branch EPB's between 1997 and 2000" (U.S. Embassy 2002). The situation in Anhui is not unique. Comparing the total number of enterprises in China with those that are included in environmental statistics highlights the insufficient monitoring capacity of local environmental protection bureaus. In 2002, the National Bureau of Statistics reported that there were more than 181,000 industrial enterprises in China. However, less than 71,000 were included in the environmental statistics. The implication is that less than 40 percent of industrial enterprises were included in the monitoring activities of environmental protection bureaus (Shi and Zhang 2006, 278, table 1).

China has earmarked $164 billion for environmental protection for the Eleventh FYP, which is equivalent to 1.5 percent of the GDP. This marks a significant increase over previous years. In 1989, spending was only 0.6 percent of the GDP and a decade later only 1 percent (Carter and Mol 2006, 154). But even the current figure is well short of the 3 percent most experts believe is necessary for genuine improvements in the state of the environment (Reuters 2005). In 2007, Beijing announced that it would dedicate $250 million toward "measuring pollution and enforcing controls" against Chinese factories, but it was not clear whether this represented additional money (Reuters 2007). International aid helps fill funding gaps, but the fact remains that China's environmental protection officials operate on sparse budgets. Not surprisingly, given the scarce funding, China's environmental protection bureaus are generally considered understaffed. As mentioned above, the MEP in Beijing employs roughly 300 personnel. If one includes the five regional inspection offices and affiliated agencies such as research institutes, the number grows to approximately 2,600. This compares with the more than 17,000 employees in the U.S. EPA (Gang 2008). Although one would not expect China to have as many environmental bureaucrats as the United States, the fact remains that China is trying to tackle a far more serious pollution problem than that of the United States, with only a fraction of the trained professionals.

The weak capacity of environmental officials is exacerbated by the corruption that is endemic in China (Wedeman 2004). While it is difficult to estimate the precise cost of corruption to environmental protection efforts, senior environmental officials have made clear that the malfeasance of government officials poses a major obstacle to more stringent enforcement. In 2006, SEPA director Zhou Shengxian indicated that a government investigation of pollution control approvals for construction projects found violations in approximately 40 percent of the cases examined. Zhou stated: "It is clear the conflict between economic growth and environmental protection is coming to a head. . . . Fraud in project approval was prominent with many projects passing their environmental assessment without fulfilling the necessary criteria" (Lague 2006). In 2007, the Chinese Academy for Environmental Planning estimated that only half of the national budget for environmental protection was spent on legitimate projects (Economy 2007b). Improper land allocation, which typically involves government officials acquiring land at low prices and then selling it to developers at market price with a bribe attached, is one of the most common types of corruption. A Chinese government official estimated there were more than a million of cases of illegal land acquisition between 1996 and 2005, and a survey by the Ministry of Land and Natural Resources found that in 2005 half the land used for development was obtained illegally. A related problem is the theft of public funds. China's National Audit Agency estimated that more than $170 billion, or 8 percent of on-budget government spending, was misused between 1996 and 2005. On average, more than six thousand senior local officials are prosecuted for corruption each year, and Minxin Pei estimates that the cost of corruption in 2003 alone was possibly as high as 3 percent of government GDP. This translates into $86 billion and is almost half the amount allocated for environmental protection for the entire Eleventh Five-year Plan (Pei 2007, 2–3). In a country with an underfunded environmental protection regime, the loss of public funds to official graft clearly aggravates the challenge of implementing environmental law.

Weak Courts

The State Council has called for the "perfection of the legal assistance system for pollution victims," but China's courts remain weak (Alex Wang 2007). In a context of significant local government autonomy, the impotence of the courts augments the ability of local elites to influence environmental regulation and makes it easier for firms to escape punishment. Occasionally, China's courts are used by local EPBs to coerce intransigent firms to comply with environmental regulations. In 2002, the owner of an ore-dressing plant was sentenced to five years in prison and fined 100,000 RMB (Renminbi) for polluting the drinking water in his village, which led to arsenic poisoning of 334 villagers (Warwick 2003, 50n86). Pollution victims also sporadically sue companies that are alleged to be violating environmental standards. The Center for Legal Assistance to Pollution Victims (CLAPV), one of China's most well-known NGOs, has handled almost eighty cases since its establishment in late 1998. Thirty-five of the cases involved damages to human health, and CLAPV won twelve of them.[5] In one of its more notable successes, CLAPV helped 1,800 farmers from Fujian win a judgment against a chemical plant. This victory is impressive because the factory accounted for 25 percent of local county revenue. Other similar organizations exist, such as the All-China Environment Federation, which has taken on twenty-three environmental matters since 2005 (Alex Wang 2007). The Natural Resources Defense Council and the American Bar Association, as well as several European and EU-sponsored organizations, are also active in China, although they have typically focused more on education and environmental legal training than advocacy. Beijing has also encouraged citizens to make greater use of the courts. For example, in 2008 China forwarded a plan to increase government accountability in the environmental arena by making it easier for citizens to use the courts to seek compensation for water pollution. According to Xinhua, "a new law effective June 1, 2008, allows for fines against the heads of polluting enterprises for up to half their annual income" (Xinhua 2008a, 2008b) .

One additional legal enhancement of China's environmental governance that affects foreign investors is the inclusion of environmental protection articles in the 1997 Criminal Law of the PRC. Whereas the original 1979 Criminal Law had almost no articles related to environmental protection, Chapter 6, Section 6 of the 1997 Criminal Law, entitled "Crimes of Impairing the Protection of Environment and Resources," lists several environmental acts deemed criminal (NPC 1997, Articles 338–46).[6] This includes the import of hazardous waste (solid, liquid, or gaseous) for treatment, dumping, or use as raw material without express permission from the relevant authorities.[7] Sentences range from not less than three years to ten years. The inclusion of environmental clauses in the Criminal Law is a clear message from the central government that environmental issues are an increased priority, but to date it is still uncommon for enterprise managers or government officials to be brought up on criminal charges for environmental incidents.[8]

These developments represent important first steps in the rise of environmental litigation as a restraint on industry's pollution discharges. However, when one compares the small number of court cases and organizations that provide legal advocacy with the large number of industrial accidents and environmental protests, which totaled roughly 51,000 in 2005 alone, it is clear that environmental litigation is not yet a central part of industrial environmental regulation. Not only are China's environmental legal advocates few in number, but they remain under state control. In March 2006, the All China Lawyers Association, which is essentially China's bar association, issued the "Guiding Opinions of the All-China Lawyers Association on Lawyers Handling Mass Cases." This document instructed lawyers handling cases of mass litigation, defined as involving ten or more plaintiffs and specifically applicable to environmental cases, to seek the "supervision and guidance" of judicial administrative bureaus (Human Rights Watch 2006). Only "politically qualified lawyers" are to work on large, class action cases, and any lawyer taking such a case must work with at least two other lawyers. These rules were largely interpreted as a means of controlling and possibly deterring lawyer involvement in environmental litigation.

Aside from state control of legal advocates, another factor that limits the role of the courts in controlling industrial pollution is that, much like environmental regulators, local courts are heavily reliant on the local government. Alford and Shen note that "subnational judicial salaries and court operating expenses come from subnational, rather than national, funds, leading some observers to question their capacity to maintain a high degree of independence from local officialdom" (1998, 416). They also point out that a local government's influence on the courts can go beyond financial matters. The Chinese court system leaves room for individuals other than judges formally hearing a case to influence decisions. These other individuals can include adjudication committees (comprised of other senior judges) as well as party committees. Local government officials can also manipulate the court system to their advantage. In 2007, *Nanfang Daily* reported a case in which villagers in Duigou (Jiangsu) became concerned about pollution and had a local river tested. The results showed the water was undrinkable for both humans and animals. The villagers sued a local industrial park and chemical plants. The park's administrative committee countersued, leveling charges of blackmail against the villagers. The result was that several villagers were imprisoned for six months (Liu Yingling 2007).

A further impediment to environmental litigation is that many judges still lack legal training. According to Ferris and Zhang (2003, 598–99), "individuals with formal law school training still represent a minority in the legal departments of government environmental institutions." They point out that the SEPA Law and Policy Department was staffed with fourteen people, of whom only five had law degrees. This is a problem endemic in China's legal system as a whole. As late as 1995, only 7 percent of judges in China had a college degree. By 2005, the number had increased to more than 50 percent, but the country as a whole still lacks a sufficient pool of qualified, experienced judges.

Pollute First, Pay Later

In the context of local government autonomy and a weak legal system, the work of EPB officials is often further hampered by the fact that local government elites are strongly oriented toward pro-growth policies and place environmental protection low on their list of priorities. Local government officials have been notoriously fixated on economic expansion, and it is widely accepted that the primary goal of the Chinese government over the last three decades has been fostering economic growth. Johnston summarizes the

Chinese view most succinctly when he states, "Rapid economic growth, not its quality or distribution, is the first priority of the state" (1998, 566). Johnston cites China's Agenda 21 statement, which claims that improving living standards means China must follow "the path of relatively *rapid* economic growth and *gradual* improvements in the quality of development" (emphasis added). In some cases, local government officials' concern with encouraging income growth is shared by the local community. Benjamin van Rooij's extensive and highly impressive investigation of environmental protection in three Yunnan villages (2006b) shows that in some cases local communities did not oppose violations of environmental and natural resource laws—and even benefited from them. For instance, in one village local residents earned income from leasing village land to private enterprises, even though the leases violated the 1998 Land Management Act. Economic interests often trumped environmental concerns. SEPA described the prevailing mentality in the late 1990s as: "Commodities have a high value, resources have a low value, the environment has no value" (Warwick 2003, 4). Given the endemic poverty many of China's jurisdictions confront, a fixation on increasing incomes is an understandable reaction to local conditions, but it is nonetheless frequently inimical to enforcement of environmental standards.

Sometimes stress on local officials to maintain rapid economic development comes from the center, as the national government tends to reward officials who have spurred economic growth in their region. One source of pressure is financial support; local governments can no longer rely on the central government for funds and must fend for themselves. Although in recent years the central government has placed more emphasis on sustainable development, it has throughout the reform period created "growth oriented consumerist social norms" (Jahiel 1998, 767). For more than thirty years Deng Xiaoping's "to get rich is glorious" has been the mantra of the Communist Party, which in the wake of the demise of its ideological authority has based its legitimacy largely on its ability to maintain social stability and contribute to the improvement in citizens' material lives. Faced with a huge and growing population and an economic transition that is generating tens of thousands of layoffs from the state sector each year, maintaining stability and improving lifestyles means generating rapid growth. The result is that local government leaders are prone to interfere and overrule EPB officials when enforcing environmental regulation is perceived as inhibiting economic development.

In recent years, under Hu Jintao's call for constructing a "well-off," "people-centered," and "harmonious" society, the central government has placed increased emphasis on balancing economic growth, social equity, and ecological sustainability. For instance, the Tenth Five-year Plan (2001–2006), presented by Zhu Rongji in 2001, lists "Coordinating Economic Development with Social Development" as one of its five guiding principles. Whether Chinese leaders are speaking to national leaders in Beijing or to local cadres during inspection tours, calls for "sustainable development" are now a standard element in their speeches on economic reform. In his annual government work report delivered to the National People's Congress in 2006, for instance, Wen Jiabao emphasized China's efforts in enhancing environmental governance, while admitting that it is one of the areas in which "the people's interests are adversely affected by violations of regulations and policies" (Xinhua 2006a).

Aside from hastening the development of environmental law, this emphasis by the central government on protecting natural resources has translated into several broad policy initiatives designed to compel local governments to implement environmental law more sedulously. Beijing announced a goal of reducing total discharge of major pollutants by 10 percent and energy consumption per unit of GDP by 20 percent during the Eleventh Five-year Plan (2006–2010).[9] It also declared its intention to publicize figures on energy consumption per unit of output for all regions and major industries. MEP has also experimented with a "Green GDP" plan under which local cadres would be assessed not only by economic growth in their jurisdictions, but also by measures of environmental protection.

The government has also grown increasingly open about the costs of China's failure to protect the environment. In 2006, it announced that environmental degradation cost China approximately 3 percent of its GDP, which translates into roughly $64 billion. The report itself acknowledges that the real costs are likely higher, which is almost certainly correct, as outside experts tend to place the figure in the 8 to 12 percent range (Economy 2004, 88). Such admissions are typically followed by a call for local governments to pay more heed to the task of environmental protection. In time, these changes may lead to a greater willingness among local government officials to balance economic growth and ecological sustainability, but for the present China remains a country in which development of the economy is privileged above all else, including environmental protection.

China's Corporate Watchdogs—Little Bark, Little Bite

The fragmented environmental protection regime and growth-oriented local government elites make it difficult for local EPBs to enforce China's environmental laws and for citizens to express grievances against polluters. One additional element that hinders robust industrial environmental regulation is the relative feebleness of China's environmental community in terms of its ability to monitor corporate behavior. Since the establishment of China's first environmental non-governmental organization (ENGO) in 1994, the number of ENGOs and environmental student groups has increased rapidly, and today China has a vibrant environmental NGO community.[10] The growth of environmental NGOs has occurred in step with the greening of the Chinese media, which is often the strongest ally of China's environmental activists. By any measure, ENGO activity and media reporting of environmental problems are far more extensive and outspoken than just a decade ago. Investigative reporting that uncovers incidents of corporate malfeasance is increasingly common (see Chapter 6 for an example). These developments have led one well-known Chinese environmentalist to proclaim, "China has the greenest media in the world" (Yang 2005, 56).

Despite such proclamations, the influence of the environmental community remains marginal. This is due in large part to the fact that the Chinese government remains highly sensitive to collective efforts that have the potential to criticize the government. So environmental NGOs and their allies in the media, although widely recognized as freer than those working in other issue areas, are still extremely constrained. As Palmer states, "the political and legal milieu in the PRC is inimical for indigenous NGOs. . . . Authorities are not keen to encourage an organizational form that is often associated with political dissent" (1998, 795). Registration restrictions that require NGOs to find a government sponsor and various other legal measures mean that few environmental NGOs are officially registered as public organizations (many register as businesses or simply do not register). The environmental media faces a similar mix of autonomy and restraint—a situation that might be characterized as "freedom of the state-controlled press." A 1996 State Council document called for the media to denounce environmentally destructive behavior, but environmental journalists (like all members of the media) receive normative guidance and operational rules from the state via management structures (Wang Qing-Jie 2005). Topics that have been approved tend to generate a great deal of candid coverage, while others that are deemed too embarrassing to individuals, government agents, or corporations get blocked. The result is an inevitable tendency to self-censor among the members of the environmental media. One Chinese environmental journalist summarized the situation succinctly, stating: "As long as we do not cross the boundaries and limits set by the government, we have freedom to report what we want" (Hildebrandt and Turner 2002).

Not surprisingly, given their own tenuous existence, Chinese NGOs and the environmental media are typically hesitant to engage in confrontational efforts. Although there are a few exceptions, NGOs rarely introduce court cases on behalf of citizens and typically do not organize demonstrations or protest activities.[11] One NGO leader, explaining why he chooses workshops over protests, stated: "Survival is of paramount importance. Radical actions can get NGOs killed. Chinese NGOs cannot do as they please" (Lu 2007). Organizations that do confront the government, as was the case with the NGO Green Watershed in its opposition to dams on the Nu River, face the possibility of retaliatory tactics by local governments. While Wen Jiabao ordered an investigation into the dams, the Yunnan government ordered an investigation into Green Watershed and restricted its activities as well as the travel plans of its director.

Unfortunately, such retaliation is common. Wu Lihong, an activist who worked for years to expose companies contributing to pollution in Tai Lake and whose efforts led to the shuttering of almost two hundred companies, was beaten by local thugs and arrested on trumped-up charges of blackmail by the local government. This is in spite of the fact that he was awarded a top environmental award by Beijing (Economy 2007b). Not surprisingly, most NGOs have largely limited their activities to education and raising awareness. While this educational role is undoubtedly necessary to achieving better environmental quality in China, it nonetheless means that the overwhelming majority of companies in China feel at best modest pressure of ENGOs looking over their shoulders.

This is not to say that China's environmental community is inert. In recent years, it has on occasion demonstrated an admirable willingness to take advantage of the political space afforded it and challenge corporations and government officials (Economy 2004, 131–75). Much of this increased activity has been aimed at preventing the construction of hydro-dams, but occasionally it has occurred in the area of corporate liability. Greenpeace now has an office in Beijing and, as described in Chapter 6, has worked to expose corporate malfeasance in the environmental arena. As discussed in the previous chapter, in late 2006 Ma Jun's Institute of Public and Environmental Affairs broke new ground by posting on its website a list of 2,500 companies accused of polluting China's water system. These are important efforts, but such examples remain more the exception than the norm, and there is nothing in China akin to the corporate watchdogs that exist in the West or even in many other developing countries.

Balancing State, Market, and Society:
New Directions in Environmental Governance

As in other countries, the government is the major actor in China's environmental protection. For most of the past thirty years, China's environmental protection regime has been dominated by a "command and control" approach: the national government sets standards and discharge limits, which are passed down through the various levels of administration to county EPBs, which are charged with enforcement. However, over the last decade the shortcomings of the top-down command-and-control system, particularly in the area of implementation and industrial compliance, have become increasingly clear. The failings have become evident not only in the inability of Beijing to meet stated targets for measures of environmental quality, but in the rise of environmental protests. As mentioned in the previous chapter, in 2005 the number of environmental protests increased by 30 percent to more than 50,000. China's continued environmental degradation and the social instability to which it has given rise, along with its exposure to the international community, has served to move Beijing away from end-of-the-pipe solutions and to make increased use of flexible market mechanisms to control industrial pollution (Lin Shuwen 2004). In a similar vein, Beijing has also established a number of environmental information disclosure programs, which along with the market instruments are designed to permit a greater number of actors to participate in the process of governing the environmental practices of industry. Compared to years past, citizens, the media, financial institutions, and NGOs all play a more prominent role in holding industry accountable, creating what Shi and Zhang refer to as a "multi-actor environmental governance model." They argue that "one can no longer understand China's industrial pollution control regime when civil society and markets are ignored or made solely dependent upon the state" (2006, 279). This is not to say that the state has ceded control to the market or society. Environmental protection, like all important political issues, remains the purview of state authorities. Markets and economic actors at best influence companies' environmental behavior at the margins. But the government has shown an impressive willingness to experiment with new tools in order to moderate the environmental impact of China's rapid economic growth.

The Use of Market Incentives

In recent years, China has rolled out a dizzying array of market-based environmental programs, leading one scholar to refer to China as undergoing the "economisation of environmental governance" (Economy 2006). When SEPA was promoted to MEP in early 2008, director Zhou Shengxian stated that MEP's mission is "to deal with mounting environmental woes caused by previously rapid growth, and to try innovative means and tools to curb new problems." According to *China Daily*, Zhou indicated that the solution to China's "mounting environmental woes . . . lay in measures including law enforcement and market mechanisms" (Li Jing 2008a).

Traditional market-based programs include those that use economic instruments, such as levies and taxes, to provide a financial incentive to businesses to limit their pollution. The pollution levy and discharge permit systems, which date back to the 1980s, have been the traditional heart of China's market-based strategy. (The systems are described in Table 2.2.)[12] In 2003, about 1.3 million businesses paid pollution levies, most of which were industrial enterprises violating the national pollution discharge standards (Shi and Zhang 2006, 272). There is some evidence that the pollution levy has influenced firm behavior in a manner beneficial for environmental protection (Jiang and McKibben 2002; Wang and Wheeler 2005), but the programs have well-established flaws.[13] Most notably, fees for violating China's discharge standards are insufficient to motivate industry to alter its behavior. Jilin Chemical, the company responsible for the spill that dumped one hundred tons of benzene into the Songhua River and cut off drinking water to almost four million people for several days, was fined the maximum penalty under Chinese law. This amounted to only $125,000, while the estimated cost to the government for the cleanup was $1.2 billion (Xinhua 2007). Not surprisingly, many companies simply choose to continue violating discharge standards rather than invest in pollution abatement facilities. With the revision of the Water Pollution Prevention and Control Law in 2008, fines were increased and enterprises are now responsible for 30 percent of the economic loss associated with cases of "serious" water pollution and 20 percent of the loss associated with incidents having "medium consequences" (Li Jing 2008a). It remains to be seen whether the fee increase will change the compliance calculus for enterprises in China.[14]

More recent market-based programs also include a series of policies that aim to bring financial markets and actors such as banks and insurance companies into the environmental arena to serve as an additional influence on corporate environmental behavior. In 2007, SEPA announced the launching of a "green credit" policy to prevent bank loans to industries in energy- and pollution-intensive sectors. A year later this was followed up with a "green insurance" program intended to compel companies to purchase insurance for industrial accidents. For more than a decade, China has been building a "green securities" or "green listing" program that requires companies applying to issue shares on the Chinese stock market to include in their prospectus an explanation of environmental risks associated with their investment project. Listing firms must also state whether their operations comply with national environmental standards and whether they have violated standards in the last three years (Li et al. 2008).

Historically, these listing requirements have been ignored. In 2008, an MEP deputy director indicated that only half of listed companies in China included information on environmental performance and even those that did offered "only qualitative descriptions" and "scantily useful facts" (Sun 2008b). This listing requirement was given added teeth in early 2008, when MEP indicated it was stepping up enforcement and issued the "Guiding Opinions on Strengthening the Supervision and Management of Environmental Protection of Listed Companies" (SEPA, 2008). According to this document, MEP would require all cross-provincial companies in pollution- and energy-intensive sectors to comply with the listing requirements and disclose the relevant environmental data. This included firms already listed as well as those applying for an IPO (Initial Public Offering) or seeking to refinance. At the same time, MEP announced that in conjunction with the China Securities Regulatory Commission, it had rejected the IPO applications of ten of thirty-seven companies between 2004 and 2007 (Sun 2008a).

Finally, there are market-based strategies that aim to enhance the influence of citizens and consumers over corporate environmental behavior. This includes the promotion of the ISO 14000 system, through which companies have their environmental management program certified as in accordance with international standards by external third parties. China has also spent several years building a green label system. Both programs allow companies to burnish their environmental credentials and presumably enhance their appeal to consumers. Heavily promoted by the government, these programs have expanded rapidly in recent years. When China's environmental labeling regime was first established in 1994, twelve products were selected for development of eco-label standards.[15] By 1996, that number had been expanded to forty-three, but there were still few firms applying for certification. Over the next few years the program steadily expanded so that, by 2002, three hundred firms and approximately one thousand products had been certified as eligible to use environmental labels. NGOs have joined the effort to help consumers purchase green products. For instance, one can visit the "China's Green Pages" to find information on environmentally friendly products.

Market-based strategies designed to enhance the power of consumers also include programs such as the China Green Watch, in which local EPBs rank companies in terms of their environmental behavior on a five-point color scale—from green to black—and then publish the results in local newspapers (see Chapter 6). Like many of the "name and shame" lists experimented with across China, such as those in Chongqing, Anhui, and Shandong (Guo 2005), the intended aim is to create public pressure on firms that violate the law, while rewarding those that go beyond compliance. In May 2008, MEP took the endeavor of environmental disclosure a step further when the "Measures on Open Environmental Information (Trial)" came into effect (SEPA 2007). This regulation requires governments to disclose "on their own initiative" a variety of environmental data, including information on corporate environmental behavior. EPBs must provide a list of enterprises with "severe pollution" or whose pollution discharges exceed local or national standards, as well as companies that have experienced pollution accidents or refused to act on administrative penalty decisions (SEPA 2007, Article 11, items 13 and 14). A firm placed on these lists is itself required to disclose a variety of information, including the total volume of major pollution discharges and the status of its environmental protection facilities (SEPA 2007, Article 20). All companies are "encouraged" to provide a host of information, such as their environmental management policies and annual resource consumption.

The majority of these programs are less than a decade old and it is safe to say that the use of market mechanisms in industrial environmental regulation is in an embryonic stage in China. As one might expect, these programs have yet to exert a significant influence on companies operating in China. In a survey of Chinese Fortune 500 companies, among the roughly one-third of sample firms that replied to the rather loaded question, "Why is environmental care important to you?" only 28 percent indicated customer demand had an influence (Lei et al. 2005). In another survey, 44 percent of companies engaging in environmental reporting indicated that they did so due to market pressure, and 21 percent attributed it to public pressure (Guo 2005). The firms included in these surveys represent China's largest and most visible companies. Suffice it to say that the large number of companies that escape both government and public notice feel even less market and public pressure.

The primary reason markets have yet to exert much pressure on corporate environmental behavior is that, despite the repeated calls by MEP officials for greater disclosure of information and the enhanced role of the Chinese media in reporting environmental problems, environmental information is still subject to government control, and China has a long way to go in building a culture of transparency. It is entirely common for both government agencies and enterprises to falsify or simply refuse to release information that might portray the enterprise in a negative light (Guo 2005; Li et al. 2008). In my own attempts to gather the names of firms included in the Green Watch program, I was often refused or only offered the list of green firms. The tight control of government agents over environmental data is also illustrated by the March 2007 case in which Chinese officials pressured the World Bank to remove its estimate of 750,000 pollution-related premature deaths from its report *The Cost of Pollution in China*. Similarly, in 2006, in part as a response to the Songhua River spill, the NPC considered regulations that would fine the media for reporting sudden events "without authorization," although this clause was eventually dropped. The challenge of environmental disclosure is also evident in the numerous problems with the Green GDP program, which was aimed at including environmental criteria in calculations of GDP. The original goal was to account for the costs of pollution and to spur government officials to balance economic growth and environmental protection. Highly touted as an example of China's increased concern with the environment when it was announced by Hu Jintao in 2004, the program ran into a host of political opponents, many of whom refused to release information that would show the true extent of environmental damage in their regions. The Green GDP figures for 2004, which were not released until 2007, were widely believed to underestimate the economic cost of China's pollution (Economy 2007a). The 2005 figures were never released, and the program, as of mid-2007, has been scrapped (Spencer 2007).

Aside from the sensitivity of releasing information, other factors inhibit the effectiveness of market initiatives in influencing corporate behavior. First, China's green markets are still relatively small. According to a manager of the China Consumers' Association, "a large percentage of Chinese consumers are still facing more basic concerns than questions on the environmental performance of goods and services" (Martens 2006, 221–22). Consumers' green demands are simply not a source of pressure for the vast majority of firms in China. A lack of technical personnel is also a perennial problem. This is especially the case with regard to ISO 14000 and green labeling programs, which require a large pool of experts to certify companies' environmental management practices.

The lack of qualified professionals often contributes to an additional problem—corruption. As ISO 14000 certification and green labels have gained both cachet and potential market value, counterfeits and corruption have become abundant. Firm representatives with whom I spoke about their ISO experience are dubious about the quality of the process. For instance, one representative from a domestic firm that achieved ISO certification in 1999 was highly disparaging of the current state of ISO certification in her region. She indicated that when her firm went through the process, and there were only a limited number of consulting companies from which to choose in order to aid the process, ISO certification required multiple inspections. Today, a firm can shop around until it finds a consulting company that will fill out all the paperwork and never inspect the company's production facilities. Another company had a dispute with a consulting firm that was supposed to train employees in preparation for ISO certification. The consulting firm charged 80,000 RMB (roughly $10,000), but conducted only one class and then offered to provide paperwork stating that the firm's employees were ISO qualified.[16]

The Chinese media during recent years has been full of stories lamenting the widespread use of counterfeit environmental labels and the propensity of firms to make spurious environmental claims about their product for the purpose of enhancing market appeal (Chen and Chen 2004; Wang Wei 2002; Wang and Li 2001; Ze 2004). The problem has been particularly acute in the home appliances and electronics, building materials, and food sectors. Illegal behavior ranges from outright counterfeiting of official environmental labels to false claims about products' environmental credentials (such as "health protecting" air conditioners) to fake credentialing by nonlicensed ersatz organizations with lofty environmental names.[17]

Another variant of the problem of fraudulent environmental claims, which is most common in the building materials industry, occurs when firms are compliant only with basic regulations, but deem such behavior "environmental" and so freely use eco-labels.[18] These firms are either unaware or choose to ignore the fact that environmental certification requirements are far more demanding than basic domestic law. This is not simply a problem of firm malfeasance, but often involves government, as local officials, seeking to be leaders in the environmental field, issue recommendation letters praising the environmental practices of local firms that comply with basic regulations. For instance, Chinese law requires that water-based paint should have less than two hundred grams of volatile organic compounds (VOC).[19] To be certified as "environmental," the paint must have less than one hundred grams. The problem is that firms that reach the two-hundred-gram level are sometimes awarded green labels. This problem has been severe enough to generate a series of meetings between officials from SEPA and the Commission on Product Environmental Label Certification (*Zhongguo Huanjing Biaozhi Chanpin Renzheng Weiyuanhui*). The committee conducted an investigation and found more than fifty kinds of paint that falsely used environmental labels—over half of which were from Guangdong (Jian 2002).

The problem is not limited to Guangdong but ranges across China's east coast. In the northern city of Harbin (Heilongjiang Province) the municipal EPB conducted an undercover investigation of twelve enterprises using environmental labels. Five of the firms were either using expired certificates or failed to produce evidence that their products had been officially certified (Wang Yihui 2003). Another article cites an official in the Shanghai Commercial Bureau who indicated that in a recent government crackdown, government authorities discovered more than 650 paint products with fake environmental labels. This led the reporter to conclude, "If one were to use a single word to describe China's green product market, it would be 'chaos'" (Wu and Pan 2002). Other observers reach equally gloomy assessments, such as one journalist who states: "After 10 years of development, China's green products market has basically formed. However, due to the market's disorderly development and some enterprise's false advertising, people cannot help worrying about the future development of China's green product market" (Zhao Shanxiong 2003).

The potential importance of ISO certification or a green label to a firm's bottom line, combined with inadequate government resources to govern the market and the very speed with which the government has pushed the development of market-based strategies such as green certification, has undermined some of the success achieved in firm environmental management. It is too early to tell if the growth of counterfeit certifications will completely undermine the value of being certified, but clearly some in the media are not optimistic. It is possible that in the absence of greater government oversight, market-based mechanisms such as ISO certification and green labels will be of modest use either as an indicator of a firm's environmental management or in pushing companies in China to place greater stress on pollution abatement.

The Power of Participation

As with market-based incentives, public participation is becoming an increasingly important element in industrial environmental regulation. Although China has a long tradition of offering government-sanctioned and controlled outlets for citizens to voice grievances, in recent years Beijing has experimented with new mechanisms to promote citizen input into environmental protection. Compared to any time in China's past, citizens today have a greater variety of channels through which to voice their opinions about the environmental practices of local companies.

Among the most widely hailed developments is the public participation requirement of the Environmental Impact Assessment Law, which took effect in 2003, and its implementing measures, which were issued in 2006. These laws mandate public participation in the EIA approval process for industrial and government projects that have a major environmental impact. They also require that the developer and EPB disclose key information to the public at relevant points during the EIA approval process and oblige the government to institute a mechanism for collecting public opinion. Although still in its infancy, the EIA Law has allowed the public to exert some degree of influence. Perhaps most famously, in 2005 the Beijing municipal government was forced to alter its plan to line lake bottoms in the Old Summer Palace with plastic to prevent unwanted drainage. First noticed by a professor visiting the Old Summer Palace, the local EPB concluded that the park administration had conducted its lake-lining project in violation of the EIA law. This eventually led to a public hearing in which seventy-three members of the public participated.

Despite these advances, the ability of Chinese citizens to influence corporate behavior via the EIA public participation mechanism remains of modest influence. A number of obstacles hamper its effectiveness. For example, the standard under which the government should accept or reject public concerns remains unclear. Government officials are more prone to use public hearings to justify decisions already made than to attempt to incorporate public opinion, a phenomenon sometimes referred to as "hearing held, final decision approved" (*feng ting bi guo*) (Moore and Warren 2006, 16). A lack of NGOs in China to represent citizen interests and provide expertise also hampers public input in the EIA process (Gu and Sheate 2004, 138–39). Also, environmental authorities still typically fail to make EIA reports publicly available, even when explicitly requested. The more significant and controversial the environmental impact, the less likely they are to disclose the EIA. It took more than two years of NGO pressure for the government to release the EIA for the series of dams on the Nu River. Often, EIAs are made public only after construction has begun, which defeats the purpose of allowing public concerns to be incorporated into the design of the project (Moore and Warren 2006).

Another relatively new mechanism for citizen input is the environmental complaint system, through which citizens can voice concerns about pollution via petitions, letters, and phone calls. Formally established in 1990, the program has expanded substantially over the last two decades. In 2004, the number of people sending letters and visiting EPBs was more than 726,000, an increase of 410 percent over 1991. Between 2001 and 2005, SEPA received 2.53 million letters and 430,000 visits from 597,000 petitioners seeking compensation for pollution damage (Alex Wang 2007). Approximately two-thirds of local EPBs have established hotlines to facilitate environmental complaints (Brettell 2008). For instance, since 2000, Shanghai has maintained the "Green 110" hotline. The former director of the Shanghai EPB (SEPB) called it "SEPB's most important enforcement tool" (Warwick and Ortolano 2007, 241). After receiving a complaint, the EPB uses an in-house global information system to locate the address at which the problem has been discovered and then searches a database for nearby enterprises so that possible pollution sources are identified before the inspectors reach the scene. In 2001, the SEPB received almost 28,000 calls, more than 76 per day, which resulted in just under 3,400 inspections and the discovery of 430 violations (Warwick and Ortolano 2007).

Clearly the expansion of the complaint system is a positive development that has the potential to compel companies to place greater stress on environmental protection. As Warwick and Ortolano note (2007, 259), "the establishment of a complaint system is an important step towards greater transparency and citizen involvement in environmental protection in China." There are still several problems, however, that limit the ability of citizen complaints to influence government enforcement and company environmental practices. The most prominent is the frequent failure of the government to respond to citizen complaints. For every anecdote highlighting how the complaint system has contributed to stronger enforcement, there seems to be one in which petitioners were stifled or made the object of retribution (Brettell 2008). In a survey in Anqing (Anhui), 75 percent of respondents indicated that they had declined to take action to address a known environmental problem. Among these respondents, 50 percent indicated that taking action was useless. As citizens are well aware, if local government authorities are loath to take action, complainants have little recourse. A lack of awareness of the complaint system also hampers its effectiveness, as 50 percent of Anqing residents indicated they failed to take action because they were unaware of what to do (Alford et al. 2002, 506–7). The result is that the citizen input mechanisms have failed to have a demonstrable effect on environmental protection. Brettell (2008) looks for correlations between the number of complaints and various measures of pollution and finds no relationship. This statistical finding, along with the various problems associated with the complaint system, leads her to conclude that a lack of citizen input remains a major obstacle to implementation of China's environmental laws.

Conclusion

China's environmental protection system, like the larger state in which it is situated, is one in which there is overlapping authority between bureaucracies and a prominent role for local governments, which are not always inclined toward stringent environmental protection. Despite the progress in recent years, China's courts, social organizations, and citizens are unable to serve as a consistently effective safeguard against companies that violate pollution standards or against government officials who fail to implement China's environmental regulations. Beijing has trotted out a wealth of new initiatives designed to increase the power of markets, economic actors, and average citizens vis-à-vis industrial enterprises. But for a number of reasons ranging from insufficient capacity to local government intransigence to outright corruption, these programs have yet to become a consistent source of pressure on corporate environmental behavior. In terms of industrial environmental regulation, companies in China operate in a permissive regulatory setting.

Although this chapter paints a rather grim picture of China's environmental protection system, it should be placed in a proper context. First, as noted at the outset, in a little less than three decades China has built an environmental protection regime virtually from scratch. Despite the shortcomings of the system, China has achieved some noteworthy successes. For instance, China has lowered the gross output of key pollutants, such as SO_2 and soot, which is a noteworthy accomplishment considering the speed of China's economic expansion (Ho and Vermeer 2006, 258, table 1). It is also managing to meet its commitments to international environmental agreements, such as promises to reduce or eliminate ozone-depleting substances made under the Montreal Protocol (Zhao Jimin 2005). Accomplishments such as these are discussed further in Chapter 4, which focuses more on implementation of environmental law, but for the moment the point is that China's successes in environmental protection should not be overlooked or discounted.

Second, it should be pointed out that a weak regulatory setting is not unique to China. Indeed, most developing countries face formidable challenges in controlling environmental degradation. Comparative cross-national studies of environmental performance have, not surprisingly, shown that factors commonly associated with developing countries, such as low per capita income and ineffectual judicial systems, are associated with weak environmental protection (Dasgupta et al. 2001). Many developing countries, cognizant of the fact that environmental problems cannot be solved in the context of poverty, are unwilling to sacrifice economic for environmental interests. Newly industrialized Asian countries, much like China, have shown a particular reluctance to crack down on polluting industries when it means forfeiting economic development (World Bank 1997).[20] Thus, it should not be assumed that the problems described in this chapter make China singular. The problems China faces with regard to regulating the pollution output of industry are similar to those faced by many developing countries.

This chapter has shown that China has constructed an impressive foundation for environmental protection, but enduring flaws provide ample opportunity for companies, including foreign-invested enterprises, to evade environmental regulation. The questions that remain are: Given this permissive domestic setting, what effect does opening the economy to foreign investors have? Does competing for foreign investment make local governments more apt to ignore environmental rules in order to attract investors? Do foreign firms aid or hinder local EPB officials in their effort to protect the environment? How does interaction with foreign firms affect the behavior of domestic firms? It is to these questions that the remaining chapters turn.

3 Greening Foreign Investment: China's Legal Framework

Why Start with the Legal Framework?

To what extent do foreign-invested enterprises comply with China's environmental laws? Do government regulators enforce regulation or does the desire to attract foreign capital take precedence over and undermine environmental protection laws? Before we can answer these questions, we must know more about the laws China has developed to control the pollution impact of foreign investment. In other words, it is necessary to analyze the specific legal framework in which foreign investment occurs. The previous chapter began this process by broadly introducing China's environmental laws and organizations. This chapter continues the discussion by analyzing in greater detail the regulatory framework that polices the environmental protection aspects of foreign investment in China.

The concern of this chapter is not only with introducing the legal regime governing environmental aspects of FDI, but also with showing how this regime has developed over time and, more importantly, how it reflects the problems confronting Chinese regulators in the process of governing FDI. Specifically, this chapter answers questions such as: How has the Chinese central government responded to the need to regulate the environmental behavior of foreign firms? What are the principal challenges and concerns that national environmental authorities face in regulating the environmental aspects of FDI, and how have these challenges evolved over time? To what extent does the development of China's environmental law reflect the expectations of scholars concerned with the potential negative effects of global investment on environmental protection? Has China experienced a regulatory chill in industrial environmental regulation that has served to turn China into a pollution haven? The focus here is on legislation (i.e., the creation of law), which is a necessary precursor to the discussion of enforcement and compliance that follows in subsequent chapters.

The analysis below relies primarily on an analysis of Chinese-language legal texts published since the start of the reform period in 1978.[1] To a lesser extent, it also utilizes comparative environmental law scholarship and Chinese-language secondary sources. There is a relatively large Chinese-language literature dealing with trade, FDI, and the environment, a portion of which addresses the legal aspects of FDI environmental governance. Yet this Chinese literature tends to focus attention more on firms and less on the actions of the government. On the issue of government action, the analysis tends to be highly positive and somewhat superficial. As such, it is a challenge to uncover the principal concerns and issues Chinese environmental authorities face in governing foreign-invested enterprises.

However, the basic texts of Chinese law offer insight into the path of China's legal development and provide a sense about the extent to which the governance of foreign investment has been a concern for environmental authorities. In the late 1970s, China had virtually no laws regulating foreign investment. Since the start of the reform period, China has issued hundreds if not thousands of legal documents dealing with foreign capital and investment (including those issued at the local level).[2] As one might expect, most have little to do with environmental protection and are related to the technical, economic, and administrative aspects of investment. There is nonetheless a growing body of law that deals with the environmental elements of foreign investment in China. These regulations reflect the concerns of central government authorities and are designed to address the chief environmental problems related to foreign firms. Therefore, China's legal texts are useful both for analyzing the issues confronting government regulators and for tracing official responses to the evolving challenge of governing the pollution control practices of foreign-invested firms.

The sheer variety of Chinese legal instruments also aids in the process of tracing the government's response to the environmental challenges of increased foreign investment. China's complex legal system is comprised not only of statutes created by the central government bodies such as the National People's Congress, the State Council, and the administrative bodies of the State Council such as MEP, but also a variety of other secondary legal instruments. This includes notices (*tongzhi*), opinions (*yijian*), directives (*zhishi*), catalogues (*mulu*), decisions (*jueding*), and many other similar types of circulations. The secondary instruments are typically released by the State Council, but are often issued by specific administrative departments within the State Council, such as MEP or the Ministry of Commerce. On occasion, the Central Committee of the Communist Party also issues a public notice. These instruments typically address gaps or ambiguities in the existing law, provide guidelines for implementation, or simply speak to a particular legal issue. Quite often, legal notices related to environmental protection introduce no new decrees, but serve to identify a problem and to remind lower-level government organs of the need to implement existing laws. As such, they are a reflection of central government concerns and responses to the twin challenges of protecting the environment and attracting foreign investment.

The argument of this chapter is straightforward. Over the last quarter century China has developed an increasingly stringent and detailed set of guidelines for governing the environmental protection component of foreign investment. In the early 1980s, China's foreign-investment laws contained few provisions dealing with pollution control. Today, there is a relatively comprehensive set of rules and guidelines designed to increase the likelihood that foreign-investment projects address environmental protection in their design and operation. These rules are based on two main regulatory pillars—the foreign-investment approval process and technology or production process guidelines. In both of these areas, China has made significant strides in developing legislation that guards against environmentally harmful foreign-investment projects. China's progress in creating laws to control foreign firms' environmental practices is notable because it has taken place in a climate in which foreign investors have been granted a host of legal privileges vis-à-vis domestic firms. Since the early days of the reform era, Beijing has forwarded numerous legal incentives and protections that collectively serve to favor foreign investors over domestic firms. Yet it has not extended foreign privileges to the arena of environmental regulation. Domestic and foreign firms face a similar environmental legal regime. Further, China's progress in establishing a legal environmental framework compares favorably with other countries at a similar income level. The conclusion is that China has made both absolute and relative progress in the development of environmental law. At least in terms of legislation at the national level, there is little evidence that foreign investment has had a chilling effect on environmental protection. Put another way, when one looks at trends in environmental law, there is little evidence that the quest for FDI is turning China into a pollution haven.

The Early 1980s: An Absence of Pollution Control

At the onset of the reform period, there were only a handful of clauses in China's domestic law that put restrictions on foreign (or domestic) firm environmental behavior. The 1979 Law on Chinese-Foreign Equity Joint Ventures had merely two clauses tangentially related to environmental protection (NPC 1979a).[3] Article 2 stated that all joint venture activities are subject to the laws of the People's Republic of China, and Article 5 stated: "The technology or equipment contributed by any foreign party as investment shall be genuinely advanced and appropriate to China's needs. In cases of losses caused by deception (*jinxing qipian*) through the intentional provision of outdated equipment or technology, compensation shall be paid" (NPC 1979a). The "Implementing Regulations" for the JV Law, issued four years later in 1983, specified that projects should not be approved if they are polluting. But nowhere in its 118 articles did it offer clues as to what sort of projects should be deemed polluting (State Council 1983a).

The Implementing Regulations specified three categories for which joint ventures were permitted, the last of which was those "clearly capable of saving raw materials, fuel, or power" (State Council 1983a, Article 28). But beyond these broad statements, the joint venture laws offered no guidelines concerning the environmental requirements of foreign investment. Moreover, although the Implementing Regulations listed the required information a foreign partner must submit for approval of a joint venture, including detailed information about the project's technology, it notably did not stipulate investors tender an environmental impact report. In fact, despite several clauses describing the investment approval process, there is no mention of the environmental protection criteria needed for project approval.

This lack of mention of an environmental impact assessment in the Implementing Regulations is noteworthy because it demonstrates the weakness of the environmental impact assessment (EIA) requirement during the early reform period. In 1981, the State Planning Commission, State Economic and Trade Commission (SETC), and State Council Environmental Protection Leadership Small Group passed the "Administrative Measures for Basic Construction Projects' Environmental Protection" (State Planning Commission et al. 1981).[4] This "Measures" document is important because it laid the foundation for one of the main pillars of Chinese law governing firm environmental behavior—the environmental impact assessment system. Yet at the same time it was also relatively feeble and reflective of the virtually nonexistent environmental oversight of foreign firms in the early reform period.[5]

Designed when the Chinese industrial economy was still overwhelmingly driven by central planning, the Measures were directed principally at local governments rather than firms. The Measures required an environmental impact assessment report be included as part of the feasibility study report (FSR), which is the principal document requiring approval from government bodies prior to an investment project. The FSR is typically approved by the industrial bureau (and at that time the planning bureau) overseeing the project. Therefore, the local bureau of the Chemical Ministry would approve the FSR for a project to produce dye. According to the 1981 regulation, the EIA section of the FSR should be approved by the local environmental protection bureau (EPB), but there were few details about the approval process. Rather, almost every major decision was left to the discretion of local industrial bureaus.

For instance, there was no indication in the Measures whether the government organ receiving the FSR, or the construction enterprise itself, was responsible for giving the FSR to the EPB. The law merely stipulated that the planning and industrial bureaus "exchange views" (*cuo shang*) with the EPB during the process of approving the various required documents, which at best is a weak condition and easily allowed EPBs to be shut out of the process. There was also minimal discussion of penalties for failure to obtain EPB approval. Also, the Measures applied only to large-scale projects; the method for governing environmental management practices for all other types of projects were explicitly left to the preferences of local governments (State Planning Commission et al. 1981, Article 5). "Large-scale" was not defined. In short, there was ample room for local interpretation of the environmental protection requirements of investment projects.

Interestingly, there was no mention in the Measures of whether the regulation applied to foreign-investment projects. Given the requirement in the Joint Venture Law that JVs abide by Chinese laws, the applicability of the Measures would not seem an issue. By contrast, subsequent Chinese laws typically stipulate specifically and unequivocally the law's application to foreign-invested firms, including those from Hong Kong, Taiwan, and Macau. Moreover, the absence of the EIA requirement in the 1983 Implementing Regulations casts doubt as to whether the Measures applied to foreign firms. In short, although an important foundation for future EIA regulation, in the early 1980s the existing EIA requirements were weak, vague, and of questionable applicability to foreign-investment projects.

Another aspect of China's early environmental law that left foreign firms largely unregulated is that, although early JV laws stipulated foreign-invested enterprises were formally subject to Chinese law, there were few existing environmental statutes in the early 1980s. Only a handful of China's main environmental laws were created before the late 1980s (see Chapter 2, Table 2.1). The Pollution Levy System was not established until 1982 and prior to 1984 China had no forestry, air, water, soil, or solid waste laws. Only the Measures and the broad outlines of the 1979 Environmental Protection Law (EPL) regulated foreign-firm behavior (NPC 1979b). The 1979 EPL formally introduced the "three simultaneous program" (*san tong shi*) and the "polluter pays" principle. It also prohibited certain actions, such as the establishment of polluting industries in residential areas and dumping garbage into water. But for the most part the EPL simply promoted broad guidelines such as urging enterprises to "Strengthen business management and carry out civilized production" (NPC 1979b, Section 3, Article 18). The lack of emphasis among regulators on governing the environmental behavior of foreign investment is also seen in the fact that during the first half of the 1980s several directives related to foreign investment were dispensed, but none focused on environmental issues. One 1983 State Council document, entitled "Directive on Work Related to Enhancing the Use of Foreign Capital," is similar to the aforementioned Implementing Regulations of the JV Law and typical of the period in its lack of environmental protection content (State Council 1983b). The "Directive," more a political than a legal text, put forward the argument that FDI and foreign capital are beneficial for China and aid the process of development. Even though it specified ten areas in which China should improve the use of FDI, all of them had to do with the economic aspects of attracting FDI (such as preferential policies, import quotas, and market opening). There was no mention of environmental protection or pollution abatement, which stands in stark contrast to later State Council notices concerning foreign investment.

In large part, this absence of environmental protection provisions reflects the earliest stages of the reform period, when investment levels were low and the foremost concern of China's leaders was assuring capital inflow and maximizing technology transfer. But as is the case with the Equity Joint Venture Law, the Directive is symbolic in that it shows that through much of the 1980s there was little environmental regulation to shape the operations of foreign enterprises. By 1985 China utilized roughly $5 billion in FDI and by 1989 over $16 billion, which is equivalent to approximately 22,000 contracts (U.S. Department of State 2005; US-China Business Council 2006). For most of these investors, pollution abatement was largely voluntary.

The Mid-1980s and Early 1990s: More Recognition than Action

Throughout the course of the 1980s and early 1990s, Chinese authorities became increasingly aware of the environmental hazards of unsupervised foreign investment. In 1986, China issued the first directive dedicated principally to problems with foreign investment and environmental protection, entitled "Temporary Regulations on Environmental Management in Economic Development Zones" (State Council 1986). Approved by the State Council and issued by the National Environmental Protection Administration (NEPA), the document was aimed principally at the local government officials overseeing the construction of Economic Development and Technology Zones (EDTZs).[6] It contained no new regulations, but rather served as an admonition to local governments and investing enterprises to obey existing law.

For instance, the "Temporary Regulations" reaffirmed that local governments must treat environmental protection as one of their primary goals and that pollution-intensive projects are forbidden in certain areas (e.g., residential areas, nature reserves, and areas close to water sources). These clauses were taken almost verbatim from the 1979 Environmental Protection Law. The 1986 notice also made clear the requirement that enterprises gain approval for their environmental impact report and submit information about pollutant discharges (e.g., type, amount, concentration, and abatement measures) to the relevant local environmental authorities. The notice reiterated that both sides (firms and local government) must be clear about their environmental responsibilities prior to the signing of any contracts. The wording of these clauses was virtually the same as various articles in the 1979 EPL and the State Council document discussing the 1982 Pollution Levy System (State Council 1982). The fact that this document repeated word for word clauses from existing environmental law, and then tied them to the environmental management practices of investment projects in zones set up for foreign companies, is one early indication that the central government was increasingly aware that China was having problems controlling pollution as it eagerly sought to lure foreign investment.

Other documents from this period reveal a growing concern with FIEs' environmental behavior. In 1986, China passed the Law of the People's Republic of China on Foreign Capital Enterprises (NPC 1986b). Much like the 1979 Equity Joint Venture Law, the Foreign Capital Enterprise Law laid out the basic rights and obligations of foreign-invested firms and offered a broad outline of the investment process. Many of the critical details of the Foreign Capital Enterprise Law were not codified for another four years, when the State Council released the "Detailed Rules for the Implementation of Wholly Foreign-owned Enterprises Law" (State Council 1990). Unlike FDI governance documents in the first half of the 1980s, the "Detailed Rules" had some environmental content. For instance, it listed five broad conditions under which a foreign-invested project should be rebuffed, one of which included projects that "can possibly produce environmental pollution" (*keneng zaocheng huanjing wurande*). Much like the 1979 JV Law, it gave no specific indication of what sort of projects should be deemed polluting, but it nonetheless strengthened the foundation for incorporating environmental governance into the oversight of foreign investment.

Also in 1986, NEPA amended the "Administrative Measures for Basic Construction Projects' Environmental Protection"—the previously discussed document that had originally established China's environmental impact assessment system in 1981. Not only was the Measures document strengthened and clarified on a number of fronts, it also was modified so that it explicitly stated that EIA requirements apply to foreign-invested projects (State Council Environmental Protection Committee et al. 1986, Article 3). Shortly after the release of the amended Measures, the central government issued a flurry of other regulations that clarified and enhanced various aspects of the EIA system, including licensing requirements for organizations hired to conduct EIAs on behalf of construction projects, regulations governing fee collection for EIAs, and detailed descriptions of the EIA approval process. The result was that foreign firms were now, at least on paper, firmly included in China's increasingly robust environmental impact assessment system.

Over the course of the early 1990s, the central government continued to show growing concern with foreign investors' environmental management practices. In 1992, NEPA and MOFERT (Ministry of Foreign Economic Relations and Trade) released the "Notice on Strengthening the Environmental Management in Foreign Investment Construction Projects" (NEPA and MOFERT 1992).[7] Like many previous environment-related announcements, the 1992 "Notice" contained nothing new in terms of requirements for foreign-invested enterprises. Rather, it was another in a series of central government warnings to firms and especially local governments to place greater stress on the pollution abatement practices of foreign-invested enterprises. The notice, less than a page long, reiterated existing aspects of Chinese law such as: the requirement that foreign firms abide by Chinese laws and environmental programs such as the "three simultaneous," the prohibition of foreign investment in heavily polluting projects, and the obligation of FIEs to submit environmental impact reports for approval by government authorities. The notice also reminded local governments that no project is to be approved or initiated in the absence of an environmental impact report. Notably, it specifically mentioned that Hong Kong, Taiwanese, and Macau firms are subject to the same requirements as other foreign investors.[8] As was the case with previous documents, the language was familiar and much of the document was drawn directly from existing law. Although the notice was short and offered no new rules, it makes clear that Chinese regulators were increasingly worried about the lack of attention to environmental protection in the foreign-investment process.

Some of the environment-related secondary legal instruments released in the early 1990s help demonstrate the particular issues facing environmental regulators. One was the tendency of foreign firms to invest in pollution-intensive sectors. For instance, in 1993 Chinese authorities issued regulations related to the reprocessing of imported waste metals for export. Noting that in "recent years China has seen a relatively large increase in foreign-invested projects" of this kind, it reminded local governments that foreign investment in this area is "restricted" and should be managed stringently, and decreed that it is deemed "not suitable" (*bu yi*) to approve such projects (MOFTEC 1993).[9] A second problem was an abundance of projects that use outdated, heavily polluting technologies. For instance, a 1993 State Council document on how to improve the use of foreign investment warned that when the foreign side is investing technology and equipment, it is important to prevent the foreign partner from seeking unreasonable profits from "pretending good from inferior, pretending new with old" (*yi ci chong hao, yi jiu ding xin*) (State

Council 1993). As in many previous notices, the State Council emphasized that the way to solve this problem is to make sure the project goes through all the required approval channels.

Secondary legal instruments also indicate that in the late 1980s and early 1990s there were significant problems with the expanding environmental impact assessment system. In 1988, NEPA released "Some Opinions Concerning the Environmental Management of Construction Projects" (NEPA 1988). Although the "Opinions" document is not directed specifically to the issue of foreign investment, it is one of the more candid assessments of implementation problems in China's recent history of environmental legislation and highlighted many weaknesses in the EIA system. For instance, it discussed problems with EIA service agents, which are domestic organizations contracted by investors to conduct the EIA. With regard to the quality of EIA reports, it states: "In compiling the environmental impact report, because of the influence of traditions, there typically exist many practical weaknesses. . . . The evaluation's methodology is impractical, the evaluation period too long, the investigation of the pollution sources superficial, pollution prevention recommendations are not concrete, and the conclusions not clear." It notes that many government organs and EIA agents engage in "covert subcontracting" (*bianxiang zhuan jie zhuan bao*), whereby EIA agents give their EIA license to other organizations or government officials allow nonlicensed organizations to conduct EIAs. Other problems included government officials compelling investors to choose a particular EIA agent. The reason for this behavior is that government officials do not want "fertile water to flow away" (*feishui bu wai liu*) (NEPA 1988, Section 2.2). EIA fees, especially for large projects, can be considerable, and often the government officials who are approving projects want to make sure the fees remain within their own jurisdiction and flow to organizations in which they have a personal interest.

A subsequent 1993 document entitled "A Few Opinions on Making Progress in the Work of Administering the Environmental Protection of Construction Enterprises" reiterated some problems with the EIA system and added new ones such as the tendency to "construct first, approve later" (NEPA 1993). Most importantly, it explicitly addressed EIA issues related to foreign investment, imploring local governments to "prevent the transfer of pollution to China" by making sure that foreign-investment projects meet environmental standards and abide by national laws (NEPA 1993, Section 1.5). This emphasis on problems with pollution by foreign investors was further underscored by a discussion of problems with implementing environmental regulations in economic development zones, which particularly in the 1990s were the chief locus of foreign investment. Clear from these documents is that, despite the fact that China's EIA system underwent rapid expansion in the late 1980s, implementation was sporadic, and foreign (and domestic) firms often failed to comply.

In sum, evident in the Chinese legislation in the late 1980s and early 1990s is a growing concern among central government authorities with the environmental compliance of FIEs and especially local governments approving foreign-investment projects. The repeated publication of notices reminding local officials and enterprises of existing environmental protection requirements, and recurring exhortations to assure investment follows proper channels, point to the growth of a problem in the environmental management of FDI. At the same time, the lack of specificity in these documents suggests that central government authorities were either unwilling or unable to take additional steps to coerce local governments and foreign investors to make greater efforts toward pollution abatement. Local governments were told to reject projects that contribute to pollution, but the legal documents offered no specific criteria about what sorts of projects were permissible. Only the most basic penalty schedule was put forward for those who failed to submit environmental data or to gain approval for environmental impact reports. Much of the concrete information needed to implement the spirit of the law was missing, which meant that in practice discretion was left to firms and local governments.[10] It is clear from the documents that central government officials unquestionably recognized lack of local government enforcement as a fundamental problem in implementation. Thus this willingness to leave decision-making power in the hands of local governments shows a lack of power or desire to enhance environmental governance. In short, prior to the mid-1990s, among China's central government authorities there was recognition of a problem concerning FDI and the environment, but not much action.

The Mid-1990s to 2007: Establishing a More Robust Legal Framework

In the mid-1990s, matters began to change as Chinese authorities started creating a more comprehensive set of concrete regulations to oversee foreign investment. This period marks a significant tightening in the supervision of the environmental protection practices of foreign investors and economic development zones.

In 1995, the State Planning Commission, the State Economic and Trade Commission, and the Ministry of Foreign Trade and Economic Cooperation (MOFTEC) issued the "Provisions on Guiding the Orientation of Foreign Investment" (State Council 1995b) and the "Catalogue for the Guidance of Foreign Investment Industries" (State Council 1995a).[11] These documents in some ways completed the 1986 Foreign Enterprise Law, which had indicated that the State Council would issue guidelines concerning areas restricted for foreign investment. Both the "Provisions" and "Catalogue" were breakthroughs because they provided an appreciably more detailed overview of China's priorities in seeking foreign investment. This was accomplished through the categorization of over three hundred industries as either "encouraged," "restricted," or "prohibited." Sectors not in the Catalogue are deemed "permitted." In the wake of these documents, sectors labeled "encouraged" are eligible for preferential policies such as tax reductions.[12] Those that are restricted have to go through a more rigorous approval process involving either central government or local government inspection (depending on the size of the investment).[13]

As is evident in Table 3.1, the release of the 1995 Catalogue offered a dramatic increase in the amount of detail concerning central-government goals in inviting foreign investment. Prior to 1995, Chinese law specified only about 25 types of industries that were either encouraged or restricted and some of the categories, such as "chemical industry," were exceedingly broad. With the circulation of the 1995 Catalogue, 317 industries were divided among the three categories of "encouraged," "restricted," and "prohibited." This figure was later expanded to over 360 with amendments in 2002 and 2004. Admittedly, some of the industries listed in the 1995 Catalogue were still ambiguous, such as "special cement," but it represents a clear step forward in the development of China's legal framework for governing foreign direct investment.

The 1995 Catalogue and subsequent amendments had significant implications for the environmental governance of FDI. This point, however, should not be exaggerated. Both the Provisions and the Catalogue, like virtually all China's foreign-investment policies, were designed chiefly for the purpose of harnessing foreign capital toward the goal of developing China's national economy. Environmental protection was undoubtedly a considerably less im-

TABLE 3.1 China's expanding legislative framework governing FDI

Legal document	Year	Encouraged industries (#)	Restricted industries (#)	Prohibited industries (#)
Detailed Rules for Implementing Foreign Capital Enterprises Law	1983	20 broad categories[a]	5 broad conditions[b]	—
Catalogue for the Guidance of Foreign Investment Industries[c]	1995	172	114	31
	1997	185	111	30
	2002	262	80	32
	2004	256	77	33
	2007	351	87	40

[a]For instance, "energy development" and "chemical industry."
[b]For instance, "can possibly produce environmental pollution."
[c]The Catalogue was amended in each of these years, and the number of encouraged, restricted, and prohibited industries for each year was adjusted. The numbers are cumulative totals.

portant priority in drafting the Catalogue. Industries labeled "encouraged," such as ethylene projects of more than 600,000 tons annual capacity, are usually those deemed key to the industrialization process and in which China seeks modern technology (or simply lacks the means to develop alone). Restricted industries tend to be those the government seeks to protect from international competition, such as the production of Chinese tea. This is why one can see in Table 3.1 that after 1995 there is a decreasing number of restricted industries as China liberalized its market in preparation for WTO membership.

It is virtually impossible to know the range of motivations and bureaucratic battles behind each industry or product included on the list. To what extent did environmental protection concerns influence the content of the Catalogues? In large part, the answer to that question may depend on a second question. What input did SEPA and other environmental authorities have in determining which industries were classified as encouraged, restricted, and prohibited? Given the black box that is the Chinese policy-making process, it is unlikely that anyone outside the immediate policy-making circles knows.[14] Traditionally SEPA's influence has been minimal in bureaucratic infighting. It was not until the 1998 government reorganization that SEPA was even promoted to State Council status, and only in 2008 did SEPA get fully promoted to the level of ministry (when its name was formally changed to the Ministry of Environmental Protection). Given that foreign-investment regulation falls outside of SEPA's immediate bureaucratic profile, it is unlikely that SEPA was able to project much power in the drafting of the Catalogue.

But whether or not SEPA and other environmental authorities had a strong influence in creating the Catalogue, the document reflects Beijing's increased emphasis on the goal of environmental protection and has laid the groundwork for stronger control of the environmental aspects of foreign investment. Many production activities potentially damaging to the environment have been deemed restricted and are now subject to increased scrutiny in the approval process. This includes such sectors as "the processing of rare species of trees," "reconditioning old tires," or the production of many kinds of chemicals such as benzidine.[15] The production of caustic soda, which is an energy- and pollution-intensive chemical product used in a variety of industries such as the pulp-and-paper and textile sectors, was added to the "restricted" list in 1997.[16] In 2002, the production of persistent organic pollutants (POPs) and genetically modified organisms (GMOs) were added to the "restricted" list, although it is likely that the latter was added because it was deemed a strategic industry of the future and the government sought to protect it from foreign competition. Pollution-intensive industries, such as pesticides and fertilizers, were removed from the "encouraged" category. Likewise, in 2004 "tamp tar and dry-cooling tar processing" was removed from the "encouraged" list due to its high energy requirements.

At the same time, a number of environmentally friendly industrial processes and products have been labeled "encouraged," thereby making them eligible for preferential policies. This includes specific items such as lithium batteries, freon-substitution technologies, and ionic membrane for caustic soda, as well as broader categories such as "technology for recycling and comprehensive utilization of resources" and "energy-saving technology."[17] In 2002, Beijing began encouraging investment in chlorofluorocarbon (CFC) substitutions, and the 2007 Catalogue went a step further by restricting investments in CFCs for the first time. By publishing more detailed descriptions of favored and nonfavored investment projects, the central government signaled its increased stress on the environmental aspects of FDI while giving authorities a tool to prevent several pollution-intensive foreign-investment projects. The Catalogue represents a clear enhancement of China's environmental control over foreign investment.

In the period after 1995, not only did the Chinese government become increasingly concerned with preventing foreign investment in industries deemed excessively polluting, but it also focused attention on the ecological impact of FIE technology and production methods. This is evident, for instance, in a key difference between the Provisions published in 1995 and amended in 1997, and the 2002 and 2004 amendments. In each edition of the four issuances of the Provisions, there is listed a set of broad categories that are deemed restricted or prohibited. In the original Provisions and in the three amendments, two of the six prohibited (*jin zhi*) categories of projects are related to environmental pollution. However, starting in the 2002 amendment, the "restricted" (*xian zhi*) category is more explicit in pointing to the problem of outdated technology. In fact, in the 2002 and 2004 amendments, included in the five general categories of restricted investments are projects classified as "using backwards technology" (*jishu shuiping luohuo de*). In the earlier versions, there is no mention of backwards technology. This almost certainly reflects a decision on the part of Chinese officials to tackle the use of pollution-intensive production processes, which had been recognized as a problem in the late 1980s.

Further evidence for a desire to reduce investors' use of outdated technology can be seen in other regulations. In 1999, the State Economic and Trade Commission established another important tool for regulating the environmental protection elements of foreign investment with the circulation of the "Catalogue of the Backward Production Capacities, Processes, and Products to Be Eliminated." Two more batches (*pi*) were issued in 1999 and 2001 (State Council 1999a, 1999b, 2002). Together these three documents create an inventory of productive processes, equipment, and products that are no longer permitted in China. In total, they ban 353 products and processes, covering sectors such as mining and mineral extraction, as well as a range of specific products in various manufacturing sectors, including certain kinds of textiles, chemicals, pulp and paper, and leather products. Many of the eliminated products and processes are pollution- and/or energy-intensive. The focus, particularly in the first guideline, is on closing down small, inefficient enterprises. For example, pulp-and-paper producers with an annual production of less than 5,000 tons are required to cease production, as are cement plants producing less than 44,000 tons annually. Certain types of equipment are also banned, such as blast furnaces measuring less than fifty square meters.

The "Elimination Catalogues," although almost certainly oriented more toward domestic than foreign firms, clearly seek to prevent foreign firms from investing with pollution-intensive technology. This is evident from the fact that they explicitly outlaw not only the use of listed technologies, but also their transfer, import, and distribution. Interestingly, only "transfer" was included on the first batch, while "import" was added to the second and "distribution" added to the third. Still, the Elimination Catalogues are somewhat unclear on how to deal with FIEs that had already invested using the banned technologies at the time of the regulation's issue. They merely state that FIEs that were legally established and are using the now-illicit technology should work with the State Economic and Trade Commission and local governments to handle (*chu li*) the situation. By contrast, domestic firms are ordered to cease production, and those that do not cooperate are to lose their business licenses and permits, as well as be cut off from any new loans (State Council 1999a, Sections 4 and 5). So although the publication of the Elimination Catalogues represents an overall strengthening of China's environmental FDI governance, the lack of clarity leaves room for maneuver among local governments.

While regulations restricting certain types of investment and technology have enhanced the legal framework for governing foreign-investor environmental behavior, these investment regulations have themselves been enhanced by the continued development of China's environmental impact assessment system since the latter half of the 1990s.[18] This process culminated in 2002 with the passing of the Environmental Impact Assessment Law, which took effect a year later. This law has garnered a great deal of attention inside and outside China, both because it greatly expands the scope of the EIA system by requiring government development plans to include EIAs and because it contains several clauses stipulating public participation in the EIA process. The EIA Law requires certain kinds of government plans be subject to outside scrutiny, and construction projects (for which an EIA report is required) must hold evidentiary meetings or testimony hearings, or adopt some other form of soliciting opinions from relevant government units, experts, and even the general public (NPC 2002, Article 21).

The emphasis on public participation in the EIA Law is a potential watershed in China's environmental governance. Although public participation requirements can be traced back to the early 1990s in projects with the Asian Development Bank, none of the major EIA laws prior to 2002 placed significant emphasis on public participation. The 1998 precursor to the 2002 EIA Law, entitled "Administrative Regulations for the Environmental Manage-

ment of Construction Projects," made no mention of public participation requirements (State Council 1998). As discussed later in Chapter 6, increased
public oversight of investment projects has put significant pressure on foreign
firms in other Asian countries, especially Taiwan.

Although they are less often discussed, the recent steps to enhance the
qualifications and the professionalism of China's EIA service agents have
been an equally important aspect in the strengthening of China's EIA system.
If the inclusion of the general public and outside experts in the EIA process
represents a new direction in China's EIA system, the professionalization of
EIA service agents is a forceful attempt to solve an old problem. As noted previously, there have been numerous problems with corruption and the quality of domestic EIA service agents. While earlier legal documents consisted
principally of entreaties to local governments to increase supervision of EIA
service agents, toward the end of the 1990s SEPA began moving to set up a
systematic means of managing EIA agents, through the creation of an EIA
certification program.

In 1989, the central government issued the first regulation for certifying
EIA service agents (NEPA 1989). This regulation laid out the basic requirements and process for an organization to obtain a license to conduct EIAs on
behalf of investment projects. Problems with EIA quality continued through
the 1990s, and the central government responded by twice strengthening the
principal certification requirements and more recently by establishing a national testing program for licensing EIA engineers (SEPA 1999, 2005).[19] Evident in these laws is an increased desire to improve government supervision
of EIA agents while increasing EIA agents' autonomy (from government), legal liability, and professionalism. For instance, the original 1988 Certification
Law required that all EIA agents be part of a government bureau, and there
was little distinction between types of EIA agents. By 1998, the government
recognized the conflict of interest involved in having government organs produce EIAs for approval by other government organs and thus the requirement
was dropped. In 2005, a new clause was inserted that expressly forbade environmental monitoring institutions (which are typically part of the local EPB)
from applying for EIA licenses.

At the same time, EIA licenses are being issued along increasingly specialized lines. In the 1998 amendment EIA licenses were divided into two
classes. Only class "A" licensed agents can conduct EIAs for projects that are
approved by the State Council, while "B" licensed organizations are limited

to conducting EIAs approved at the provincial level or below (i.e., smaller investment projects). In 2005, this classification was further divided into eleven fields, and EIA service agents are now typically restricted to conducting EIAs for projects in their particular area of specialization (e.g., textiles). Another example of the increased emphasis on EIA agent specialization is evident in personnel requirements. In 1988, the principal requirements for applying for EIA certification were technology and equipment. By 1998, the emphasis had shifted to the applying agency's personnel. For instance, in the 1998 amendment all "A" license applicants had to have at least ten personnel with an educational background in technical fields. By 2005, the standard had been raised to twelve specialists at least six of whom must be certified as EIA engineers.[20] All of this is designed to improve the quality of EIAs and has been backed by periodic crackdowns on EIA agents that conduct substandard investigations. For instance, in 2002, after investigating more than seven hundred agencies, SEPA revoked the licenses of eighteen organizations, and punished another twenty-three, for producing shoddy EIAs (Wang et al. 2003, 561).

Although none of the changes in the EIA laws are aimed specifically at foreign firms, there are nonetheless clear implications of a tightening EIA system for the governance of foreign investment. By obliging local governments to include EIAs in their development plans and by bringing the general public into the EIA process, the central government has sent a clear message that it seeks to strengthen the environmental governance of all investment and construction projects. The expansion of the EIA system has also lifted MEP's status within the government. This impact is demonstrated by the "EIA Storm" initiated in the winter of 2005 when environmental officials issued work-stop orders to thirty-one projects, including some related to the powerful Three Gorges Dam Corporation, for failing to complete EIAs. Thus, foreign investors in China today face both a more complete set of environmental guidelines and an environmental bureaucracy with modest, but increasing, authority.

However, one recent change in Chinese law does not necessarily equate with more stringent environmental governance of foreign-investment projects. In late 2004, as part of a much-needed attempt to streamline the bureaucratic approval process, the central government reduced the size of investments requiring central government approval, which gave local governments greater authority to approve investment projects. Local governments can now approve investments of less than $100 million in the "encouraged" or "permitted" categories and less than $50 million in the "restricted" category. Although this may hasten the often lengthy approval process, it also places more power and autonomy in the hands of local governments (Ian Young 2005). China's secondary legal instruments repeatedly include pleas to local governments to refrain from lowering the threshold for foreign investment and make sure environmental considerations are weighed appropriately in the investment approval process. As such, increasing local government autonomy in the approval process may hasten the investment approval process, but undermine environmental governance.

In conclusion, starting in the mid-1990s Chinese law governing the environmental protection side of FDI became much more comprehensive and detailed. To a far greater extent than in the previous decade and a half, the central government laid out the types of investment it sought and, perhaps more importantly, did not welcome. These guidelines for foreign investment created a set of legal instruments to tackle some of the problems that appeared in the secondary legal documents in the late 1980s and early 1990s, such as investment in pollution-intensive industries and the use of outdated technology. At the same time, the continuing enhancement of the EIA system makes all construction projects, including those using foreign capital, subject to an approval process that places increased stress on the environmental implications of the investment. The combination of the EIA regulations with the guidelines on foreign investment provides Chinese authorities with a more solid legal footing for governing the environmental behavior of foreign-invested enterprises.

China in Comparative Perspective: Evidence of a Regulatory Chill?

The previous sections argued that over the course of the reform period Beijing has developed a strong set of environmental standards to guide the environmental practices of foreign investors. Yet one may ask to what extent do the changes in the environmental regulation of foreign investment mirror developments in industrial environmental law more broadly? And how does China's environmental regulation compare with other countries? Someone sympathetic to the regulatory-chill argument might point out that, even if in *absolute* terms China has strengthened environmental supervision of foreign investors, in *relative* terms the increase in stringency for foreign firms may have lagged behind domestic firms. If the situation today is one in which foreign enterprises face a less stringent set of environmental standards than domestic companies, it lends credence to the regulatory-chill argument that the desire for foreign capital induces governments to keep standards "stuck in the mud."

Along the same lines one might point out that, when it comes to informing the regulatory-chill or pollution-haven argument, the trends in China's environmental law are only meaningful when compared to other countries. After all, the thrust of the argument is that it is the competition between countries that leads to lax environmental standards. Again, China's environmental law may have tightened over time, but if the pace of tightening lags behind other countries (and one can prove that the reason for the lag is concern about loss of investment), then there is still evidence for the regulatory-chill argument.

In terms of the former issue (i.e., the relative treatment of domestic and foreign firms in China's environmental law), there is no indication that Beijing ever promulgated different sets of environmental standards for foreign-invested enterprises and domestic firms. The enhancement of the environmental control of FDI has kept pace with that of industrial pollution control laws more generally. At least on paper, foreign and domestic enterprises have consistently faced a similar environmental legal regime (Richardson 2004b, 134; Ross et al. 1990, 40). As indicated in the section of this chapter about the early 1980s, at the start of the reform era foreign investors faced an exceedingly weak and vague set of environmental requirements, but so did domestic companies. China's major environmental laws do not distinguish between foreign and domestic firms. For example, the Environmental Protection Law (1989), as well as resource-specific laws such as the Water Pollution Prevention and Control Law (1984), typically state that "all units and individuals shall have the obligation to protect" the environment. Likewise, the EIA Law indicates that "construction units" are responsible for conducting environmental impact assessment and does not distinguish between types of firms based on nationality or ownership.

One could even argue that the Catalogue for the Guidance of Foreign Investment Industries, first issued in 1995 and most recently updated in 2007, has subjected foreign-investment projects to a stricter set of environmental requirements. The Catalogue is one of the tools Beijing employs to steer foreign investment toward national development goals. Over the last decade, and particularly since the start of the Hu-Wen era, Beijing has placed greater attention on environmental problems, so it is no surprise that environmental items have become more prominent on the Foreign Investment Catalogue. The result is an investment climate in which foreign firms are more environmentally controlled than domestic enterprises.

For instance, in the 2007 Catalogue foreign investment is prohibited in "paste-type zinc-manganese batteries" due to their impact on the environment (Man et al. 2008). The principal environmental problem with paste batteries is their use of mercury. In 2004, sixty factories in China produced roughly nine billion paste batteries, of which 80 percent were exported to the developing world, and in the process consumed more than thirty-four metric tons of mercury. Although foreign companies are not allowed to invest in paste battery facilities, as of 2005 there was little indication that paste battery factories would be targeted for elimination (as is the case with the even more environmentally harmful mercury oxide battery facilities). Nor did Beijing issue any restrictions on domestic investment (Natural Resources Defense Council 2006). In a similar example, the 2007 Catalogue restricted foreign investment in polyvinyl chloride (PVC) facilities that use the "carbide" method. The carbide method uses calcium carbide, which itself is produced from coal, to manufacture PVC. Compared to production techniques that use alternative feedstocks such as ethylene, the carbide method is less technologically advanced, more pollution-intensive, and generally results in lower-quality PVC. Given the rise in oil prices in recent years, it is a far less expensive means of production, and in 2006 the carbide method increased its share of China's PVC market to almost 69 percent, up from 59 percent in 2004 (Gu Yao 2005, 2007). China's ample supply of coal means that the carbide method will likely retain its dominant position for the foreseeable future. By limiting foreign investment in these two sectors, Beijing has increased the probability that foreign companies seeking to grab a share of China's battery or PVC market will use less pollution-intensive production methods. In that sense, foreign firms investing in China can be considered more environmentally regulated.

The facts that foreign and domestic firms have faced the same basic corpus of environmental law and that foreign investment is increasingly environmentally restricted are noteworthy because, as Huang Yasheng has cogently argued, Beijing spent much of the reform period constructing a dualist legal regime that favored foreign investors over domestic companies.[21] This goes beyond preferential policies such as corporate tax reductions, which are common throughout the world and have been a primary method of attracting foreign investment since the early days of the reform era.[22] Rather, Huang argues that the legal bias toward FIEs is far more extensive. Over the course of the reform era Beijing extended a host of lawful protections such as legal independence, as well as ownership and decision rights, to foreign investors years before they were granted to private or state-owned firms. Looking at the sum of FIE privileges across multiple issue areas, Huang concludes: "Compared to the FIEs, the legislative and regulatory treatments of domestic private firms have been far less transparent and more restrictive" (2003a, 407).[23]

Yet Beijing never extended this preferential legal treatment to the environmental arena. Even as Beijing mandated that foreign investors could enjoy lower corporate taxes than domestic companies, it never established a weaker set of requirements for foreign investors' environmental impact assessments. It never passed a standard that indicated foreign enterprises were exempt from pollution monitoring in their first year of operation, as they typically have been for certain taxes, nor did it issue different discharge standards for foreign and domestic firms. It should be pointed out that this has not always been the case in other countries. A controversial aspect of Korean law allows authorities to reduce or waive pollution levies, environmental improvement charges, or water-use fees where it is deemed necessary for "smoothly carrying out the development project of any free economic zone" (Richardson 2004a, 234). Outside Asia, other countries such as Costa Rica and Belize also exempt investment within free-trade or export-processing zones from certain environmental regulations (221). In short, in contrast to the expectations of the pollution-haven argument and to the experience of some other countries, there is little evidence that Beijing has been willing to play the pollution card by creating a different set of environmental standards for foreign investors.

The previous paragraph touched on the second critical question about China's environmental protection development: How does China's environmental law compare with that of other developing countries? If the pollution-haven argument is correct, then China's great success in attracting foreign investment should at least in part be based on China's willingness to keep environmental standards lower than other developing countries with whom China competes to attract FDI. If there is a regulatory chill occurring in China, then one would expect China to be falling behind other developing countries in building up its environmental protection law.

A detailed country-by-country comparison of the industrial environmental standards of China and other developing countries is clearly beyond the scope of this chapter or, for that matter, this book. To conduct such an evaluation would require looking at emission limits, reporting requirements, and penalty schedules for the numerous individual pollutants regulated within the broad categories of industrial water, air, and solid-waste pollution. Further complicating matters is the fact that, like many countries, China issues sector-specific discharge standards. For instance, China has issued water discharge standards for more than twenty different industrial sectors, and standards for chloro-alkali producers are not the same as those for manufacturers of textile dyes or ammonia. In calculating discharge levies, China uses a mix of concentration and mass-load (volume) standards (Dean and Lovely 2005), which also makes it difficult to compare with other countries. Even within a given sector, standards may diverge depending on factors such as the firm's location and proximity to protected areas, particular production method, or age of the facility, as newer factories are required to meet more stringent standards.[24]

All these factors make it exceedingly difficult to craft precise estimates about the extent to which China's environmental standards are stronger or weaker than other countries'.[25] But that does not mean we have to set aside the question entirely, as there are ways to obtain at least an informed estimate about the comparative stringency of China's industrial environmental law. First, one can get a broad sense from the scholarly work on China's environmental law and comparative environmental politics.[26] This work indicates that the strength of China's environmental legislation today compares favorably with other developing countries and that, over the course of the reform era, China has kept pace with many other industrializing nations in East Asia. Put another way, in terms of extent of coverage, detail, and overall stringency, China's formal environmental law is weaker than that of OECD (Organisation for Economic Co-operation and Development) countries (Dean and Lovely 2005; Lin 2004; Nagle 1996), but is on par with other countries at China's income level. Ross, for instance, praises the Chinese environmental protection regime, stating, "While the pace and breadth of China's policy changes are far from sufficient, they constitute substantial progress and are occurring at an earlier stage of economic development than has generally occurred in advanced industrialized countries" (1998, 834). Klee and Thomas indicate that recent developments in China's environmental regime are bringing it "closer in line with Western environmental control systems. The Chinese framework is now comprehensive, increasingly detailed, and similar in concept and approach to the environmental regulatory path taken in the United States" (1997,

34). Boxer goes a step further in his praise, stating: "In no other developing Asian country over the past 20 years has there been a greater outpouring of creative ideas and strategies for legal, technical, and scientific approaches to environment and resource protection" (1989, 669).

The few existing comparative works on environmental protection in East Asia lend credence to the notion that the enhancement of China's environmental law has kept pace with other developing countries. Rock (2002), although not focusing on legislation per se, ranks China's pollution management between the successes of Singapore and Taiwan and the failure of Thailand.[27] Richardson (2004a) conducts an extensive comparison between East Asian countries and, like Rock, places China's progress in between the two poles of environmental leader and laggard. At one end are Singapore and Taiwan, which have made rapid improvements in environmental legislation in recent years, and at the opposite side of the spectrum are countries such as Thailand, Indonesia, and Vietnam. Richardson concludes: "Environmental law reform in China has not matched efforts in South Korea or Taiwan, but has nevertheless been quite extensive. Ostensibly, the PRC boasts a laudable array of environmental laws and institutions—comparable to that in many Western countries" (189–90). Perhaps most importantly, other East Asian nations have taken fewer measures than China to develop environmental regulations tailored to special economic zones, which are set up specifically to attract foreign capital. Thailand, Vietnam, the Philippines, and even South Korea all have less comprehensive guidelines for controlling the environmental implications of investment in special economic zones (217–22). The indication is that, not only has Chinese environmental regulation advanced in absolute terms, as described in the previous sections, but it has also kept up in relative terms with many of its Asian neighbors.

One can also get a sense of the comparative stringency of China's environmental regulation through surveys of business executives. Since 2000, the World Economic Forum (WEF) has conducted an annual survey of business executives that includes questions about environmental regulation.[28] The survey targets firms in dozens of countries and in each firm aims for executives who have international experience. The companies surveyed vary across each country in terms of size and ownership (e.g., private vs. public, domestic vs. foreign). Over time, the survey has expanded its scope to include more firms in a greater number of countries. For instance, the 2000 survey included interviews with executives in 59 countries, while the 2007 survey more than doubled the number of countries covered to 131. In China, over the same time period the number of executives interviewed increased from 116 to 344 (World Economic Forum 2000–2007).

Since 2000, the WEF survey has asked executives the same question: "How stringent is your country's environmental regulation?" Responses range from 1 (lax compared to other countries) to 7 (among the world's most stringent). Responses are averaged to produce a country score—the higher the score, the more stringent the regulation. Because the question is phrased in a comparative fashion, it offers insight into how China's environmental regulation has evolved in recent years in relation to other countries. Of course, the data must be interpreted with caution as there are many factors, such as firm size, sector, and ownership, that may influence perceptions of stringency but are not discernible in the aggregated results. Sample size varies considerably as well, which may also affect the reliability of the data. In 2007, 344 firms were interviewed in China, but only 68 in India. Finally, it should also be pointed out that the sample populations are different across countries and that the executives are not asked to rank order a list of countries in terms of their stringency, but only to compare generally the country in which they operate to the rest of the world. This means that the survey shows, for example, how executives in China perceive China's environmental regulation versus how executives in Indonesia rank Indonesian regulation. Despite these caveats, the survey results are still valuable if for no other reason than they represent the views of those with firsthand experience with each country's environmental law. Moreover, the survey targets companies with an international orientation and executives who possess broad global experience. Roughly 10 percent of the executives in the Chinese sample work in foreign firms. This facilitates comparisons across national settings.[29]

The survey data indicate that China has slightly below average environmental regulation both in terms of its current position and its improvement over time. Over the seven years of the survey, executives perceived China as increasing its stringency vis-à-vis the rest of the world, but the increase has been modest compared with some of its Asian neighbors. This is evident in Figure 3.1, which shows the percentile rank of China compared with several Asian countries that are similar in terms of per capita income (PPP).[30] The percentile ranking represents the proportion of countries that were deemed by business executives as possessing weaker environmental regulation.[31] For example, in 2007 China's stringency score was 87th out of 131 countries, which placed China in the 33rd percentile. This means that executives working in 66 percent of the countries in the sample considered their country's

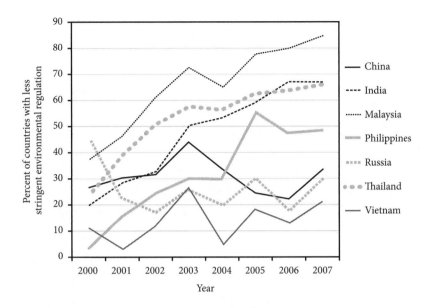

Percent of countries with less stringent environmental regulation

Year

China
India
Malaysia
Philippines
Russia
Thailand
Vietnam

FIGURE 3.1 Perceptions of China's environmental regulation vs. its Asian neighbors. Data for Figures 3.1–3.5 are taken from World Economic Forum 2006–2007. The rankings are based on the executive survey, which asks, "How stringent is your country's environmental regulation?" (1 = lax compared to other countries, 7 = among the world's most stringent). Based on an average of responses, countries are given a score between 1 and 7 and then ranked numerically in terms of stringency. For each country in the figure above, the percentages represent the number of countries with lower scores and are calculated according to the following formula: 1 − (country rank/total no. of countries in the sample).

environmental regulation more stringent than executives working in China considered China's environmental regulation. Over the seven years of the survey, China's percentile ranking has increased modestly from 27 to 33 percent, although its current rank is lower than the high of 44 percent achieved in 2003.[32] It is difficult to know the reason for the decline since 2003, but one possible explanation is the fact that the landmark EIA Law was passed the previous year, which may have affected executives' opinions of China. Among the seven Asian countries included in Figure 3.1, China was ranked third in 2000. Over the last seven years, China's rank slipped to fifth as it was surpassed by Thailand, India, and the Philippines, while it overtook only Russia. China has consistently been perceived as more stringent than Vietnam.

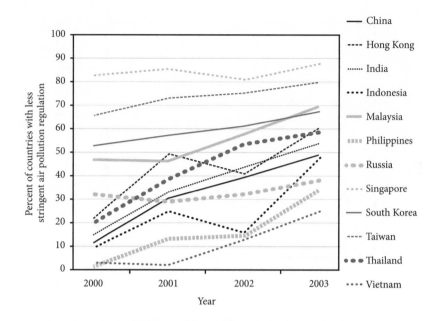

FIGURE 3.2 Comparisons of perceived stringency of air pollution regulations.

From 2000 to 2003, the survey included questions about specific types of regulation including air, water, and chemical pollution. For each type of regulation, the questions and answers were phrased the same: "How stringent is your country's air/water/chemical pollution regulation?" Again, responses range from 1 (lax compared to other countries) to 7 (among the world's most stringent). Figures 3.2–3.4 show the survey results for each issue area for China and eleven other Asian countries. Although the number of years is limited, the survey results again point to a steady rise in perceptions about the relative stringency of China's environmental regulations. China's air pollution regulations ranked in the 12th percentile in 2000, but four years later China was up to the 49th percentile and had considerably narrowed the gap with top Asian performers such as Singapore, Taiwan, and South Korea. Water pollution regulations shifted from the 9th percentile to the 46th, while chemical regulations rose from the 14th to the 50th.

China is also slightly below average when one extends the comparison beyond East Asia and instead looks at countries within China's income level. This is illustrated in Figure 3.5, which shows how China ranked in 2007 compared to ten countries immediately above and ten immediately below China

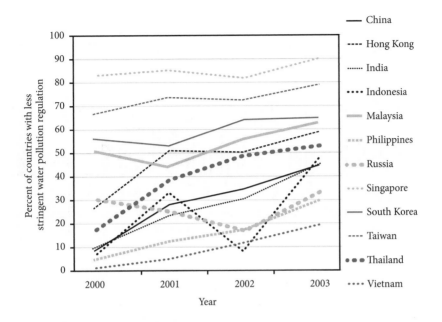

FIGURE 3.3 Comparisons of perceived stringency of water pollution regulations.

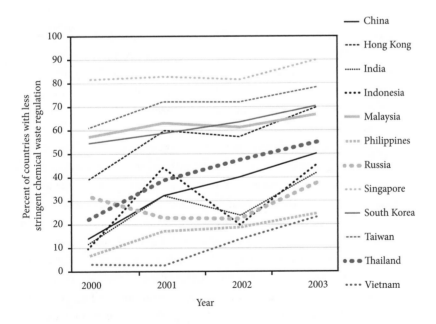

FIGURE 3.4 Comparisons of perceived stringency of chemical waste regulations.

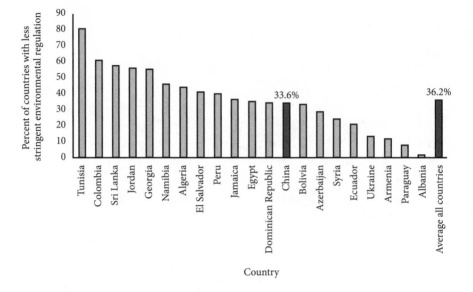

FIGURE 3.5 Perceptions of China's environmental regulation vs. countries with a similar income level, 2007.

in terms of per capita GDP. In this sample, China's environmental stringency ranks thirteenth (out of a total of twenty-one countries). China's environmental stringency in 2007 was 33.6 percent, while the average of the twenty other countries was 36.2 percent. Put differently, by 2007 the stringency of China's environmental regulation corresponded with other countries at China's same level of development.

What this information tells us is that business executives in China deem environmental regulation somewhat less strict than executives in comparable countries. Does this indicate that China's success in attracting FDI has served to weaken environmental regulation? Of course, one cannot dismiss the possibility entirely. If the executive survey is a reflection of reality, then China has lost ground to some of its Asian neighbors. However, it seems unlikely that China has undergone a regulatory chill given the numerous other factors that can influence industrial environmental regulation in a country. For instance, it is generally accepted that democratic institutions exert a positive influence on environmental protection and that greater public participation in the political system strengthens a country's environmental regulation. Hence, it is not surprising that India and the Philippines have outperformed China. Without being able to control other factors, it is difficult to pinpoint the precise reasons why some of China's neighbors have been perceived by executives as ratcheting up environmental regulations more quickly than China.

Regardless, the basic trend apparent in the survey should not be overlooked—over the last seven years China has increased its ranking relative to other nations whether one looks at environmental regulations broadly or specific types of regulations such as chemical waste standards. Moreover, China's 2007 ranking is scarcely different than the average of twenty other countries at a similar income level (33.6 vs. 36.2 percent). Given the absence of evidence pointing to a pollution-haven strategy on the part of government officials, along with the continuous progress in the development of China's environmental regulation of foreign investment, it is hard to conclude that China has experienced any kind of regulatory chill in its environmental law. From the perspective of formal law on the books, China looks little like a pollution haven.

Conclusion

This chapter began by tracing the development of the legal framework that governs the environmental policies of foreign investment and firms in China. It argued that on the legislative front China has made steady progress in its governance of FDI with momentum gathering particularly in the latter half of the 1990s. With regard to the environmental regulation of foreign investment, the tenor of Chinese law has evolved from indifference in the 1980s to muted concern through the early 1990s to active interest over the last decade. China's legal efforts have progressed from half-measure attempts and beseechments to investors and local governments to abide by the law toward a more active approach marked by the development of concrete systems to control the environmental impact of FIEs. Although Chinese law is far from perfect and continues to be plagued with problems of ambiguity, inconsistency, and lack of clarity and transparency, Chinese environmental authorities today have a far greater choice of legal instruments with which to control the impact of foreign investment on China's natural resources. China's increased control of foreign investors is all the more impressive as it has taken place within a legal climate that largely favors foreign firms. Although Beijing granted foreign investors legal privileges in everything from taxes to protection of private property, it did not create a separate legal framework for environmental protection. On the contrary, with the publication of Foreign Investment Catalogues starting in the mid-1990s, Beijing has set about establishing a more stringent set of environmental standards for foreign investors.

When placed in comparative perspective, China's accomplishments in environmental regulation are also clear. Although a lack of comparable data on the industrial environmental standards of China versus other countries warrants caution in drawing conclusions, scholarship on China's environmental law lends support to the assertion that China's formal environmental law is on par with other developing nations at a similar income level. While noting the many problems in implementation, scholars typically compliment the extent of China's legislative development in environmental law. Furthermore, comparative scholarship shows that China's progress in environmental law is similar to that of other Asian countries. Surveys of business executives asked to compare the stringency of China's environmental law with other countries also indicate a strengthening of China's environmental law relative to other countries, although China's gains are relatively modest. In sum, from a legislative standpoint China's reliance on foreign investment has not prevented or postponed the development of more comprehensive environmental protection laws. There is little evidence that the decision to seek development via foreign investment has led to a regulatory chill in environmental regulation or that Beijing has pursued a pollution-haven strategy.

This raises one final question: How much do China's environmental laws matter when it comes to actual implementation on the ground? In order to address the pollution-haven argument, which has traditionally focused on trends in legal standards, this chapter has attempted to set aside issues of compliance and enforcement and keep the focus on legislative developments. However, it is axiomatic that in the absence of enforcement, strong legislation will not translate into a robust environmental regulatory system. Although concentrating on legislation, the discussion in this chapter has nonetheless touched on issues of implementation. It has shown that throughout the reform era, regulators have faced a simmering problem with the environmental compliance of foreign firms as well as with local governments' supervision of foreign investment. A recurrent theme in China's legal documents, particularly in the various legal notices, is a concern about the failure of local governments to supervise the environmental aspects of foreign investment and instead to short-circuit the required approval channels for investment projects. On numerous occasions, Chinese officials have also expressed concern about the use of "backwards technology" and the tendency of foreign firms to invest in pollution-intensive sectors. The fact that over the last two decades legislation and secondary legal notices have been created specifically with the aim of improving the pollution control aspects of foreign-investment projects indicates that not all foreign firms have implemented robust environmental protection policies.[33] Furthermore, the fact that the notices have been issued by the State Council and other central government organs indicates that the problem has been sufficiently widespread to gain the attention of China's national leaders.

This hints at the idea that, when it comes to enforcement and compliance, the worries of scholars concerned about the negative impact of foreign investment on environmental protection perhaps have some relevance. But tracing China's legal development can only offer hints about an implementation problem and does not provide specific information about the conditions under which implementation failures might occur or about the role of foreign firms. That is the task of subsequent chapters, which will address questions such as: To what extent and in what manner do Chinese authorities use available legal tools? To what extent do the existing laws guide the behavior of foreign-invested enterprises? Exactly how big is the gap between legislation and enforcement? Do enforcement patterns resemble the expectations of those concerned with pollution havens? In other words, the following chapters address issues of compliance and enforcement.

4 Patterns in Implementation: Strengthening Enforcement

The previous chapter traced the growing strength of Chinese law governing the environmental aspects of foreign investment. However, enforcement and compliance are equally important, especially for developing countries where stronger legislation does not necessarily translate into stronger governance. Chapter 2 showed that the autonomy of local governments and the fragmented nature of China's environmental protection regime provide ample opportunity for skirting environmental regulation. The findings of the previous chapter, therefore, beg the questions: How much does China's legal development matter? To what extent are the laws described in the previous chapter the reference against which regulation occurs? Answering these questions means looking at both government actors (i.e., enforcement) and industry (i.e., compliance). The remainder of this book explores enforcement and compliance and helps answer the questions of whether and how the previously described changes in legislation have altered behavior on the ground.

In this chapter I look at the government/enforcement side, while the subsequent two chapters turn attention to compliance and examine in detail the behavior of foreign firms. This chapter argues that on a broad statistical level, implementation patterns of Chinese environmental law have in fact mirrored the changes in legislation and enforcement has generally become more stringent. Moreover, in contrast to the expectations of those anticipating a regulatory chill in environmental protection standards, there is little evidence that greater levels of foreign investment or an increased presence of foreign firms detracts from enforcement. Statistical measures, such as the percent of industrial wastewater meeting discharge standards, indicate that jurisdictions with higher foreign investment tend to exhibit more stringent enforcement.

But statistics are a general, approximate measure of empirical reality. As subsequent sections show, even if from a statistical perspective there does not appear to be a widespread impact of foreign investment on enforcement patterns, the desire among government officials to spur development through the use of foreign capital and trade has created serious lapses in environmental governance. This is evident in the case of China's chemical industrial parks, which have proliferated in recent years, often with little regard for environmental regulation. Not all parks, however, have overlooked environmental law. Rather, the parks least able to attract capital have demonstrated the least stringent implementation of environmental regulation. The conclusion, then, is that the competition for capital undermines environmental regulation in China, but under a particular set of scope conditions.

China's Increasingly Stringent Enforcement

On a broad level, the legislative strengthening described in the previous chapter has led to stronger industrial environmental regulation. Trends in enforcement have generally followed those in legislation. Some evidence for this fact comes from statistics on factories closed for environmental violations. According to a white paper on environmental protection released by SEPA, the government has dealt with more than 75,000 cases of violations of environmental law and closed over 16,000 enterprises for excessive pollution discharges. It also notes that from 1996 to 2000, the state closed 84,000 "small enterprises that had caused both serious waste and pollution." The three releases of the "Catalogue of the Backward Production Capacities, Processes, and Products to Be Eliminated," issued from 1999 to 2002, led to the shuttering of 30,000 enterprises and the postponement of another 1900 projects (SEPA 2006). As described in Chapter 3, in early 2005, SEPA initiated what was dubbed in the Chinese media as the "EIA Storm," by ordering thirty-one large infrastructure projects to halt construction, including some connected to the powerful Three Gorges Dam Corporation. Although within a month all had resumed operations, this event was seen as a watershed in China's environmental protection and as evidence of SEPA's growing assertiveness. It was followed up a year later by a similar action as SEPA went after another twenty-one chemical and oil projects, again for failing to abide by EIA regulations, and refused to approve the EIA reports of seven proposed projects (*Gongyi Shibao* 2006; *Xinjing Bao* 2006). In April 2005, SEPA took the unusual step of publicly criticizing the powerful Ministry of Water Resources for determining pollution targets for the Huai River without consulting SEPA (Shi 2005a). In late 2006, SEPA closed another eight large construction projects, again for failure to meet EIA requirements (*China Daily* 2006).

Although these actions indicate an increased enforcement effort, they must be taken with a grain of salt. There are copious examples in the foreign and Chinese press of polluting companies ignoring government shutdown orders (e.g., van Rooij 2006a). As Pan Yue, vice-minister of MEP (formerly SEPA), stated, "When SEPA attempts to investigate, fine, or close down polluting facilities, localities often simply ignore them" (Bremner 2006). It is not uncommon for factories forced into closure to simply reopen once the investigating authorities have returned to Beijing or the provincial capital. Nonetheless, the increased strength and assertiveness of MEP points to a growing toughness in the implementation of environmental regulation.

Table 4.1, which presents basic indicators for environmental regulation, also shows a trend of enhanced enforcement. Though the data only go back to 1998, and one must always guard against placing too much faith in official Chinese statistics, the picture painted in Table 4.1 is of a consistent improvement in industry's compliance with requirements for discharge standards. For instance, from 1998 to 2003, the percent of industrial wastewater meeting discharge standards increased from just over 61 percent to approximately 89 percent. Over the same time period, the solid waste utilization rate increased 13 percent to just less than 55 percent.[1] There have also been modest improvements in the implementation of emission standards for some of the main air pollutants such as SO_2 and total suspended particulates (TSP). Others have pointed out that, although China's environmental problems have continued to deepen, in the second half of the 1990s China was able to obtain an absolute reduction in some industrial air and water pollutant emissions (World Bank 2004). From the late 1980s to the late 1990s, total suspended particulates and sulfur dioxide concentrations declined in most major Chinese cities (Carter and Mol 2006, 153).

Of course, there are many factors that contribute to the outcomes described in Table 4.1, and one cannot assume they are a direct result of stronger enforcement. They are suggestive of more stringent enforcement, but not

TABLE 4.1 Outcomes in China's industrial environmental governance

Year	Industrial wastewater meeting standards* (%)	SO₂ emissions meeting standards (%)	Soot emissions meeting standards (%)	Total suspended particulates (TSP) meeting standards (%)	Solid waste utilization rate** (%)	EIA implementation rate (%)
1998	61.4	—	—	—	41.7	—
1999	66.7	—	—	—	45.6	90.4
2000	76.9	—	—	—	45.9	97.0
2001	85.2	61.3	67.3	50.2	52.1	97.0
2002	88.3	70.2	75.0	61.7	52.0	98.3
2003	89.2	69.1	78.5	54.5	54.8	98.9

Data from SEPA 1998–2004.

*There is some discrepancy between reported figures in earlier editions of the Environmental Statistical Yearbook and the 2003 edition (which reports figures back to 1998). The figures offered in the 2003 edition are included in the table.

**Refers to the solid waste that is recycled, processed, or otherwise treated in a manner that allows it to be used as raw material input; the solid waste utilization rate is calculated: amount used/(amount produced).

hard proof. In addition, the question for this book is not simply, What are trends in enforcement? but rather, What are the trends in enforcement with regard to foreign-invested firms? Again, on the broadest level the evidence points to increased efforts on the part of government regulators to assure FIE compliance with environmental law. This fact is first evident in discussions with firm representatives. In total, I conducted interviews with thirty-six firms (sixteen foreign and twenty domestic).[2] With a couple of exceptions, every interviewee representing a foreign firm indicated that enforcement has become more stringent over the last several years and expected enhanced enforcement in the future.

Foreign-firm representatives tended to point out that their firms, because they are foreign, are subject to greater regulatory scrutiny than domestic firms. There is a widely held perception among foreign firms that regulators treat foreign firms as "guinea pigs" by enforcing new regulations on them first. When there is a need on the part of officials to demonstrate toughness, they turn to FIEs (McElwee 2008, 22). Floyd's survey of chemical companies finds that the perception among foreign firms is that, in carrying out the EIA approval process, local environmental regulators "appear to hold foreign companies, which are perceived to have deep pockets, more rigorously to the rules" (2002, 36).[3] Domestic firms tended to support this notion. During my interviews, when domestic firm representatives were asked, "Are there differences in enforcement with regard to domestic versus foreign firms?" several respondents pointed out that foreign firms, at least the well-known multinationals, are held to higher standards. Among domestic firms, this was perceived as perfectly fair because foreign firms are deemed rich in capital (*xionghou ziyuan*). In short, among the three dozen firms interviewed, most representatives expressed the belief that the general trend in China's enforcement in recent years is toward increased oversight of both domestic and foreign firms, but the foreign firms are subjected to a higher level of scrutiny.

Basic statistics about foreign investment and environmental regulation indicate that on a broad level foreign firms are subject to China's increasingly stringent environmental law. Although statistics cannot provide insights into the process of implementation, they can reveal broad patterns about the extent to which foreign investment is correlated with implementation. If foreign firms are able to escape regulation or if officials in multiple jurisdictions fail to enforce environmental law in an attempt to woo foreign investors, as the strongest version of the race-to-the-bottom argument expects, then one would expect to see a negative correlation between measures of environmental regulation and foreign investment (e.g., Wheeler 2001).[4] As shown in Figures 4.1–4.3, this is not the case. On the contrary, whether one looks at water, air pollution, or a combination of multiple measures, higher implementation rates tend to go hand in hand with greater levels of foreign investment.

Figures 4.1–4.3 show the relationship between the average utilized FDI and a measure of environmental governance for the years from 2000 to 2003.[5] For Figures 4.1–4.3, these environmental measures include, respectively: wastewater discharges meeting standards, SO_2 emissions meeting standards, and a combined measure that averages the first two plus the solid waste utilization rate and the EIA implementation rate. Each point on the figure represents a province or provincial-level city (e.g., Beijing). While more years would be desirable, unfortunately Chinese environmental statistics do not go back beyond the late 1990s. Evident in Figures 4.1–4.3 is the positive correlation between FDI levels and environmental governance indicators.[6] Provinces attracting a large amount of FDI typically do *not* have low compliance rates. At the same time, provinces absorbing the least amount of FDI are also those with the lowest implementation rates. For instance, in Figure 4.1 it can be seen that, in each of the eleven provinces that attracted more than $500 mil-

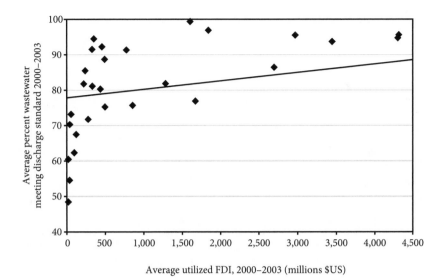

FIGURE 4.1 Provincial averages for FDI vs. percent wastewater meeting standard. For Figures 4.1–4.3, the environmental statistics are from SEPA 1998–2004, while the FDI statistics are from National Bureau of Statistics 1994–2004. Each point on the figure represents a province or provincial-level city (e.g., Beijing).

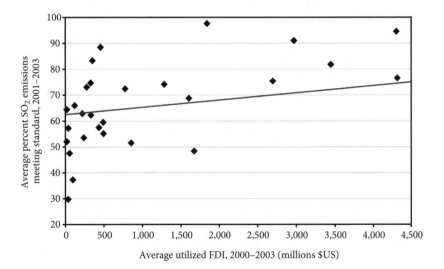

FIGURE 4.2 Provincial averages for FDI vs. percent SO_2 emissions meeting standard. Each point on the figure represents a province or provincial-level city (e.g., Beijing).

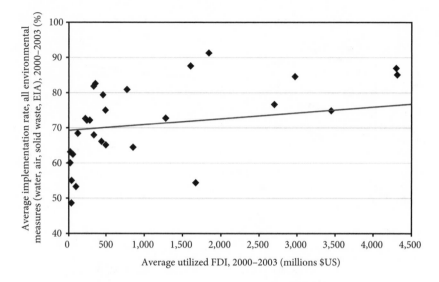

FIGURE 4.3 Provincial averages for FDI vs. environmental governance implementation rate. Each point on the figure represents a province or provincial-level city (e.g., Beijing).

lion in FDI, at least 75 percent of wastewater discharges were up to standard.[7] By contrast, the seven provinces that attracted the least amount of FDI were all under 75 percent, with two provinces close to 50 percent. The situation is similar in Figure 4.2, which shows that only three of the eleven provinces with more than $500 million had less than 70 percent of emissions meeting SO_2 discharge standards. On the other hand, only four of the seventeen provinces below $500 million in FDI achieved the 70 percent level.

What do these figures tell us about the impact of foreign investment on the implementation of environmental regulation?[8] At the very least, the data in Figures 4.1–4.3 indicate that areas with a large number of foreign investors are unlikely to experience a regulatory-chill phenomenon that leads to a failure to implement regulation. Even if the competition to attract investment leads to less implementation, and thus far this remains an "if," other factors that contribute positively to enforcement, such as income growth and enhanced government capacity, overwhelm the negative impact of competition. Put another way, even if there is a regulatory-chill *effect*, characterized by weaker enforcement than might have occurred in the absence of the pursuit of foreign capital, there is not a regulatory-chill *outcome*, characterized by a net decline in enforcement stringency and rising levels of pollution.[9]

This basic conclusion is supported by the small number of existing works probing the impact of foreign investment on environmental regulation in China. Di Wenhua (2004) looks at forty-seven prefecture-level cities and offers a statistical model of the factors influencing the performance of environmental officials. She includes FDI as a variable in her model and finds that FDI is not statistically significant. In other words, according to Di, there is no relationship between the amount of foreign investment a municipality attracts and the extent to which environmental standards are implemented. Zeng and Easton compare Chinese provinces and find that, controlling for other factors, FDI is associated with lower pollution intensities of sulfur dioxide, soot, and solid waste. They argue that FDI, along with trade openness, acts as a transmission belt for the diffusion of advanced management and technology and ultimately "encourages more stringent policy enforcement and compliance" (2007, 971).[10] Thus, the precise influence of FDI and the competition to attract it remains murky. Di's model suggests there is no effect on the implementation of environmental regulation; Zeng and Easton argue differently: there is an impact and it is favorable. But along with the data presented in Figures 4.1–4.3, both suggest that jurisdictions that obtain high levels of foreign investment do not witness dramatic decreases in the implementation of environmental regulation.

But does this mean that FDI has a positive impact on the regulatory process, as argued by Zeng and Easton? Figures 4.1–4.3 illustrate that Chinese provinces with lesser amounts of FDI display a wide range of environmental outcomes. This is seen in the large vertical distribution of the provinces clustered at the left of each figure. In the seventeen provinces absorbing less than $500 million in FDI, the wastewater discharge compliance rate varies by just over 46 percentage points (48.4 to 94.5 percent) and the SO_2 compliance rate by almost 60 points (29.8 to 88.5 percent). The indication is that an inability to draw FDI does not translate into a lower implementation rate of environmental regulation. There are several provinces clustered at the left end of the figure (i.e., that have lower FDI averages), but which sit vertically above the trend line. These provinces have achieved relative success in environmental governance without high levels of foreign investment. Intuitively this makes sense, as one can imagine several factors, including local leadership and bureaucratic capacity, that would influence implementation. But it raises the question, What explains this variance? As the subsequent sections will show, one source of variance is related to foreign capital. In some cases, the competition for foreign investment exerts a downward pressure on environmental regulation. This occurs in the jurisdictions less advantaged in the contest for foreign capital. This is shown not through statistics, but through a case study of China's chemical industrial parks.

Below the Surface of Statistics—Environmental Problems in China's Chemical Industrial Parks

The rest of this chapter focuses on the case of China's chemical parks. These parks, which have proliferated in recent years, provide evidence that the competition for external capital can undermine environmental regulation. In this sense, China's chemical parks very much fit with the expectations of the regulatory-chill scenario. However, the case of China's chemical parks also offers evidence that the downward pressure on environmental governance does not occur equally across jurisdictions. Among the key factors determining whether a regulatory chill occurs is the jurisdiction's ability to attract capital. Those parks that have less appeal to foreign investors tend to be those that display worse environmental governance.

The next section introduces China's chemical parks and provides some background about their origins and strategies behind the central government's promotion of the parks. Subsequent sections show how parks have multiplied beyond central government control and how the desire of park officials to attract capital has led to a host of regulatory problems, not the least of which has been a failure to enforce environmental law. The arguments presented are based principally on reports in the Chinese media and chemical industry periodicals and supplemented with interviews with park officials and experts on the chemical industry.[11]

China's Chemical Parks—Background

Since the 1990s, the central government has placed increased emphasis on the role of the chemical industry in China's industrial development. In response, local governments have attempted to promote development and assist chemical companies by establishing chemical industrial parks (Ian Young 2003). These parks are similar to the economic development and technology zones (EDTZs) that sprang up across China in the 1980s and 1990s. In fact, many of them are located within EDTZs. They offer both foreign and domestic investors a host of preferential policies. Firms investing in the parks have traditionally been granted significant reductions in land use fees and taxes (typically 15 percent rather than the standard 33 percent corporate tax). Administrative departments within the parks, which are often mini-governments that have been granted a wide range of authority by the local municipal government, conduct guidance, coordination, and service to foreign-funded enterprises in project approval; aid in the process of contract negotiation; and oversee construction and production within the park. They also help enterprises locate collaborative projects and partners. In building infrastructure for the parks, local governments often invest millions of RMB, and more importantly seek funds from higher-level governments, to build up the facilities necessary to attract foreign and domestic firms.

From the central government's perspective, the intent in promoting chemical parks is to consolidate China's chemical sector, which was designated a strategic pillar industry in the 1990s. Like much of China's industry, the chemical sector is plagued by the fact that it is both small and dispersed. As pointed out by Tan Zhuzhou, the head of the China Petroleum and Chemical Industry Association (CPCIA) and the highest Chinese official overseeing the chemical industry, the average sales of China's roughly 13,000 chemical firms is 50 million RMB, which is about 5.3 percent of the annual sales of foreign chemical firms. Among China's 500 biggest chemical companies, the annual sales of the 500th largest is 2 billion RMB; among the world's 500 largest chemical companies, the annual sales of the 500th is roughly 80 billion RMB (Tan 2002). Almost all the products within China's chemical industry are produced in small factories. For instance, the average size of a Chinese caustic soda operation is 40,000 tons per year, which compares with 580,000 tons in the United States (State Economic and Trade Commission 2001). While one-third of Japan's and half of Korea's ethylene is produced in one city, China has eighteen ethylene crackers dispersed over fifteen cities (Wu 2004).[12]

In response to this problem of "small and scattered," the central government in the mid-1990s began pushing for consolidation. The Chemical Ministry, which was abolished in a 1998 government reorganization, put forward the strategy of "big groups, big chemical industry" (da jituan, da huagong) (Zhongguo Huagong Bao [China Chemical News] 2003). The Tenth Five-year Plan for the Petrochemical Industry (1996–2001) put clear emphasis on modifying the distribution of the chemical industry and promoting chemical parks for the production of ethylene (Hua 2003; Xu 2002). By moving the chemical industry into parks, the government hoped to reduce the fragmentation of China's industry, generate upstream-downstream synergies among chemical firms, gain access to advanced foreign technology, and control environmental pollution (Gu Zongqin 2004; Liu Fangbin 2003; Liu and Sun 2005). The impetus to consolidate industry and increase its competitiveness gained increased urgency with China's acceptance into the WTO in 1999, which lowered the average tariff in the chemical sector from 33 to 17 percent and exposed many previously protected chemical products to international competition. So although the chemical park strategy traces its origins back to the mid-1990s, it was not until China formally entered the WTO in 2002 that the chemical park trend took off.

Most of China's chemical parks are located around Shanghai. The Shanghai Chemical Industrial Park (SCIP) at Caojing, a 22-square-kilometer facility 50 kilometers outside of Shanghai, was the first chemical park approved by the State Council and has helped to cement Shanghai's position as the center of China's chemical industry. In addition to a large portion of new greenfield investment, many domestic firms have shifted production into SCIP.[13] By 2002, SCIP had attracted $8 billion in foreign investment, and most major chemical MNCs have investments in SCIP. In part because of Shanghai's success, numerous chemical industrial parks have sprung up in surrounding areas. For instance, neighboring Jiangsu Province has at least twenty-three chemical parks. Nanjing Chemical Industrial Park, the second park after SCIP to receive approval from the State Council, is roughly 150 miles from SCIP and is China's second-largest chemical park. Other central government–approved parks include Shandong's Qilu (in Zibo), Xiamen Haicang, and Tianjin Chemical Industrial Park (*Europa Chemie* 1997). In China's west, Sichuan/Chongqing is attempting to develop its own chemical center (Reuters 1995). Gansu and Xinjiang are also attempting to woo chemical investors, often with the encouragement of the central government, which in recent years has begun to promote development of the chemical industry in China's hinterland provinces (Ian Young 1996).

Table 4.2 displays information about investment levels in nineteen randomly selected parks across five provinces/provincial-level cities. As evident in Table 4.2, there is heavy foreign investment in China's chemical parks. Each of the nineteen chemical parks had at least one foreign firm and in five parks foreign-invested enterprises outnumbered domestic firms. In eight of seventeen parks,[14] foreign investment accounts for more than half of all total investment, which reflects the larger size of foreign firms versus domestic firms. Excluding park number 19, whose large size somewhat skews the data, the average park has about sixty enterprises of which roughly 29 percent are foreign-invested. These FIEs account for 46.4 percent of all investment.

TABLE 4.2 Foreign investment levels in nineteen chemical parks across five Chinese provinces, 2004

Park number	Foreign firms (#)	Domestic firms (#)	Foreign firm investment (% total investment in park)	Domestic firm investment (% total investment in park)
1	1	33	10	90
2	2	40	10	90
3	2	51	15	85
4	2	83	0.4	99.6
5	2	18	12	88
6	5	10	65	35
7	5	50	20	80
8	5	0	—	—
9	11	26	70	30
10	12	4	90	10
11	13	3	80	20
12	13	170	49	51
13	15	60	65	35
14	20	52	52	48
15	24	54	28	72
16	38	50	—	—
17	46	10	38	62
18	96	64	84	16
19	376	705	88.4	11.6
TOTAL	688	1483	—	—
AVERAGE	36.2	78.1	45.7	54.3
AVERAGE EXCLUDING PARK # 19	17.3	43.2	43.0	57.0

Data gathered by author with the aid of a Chinese organization that wishes to remain anonymous. The parks are located in Jiangsu, Jiangxi, Anhui, and Zhejiang provinces, plus Shanghai, which is administratively equal to a province. In parks #8 and #16, representatives declined to offer investment figures.

In short, chemical parks have been built to consolidate China's industry and attract foreign investment. As Table 4.2 points out, in this latter goal the strategy has been highly successful.

An Explosion of Parks and Problems

The growth of chemical parks has gone well beyond the officially sanctioned mega-parks, and reports in the Chinese press indicate that China is experiencing a chemical park fever similar to the economic development zone frenzy of the 1990s. Because many parks have dubious legal standing, there is no record that indicates just how many exist. Although Chinese government officials typically estimate the number of parks to be around fifty, my own survey of the major chemical industry journals, various Chinese chemical association websites, and Chinese press leads me to conclude that as of late 2005 there were no less than seventy-two parks and likely many more.[15]

Regardless of the exact number, it is clear that parks have mushroomed beyond the desires of central government authorities. One expert, who has many years of working as a consultant for chemical firms in China, indicated that based simply on market demand, China needs no more than ten chemical parks and anything more represents a waste of resources.[16] He attributes the profusion of parks to two factors. First, there is the desire for consulting and approval fees by the CPCIA, which ultimately sanctions all parks. The CPCIA is the remnant of the Chemical Ministry, which, as noted, was abolished in the 1998 government reorganization. Though there were minimal changes in the staff after the reorganization, as an industry association rather than a government ministry the CPCIA receives virtually no funds from the central government.[17] This makes consulting and application fees highly valuable and, as indicated by the chemical consultant, the CPCIA simply refuses to say no when a locality applies to establish a park. The second factor is the legacy of the promotion of self-sufficiency from the Mao era. This has left industry scattered and local protectionism high. When the central government signals its emphasis on the chemical industry, as occurred frequently throughout the 1990s, every locality competes to become the newest center for chemical investment.

Articles in the Chinese media make similar claims about the undesirable profusion of parks and also point to the role of local government desires for development as a major spur to parks' profusion. (Not surprisingly, the role of the CPCIA is not mentioned in the Chinese media.) One report notes that every locality is striving to be the first to establish a park and, in a phrase that appears frequently in articles about chemical parks, concludes that chemical parks are "too numerous and too dense" (*guo duo guo mi*) (Fu 2003; Gu Zongqin 2004). Another states that chemical parks have "sprung up like bamboo shoots after rain" (*yu hou chun sun*), estimating there are almost one hundred of them (Cao 2002). Others state that parks are "coming in a continuous stream" (*fen zhi ta lai*), that China is in the midst of a "chemical park fever" (*yuanqu re*), and that chemical parks are the latest fashion (Bi 2003; Tian and Xiao 2003; Xin 2002). Tan Zhuzhou, the CPCIA head, also uses the term "fever" and states that just about every place that has a deepwater port has built or applied to build a chemical park (2003).

Also clear from the Chinese media is the fact that the race to build chemical parks has led to illegal, or semilegal, behavior on the part of firms and local governments. There is an abundance of reports in the Chinese press about unsavory activities surrounding chemical parks. As one *China Chemical News* reporter states, "from the moment chemical parks were born, problems have been exposed non-stop and debate has not ceased" (Wang Xiaoyang 2004). The crux of the problem is that the copious number of parks is spurring competition to attract capital, which is leading to blind development (*mangmu xing*) as parks hurriedly "mount the horse" (*cang cu shang ma*) (Tian and Xiao 2003).

According to Chinese media reports, facing fierce intra-regional competition, park officials are concerned solely with attracting capital (*zhao shang yin zi*), particularly foreign capital, and their principal means of doing so is the extension of preferential policies (Fu 2003). One report argues that park officials emphasize just two things—more land and more preferential policies. Park officials recognize that service is a key element of success, but they see service as simply the reduction of taxes and land prices; they believe that "yielding" is the only kind of service (Huang Cun 2003; Liu et al. 2004; Xin 2002). As Tan Zhuzhou states, "to attract capital some parks do not hesitate to hurt the country's interests by offering 'preferential policies'" (Fu 2003). One investigation concludes that chemical park administrators exist in the mind-set of exchanging land for capital. Another, more colorful report states that "the 'enclosing land' wind is blowing with increasing ferocity." It goes on to conclude that "in order to attract capital, many local governments set national laws and regulations on the side and find every possible way to enclose more land" (Zhongguo Huagong Wang 2004).

My own interviews with chemical park officials and brief trips to parks themselves largely confirm this general mind-set. Though identifying myself as a researcher and not an investor, my visits to parks in large part consisted of a tour of the park and PowerPoint presentations with detailed descriptions of plans for expansion and opportunities for future investment. In one of the parks I visited, which is widely regarded as a success story in both the domestic and foreign media, the prevalence of land issues was also clear in the farmers' protests that were taking place outside the government administration building in which I conducted the interviews. The protests, which lasted no less than ten days, involved several hundred farmers and a large number of public security officers who formed a ring around the farmers, blocked all incoming traffic, and via megaphones mounted on vans continually blasted orders to respect law and order.[18] Although such protests are hardly rare in China, the fact that one of China's most successful parks was dealing with claims of land snatching indicates the rapid growth of chemical parks has given rise to governance problems.

Chemical Parks' Missing Environmental Regulation

As parks race to attract investment and enclose more land, regulatory requirements are often tossed by the wayside. One of the most commonly cited violations of park administrators is the commencement of activities to attract capital, construction, and in some cases production prior to the attainment of regulatory approval for the park's establishment. As Chinese reports indicate, many parks have not completed a discussion over the park's feasibility, or are even still in the planning phase, when they begin large-scale activities to woo capital (Hua 2003; Liu et al. 2004). Sometimes referred to as "building the nest to attract the wind" (*zhu chao yin feng*), local governments build the park and begin the process of securing investors before even considering whether the area has any comparative advantage in the chemical industry (Fu 2003).

The bypassing of regulatory channels often means an absence of environmental protection. There are numerous reports of chemical parks failing to screen investment projects for pollution discharges and sidestepping EIA regulations. One report notes, "Environmental protection is a major reason for the grouping of the chemical industry, but presently it is also the most ignored factor" (*Zhongguo Huagong Bao* [China Chemical News] 2003). Another states, "Some of our parks do not care whether enterprises meet environmental standards and do not care whether after production there are any kinds of adverse consequences. In order to meet their goals for attracting capital, they bypass environmental protection laws and the environmental protection bureau" (Huang Cun 2003).

Many of the problems with the environmental governance in chemical parks are evident in the ongoing problems with the Shenjia Chemical Industrial Park, which is located in Quzhou City in Zhejiang Province. Shenjia Chemical Industrial Park, established in 1991 and located within the Shenjia Economic Development Zone, has roughly forty-nine enterprises and an annual production valued at approximately $65 million dollars, which indicates that it is a relatively small chemical park. Despite its small size, it has a large history of serious environmental problems. As a response to public complaints, in 2002 the park was designated a "key administrative area" by the provincial EPB, which meant it was to receive particular attention from environmental protection authorities. In 2003, seven government departments held a joint meeting focusing on cleaning up the industrial zone, which resulted in a statement that heavily criticized the park. But beyond that meeting, no other action was taken at the time.

A series of investigations in 2004 by the provincial EPB revealed grave problems with compliance and enforcement in the park. One inquiry revealed that one company was leaking poisonous chemicals inside the factory, another had not completed an EIA, while still others had not had their facilities inspected by environmental regulators prior to the commencement of production. In the local rivers, BOD (biological oxygen demand) and ammonia nitrates were well beyond permitted levels. Officials from the provincial EPBs were repeatedly blocked in their investigations and conducted some of their tests clandestinely. A representative from Zhejiang provincial government stated that, with the exception of a few firms that meet standards, most of the enterprises in the park had serious environmental protection problems.

In July 2004, provincial officials warned that the firms must fix their problems soon and indicated those that did not would have to cease production. They also sent out a warning to the local municipal government that if it is not able to solve the problem of the park's pollution and make sure the park meets its discharge standards, then the relevant government bureaus would deal with the matter seriously (Niu 2002). There was little report of follow-up until October 2004, when the Zhejiang provincial government and Quzhou city government signed an agreement on goals for repairing the environment that clearly called for the Shenjia Chemical Industrial Park to adjust its industrial structure by eliminating small, low-quality, pollution-intensive enterprises. By late December 2005, it was announced that sixteen enterprises in the park had been closed and many others were either temporarily closed or had been given a deadline to fix remaining problems. It was also announced that by 2007 all chemical enterprises would be moved out of the Shenjia Economic Development Zone (Quzhou Municipal Government 2005).

Although recent news indicates some success in enforcement in Shenjia, it is more an exception than a rule. The State Council and CPCIA have issued secondary legal instruments calling for local governments to "put in order and rectify" (*qingli zhengdun*) economic development zones and chemical parks.[19] But these urges largely resemble the empty threats of the secondary legal instruments in the 1980s described in Chapter 3, and with the exception of Shenjia there is little evidence that they led to any immediate significant action. Chinese-language chemical industry journals are full of announcements of parks opening and winning investment projects, but there is little mention of park closures.[20]

Moreover, there are still questions about the extent to which the Zhejiang provincial EPB has been able to control the activities in Shenjia Chemical Industrial Park. An investigation by the provincial EPB in mid-2005 concluded that in the park "not only has the pollution abatement not improved over last year, it has actually gotten worse." It highlighted the example of one enterprise that uses 3,700 tons of water a day, but only treats 400 tons. The investigation also found that a paint factory supposedly closed down in September 2004 was covered in paint spills and displayed numerous other signs of recent production activity. The blame was placed squarely on the shoulders of the local city (Quzhou) and park administration officials who were deemed as simply lacking the resolution to enforce environmental regulations (Li Xiaopeng 2005). Thus, the best-case scenario for Shenjia Chemical Industrial Park is that it was a serious environmental problem that took more than five years to address. The worst-case scenario is that, despite repeated investigations and much media coverage, once the spotlight fades it remains business as usual in the park.

Problems such as those in Shenjia are not limited to small parks; Shenjia is symbolic of a more widespread problem. In late 2002, Chongqing's chemical park, which was supported by the central government as a means of pushing development in China's west, was cited for failing to conduct environmental assessments prior to construction (Xiao Yunxiang 2002). In 2003, according to the supervision department head of SEPA, Liu Xinmin, across China only 50 percent of chemical parks had completed an EIA, which by Chinese law is required prior to any construction. For parks that operate at the city level and below, the implementation rate was just over 20 percent (Chen Guocheng

2004). The 50 percent implementation rate among chemical parks is roughly equivalent to the national EIA implementation rate in 1991, when the EIA program was in its infancy (Wang et al. 2003, 565, table 1). According to the 2004 China Environmental Statistical Yearbook, the 2003 national average for EIA implementation was almost 99 percent. The lowest average was in Hainan Province, 75 percent (SEPA 1998–2004: 2004, 211). While the 2003 national figures are likely inflated, the fact that chemical parks' implementation rate is far lower than even the worst provincial average is indicative of considerable regulatory negligence.

Some parks not only failed to complete EIAs, but they also did not construct the necessary environmental infrastructure. In 2004, Liu Xinmin indicated that for the majority of parks the environmental infrastructure is non-existent. He specifically noted that all parks in Hubei Province, as well as the three parks in Qinghai Province, lacked environmental infrastructure. The parks' construction was complete, but the environmental infrastructure was still in the planning phase (Chen Guocheng 2004). One report, citing the tendency of parks to allow firms to start production prior to the completion of the park's wastewater treatment facilities, noted that in 2003, in a single county the local EPB received seventy-seven complaints from the general public. One-third of these were related to chemical industrial parks (Wang Jiye 2004).

Another reporter discovered that enterprises in a chemical park are failing to treat wastewater prior to sending it off to the park's centralized wastewater treatment facility (as required by law). One firm's initial pollution treatment was to take wastewater with a high concentration of benzene, heavy metals, catalysts, and other harmful materials, put it in an iron trough, and then wait for an appropriate time to dilute it with running water. When asked about wastewater practices, a park official replied, "Right now the enterprises in the park discharge wastewater that is acidic in content, but in the future we will attract new enterprises that produce discharges with bases; we'll mix them together and everything will be fine" (Guan and Song 2003).

This phenomenon of "construct first, approve second" or "simultaneously construct and pollute" (*yibian jianshe, yibian wuran*) is both a cause and result of the organization of parks' environmental management. SEPA's supervision department head indicated that a major problem with environmental governance in the parks is the opaque nature of the parks' management, in which most of the approval processes take place within the park and are not overseen by municipal or provincial authorities. Frequently, environmental authorities within the park are appointed by the park administrators, and have little contact or relations with the local municipal EPB. Some parks have no environmental protection organization; there are no personnel whose job it is to oversee environmental protection (Chen Guocheng 2004; Wang Jiye 2004).

My own interviews with chemical park officials revealed a relatively bare-bones environmental management organization. In both of the parks I visited, the environmental protection personnel work within the park's Administrative Committee (*guanli weiyuanhui*). The Administrative Committee is technically a branch of the municipal government, but is given a great deal of autonomy and is better described as its own government. In one of the parks, which is comparably large, the Administrative Committee is comprised of approximately thirty people. One of the departments within the Administrative Committee is the Planning and Construction Bureau (PCB), which itself has five people, one of whom oversees environmental affairs. This person splits his time between the chemical park and the municipal EPB. He admitted that the PCB is stretched thin and that they do not actively monitor the environmental behavior of the hundred-plus firms in the park, but rather rely on self-reporting and the occasional spot check. Again, the parks in which I conducted interviews are national priorities for the central government, generally perceived as laudable in their environmental behavior, and have met local requirements for pollutant discharges. Given their thin environmental management, it is not hard to imagine that parks in China's hinterland that are less subject to national oversight have no environmental management system.

What Role for Foreign Investment?

Clearly, there have been extensive problems with environmental regulation in China's chemical parks. It is also evident that the neglect of environmental law is to no small extent the result of domestic officials' eagerness for development and capital combined with the increased (though ultimately limited) supply of external capital. Running throughout the narrative of the previous sections is the fact that desire for capital is driving much of the behavior of government officials who are turning a blind eye to pollution management.[21] One article summarizes the situation well, stating:

> In the process of attracting foreign investment, many local governments have little room for choice; in order to attract foreign capital they give many preferential policies among which many are related to the environment. So long

as it is foreign capital, it is categorically welcomed; everything is dedicated to attracting foreign capital and attracting more foreign capital. In this way, it is inevitable that China is becoming a pollution shelter for developed country sunset and pollution-intensive industries. (Xu and Zhao 2004)

The role that competition for mobile capital plays in environmental negligence is also apparent in government documents designed to address the problem. For instance, the CPCIA's 2003 pronouncement, "Guiding Opinion Concerning the Development of China's Chemical Industrial Parks," indicates that chemical parks have to avoid "disorderly competition" (*wuxu jingzheng*). It then forwards the recommendation that only the select few chemical parks with the requisite initial conditions should pursue investment from multinational companies. It admonishes other parks and urges them to avoid "coveting the big and seeking the foreign" (*tan da qiu yang*) and to put more of their attention on domestic investors (CPCIA 2004). Again, this points to the idea that it is the ambitious pursuit of investment, and especially foreign investment, that is driving the "disorderly" competition among China's chemical parks and undermining environmental governance.

But the competition for foreign investment does not have the same impact across all jurisdictions. The examples in this chapter indicate that it is the parks that generally lack a competitive advantage in the chemical sector that tend to exhibit the behavior that most resembles the regulatory-chill phenomenon. The four or five parks in China that because of history, location, and smart local government policies have developed a clear competitive advantage in the chemical industry are also the parks that are regarded as strongest in terms of administrative oversight and most praiseworthy in their environmental governance, and are the ones that have managed to attract numerous large-scale investments from foreign multinationals. The analysis and praise of these parks' regulatory practices fills the pages of China's industrial journals. This parallels the situation in China's special economic zones more broadly, where the zones that have enjoyed great success in wooing investment are also those that have the most stringent environmental laws. Shenzhen, in particular, has been frequently lauded for going beyond the national baseline in many of its environmental policies (Lam 1986; Richardson 2004b).[22]

By contrast, the parks that lack the initial conditions to attract investment and develop a chemical industry tend to display the weakest environmental governance. This is seen in the numerous references in Chinese articles to problems with parks in China's less developed inland provinces. It is commonly asserted that inland jurisdictions should not attempt to become a center for the chemical industry because of their unfavorable location, deficiency of technology and infrastructure, uneducated work force, absence of upstream and downstream companies, and lack of history and experience in the chemical industry (Gu Zongqin 2004; Tian and Xiao 2003). The fact that the CPCIA points out that environmental and other regulatory problems are occurring in small parks without a clear basis for the establishment of a chemical industry, and urges parks without the necessary initial conditions to give up their ambitions for attracting big projects from overseas, also indicates that it is an inability to attract capital that contributes to the neglect of environmental law. In this sense, it is not foreign investment alone that undermines environmental regulation, but the aspiration for foreign investment by jurisdictions that lack the ability to attract it. The suggestion, then, is that regulatory chill is initially most likely to occur not where foreign investment is most prevalent, but where it is strongly desired and historically scarce.

It should be pointed out that, at least in the case of Chinese chemical parks, poor environmental enforcement is an overdetermined outcome. I have indicated that areas less competitive in terms of attracting FDI are more likely to ignore environmental regulation. These areas more keenly experience inter-jurisdictional competitive pressures, as opposed to areas well suited to the chemical industry, which have the luxury of picking and choosing among investment projects. However, one of the chief determinants of a region's attractiveness to foreign investment is GDP, as wealthy areas frequently possess characteristics appealing to foreign investors, such as developed infrastructure and educated workers. The fact that FDI-competitiveness and GDP are correlated raises the question about the precise cause of weak environmental enforcement. Economic development is itself correlated with environmental protection, as high-income jurisdictions typically have a greater capacity and face increased social pressure to enforce environmental regulation (Dasgupta et al. 2002). Therefore, how do I know that it is competition for capital, as opposed to low income, that explains the weak implementation in China's chemical parks? After all, even in the absence of competition for foreign investment, one would expect poor implementation in China's poorer regions compared to the wealthier coastal areas.

The assertion here is that the competition for capital represents an *additional* causal mechanism leading to the same outcome as low income. The low-income mechanism asserts that environmental regulators in poor regions, because they lack capacity and societal pressure, do not adequately enforce environmental standards. The argument here is that environmental regulators in poor regions that are *also* competing fiercely to woo external, mobile capital face an even greater challenge in environmental protection, as the race to construct infrastructure and approve investments augments the already existing tendency to neglect environmental law.[23]

Conclusion

This chapter has shown that on the broadest level, more foreign investment is correlated with better environmental regulation. The provinces richest in foreign capital tend to be those that have the best record in implementing environmental law. The provinces with the lowest implementation rate are also the poorest in terms of FDI. This indicates that attracting foreign capital does not result in a decline of implementation as a strict interpretation of the race-to-the-bottom argument would predict. But the positive association between FDI and measures of pollution does not mean that the competition for capital is without a negative influence on environmental regulation. Provinces on the low end of the FDI spectrum display a wide range of regulatory outcomes and, as the case of China's chemical parks shows, some of this variance is explained by strategies for attracting foreign capital. The desire of local governments to build chemical parks based on foreign capital has contributed to serious problems in environmental regulation, which have taken the form of nonimplementation of standards and been particularly common in areas disadvantaged in the quest to build a local chemical industry. Jurisdictions eager for capital, but challenged in attracting it, demonstrate a willingness to disregard environmental protection requirements.

One can question how representative the case of China's chemical parks really is. To what extent are they a unique occurrence? Certainly, a particular confluence of factors have come together to create the environmental problems with chemical parks. These factors include a heavy stress on the chemical industry by the central government, combined with a high degree of decentralization that gives local governments extensive autonomy from national authorities and allows park officials freedom from the oversight of municipal governments. At the same time, China's nondemocratic political system means that local government officials, who have traditionally placed environmental protection well below economic development on their list of priorities, lack accountability to the general population. This has facilitated the enclosing of land for the construction of chemical parks and hastened the approval of pollution-intensive projects that might have generated social resistance in a more participatory political system. As evident in the Shenjia example, in which no less than five years passed from the onset of public complaints until officials took active steps to resolve environmental protection problems, local governments have also been relatively shielded from the societal repercussions arising from pollution caused by chemical parks. Finally, all this has taken place in the context of a country that is extremely eager for foreign investment. The very name of the reform period in Chinese, *gaige kaifang*, which translates as "reform and opening," points to the central place foreign capital holds in the minds of most Chinese seeking to promote economic development. As noted in the first section, a chief purpose of promoting chemical parks has been to attract foreign investment and technology. This deep-seated normative belief in the need for foreign capital helps explain how a desire for development can turn into the "chemical park fever" described by so many Chinese analysts.

The implication is that, although China's situation is somewhat unique, the basic factors giving rise to the park phenomenon—jurisdictional competition, a political system in which elites are sheltered from the public, eagerness for foreign capital—are certainly prevalent elsewhere in the world, whether one is talking about competition between states in Southeast Asia or intra-country competition in India or Brazil. The case of Shenjia presented above took place in Zhejiang Province, which is on China's coast and is one of the provinces more abundant in foreign capital. Other areas in Zhejiang (e.g., Hangzhou) have had success in balancing development of the chemical industry and environmental protection. But with a population of 43 million and area roughly the combined size of Georgia and South Carolina, there is significant room for intra-provincial competition. Indeed, one member of China's environmental media indicated that problems of competition between parks may be fiercer within provinces than across provincial boundaries. Hence, it may be possible that wherever one finds areas that are desirous of attracting capital but poorly endowed in terms of competitive advantage, there is the potential for a situation that resembles that of China's chemical parks.[24]

5 Patterns in Compliance: Multinationals as Agents of Upward Pressure

The preceding chapter showed that under certain conditions a desire to attract foreign capital has led to a neglect of environmental law in China's chemical parks. Government officials, eager to build parks and woo capital, have failed to heed basic environmental protection requirements such as the Environmental Impact Assessment Law. This phenomenon, which largely resembles the expectations of the regulatory-chill argument, is not universal, but limited principally to jurisdictions that are poorly suited to attracting external capital. However, one question was left unanswered: Do foreign-invested enterprises take advantage of the lax regulatory environment and shirk pollution abatement requirements in their China operations? The next two chapters answer this question. This chapter begins the process by analyzing the environmental behavior of multinational corporations (MNCs) in the chemical and energy sector, as well as their interaction with domestic firms and government regulators. It is well established that there is a difference in the environmental behavior of large firms versus small and medium-sized firms. Thus, there is a need for focusing separately on large multinationals, which is the task of this chapter. In Chapter 6, I broaden the focus and look at foreign-invested firms more generally.

Most of the research presented in this chapter is based on interviews with foreign-firm managers and on companies' internal environment, health, and safety (EHS) documents. I conducted just fewer than thirty interviews with representatives from sixteen MNCs.[1] This information is supplemented with discussions with twenty Chinese-firm representatives, as well as interviews with those outside the corporate world, including government officials and local experts such as environmental lawyers, NGO workers, journalists, and consultants.

The argument put forward here is that, when looking at large MNCs, there is little evidence of a firm-induced downward pressure on regulation.[2] On the contrary, most evidence points to the fact that MNCs comply with China's environmental regulations and many go beyond compliance. This is not to say that foreign manufacturing sites are 100 percent compliant 100 percent of the time. Nor is it to say that MNCs' environmental records are as good in their China operations as they are in home countries. But this difference is often as much a function of a lack of environmental infrastructure as it is firm strategy. More interesting than foreign-firm compliance is evidence that firms exercise private authority in a manner that enhances China's environmental governance. As part of their EHS practices, leading foreign companies often work with domestic firms to bring their environmental behavior into compliance with local regulation. This interaction between foreign and domestic firms takes various forms and can involve both coercion and persuasion. MNC private authority influences joint venture partners, domestic suppliers and commercial partners, and in some cases competitors. Foreign companies also work with regulators in a manner that generally enhances industrial environmental regulation. In short, to the extent that they have an effect, MNCs help narrow the gap between environmental regulation on the books and enforcement on the ground.

The next section provides a brief overview of multinationals' EHS practices and shows that, while they do not necessarily perform on the same level as they do in their home country, large MNCs in China take EHS seriously. The subsequent section focuses on the exercise of private authority, exploring MNCs' relations with, respectively, joint venture partners, suppliers and domestic commercial partners, and government regulators.

The Environmental Behavior of Multinationals in China

MNCs operate at or above Chinese regulatory standards. Because China is a country characterized by weak environmental governance, where firms can go long periods of time without oversight, and because government agencies do not routinely provide firm-level compliance data to foreign researchers, the previous statement is not based on a regulatory paper trail. Rather, as stated at the outset, it is based on interviews with a number of those involved in China's environmental governance as well as firms' EHS documents.

The first piece of evidence of foreign-firm compliance can be seen in the details of firms' corporate EHS practices. Each of the sixteen foreign firms interviewed has a highly developed corporate EHS policy.[3] Corporate EHS policies differ across firms in their wording and particular emphasis, but share many common features and tend to reflect the various global agreements on environment and safety, such as the chemical industry's Responsible Care (RC), the United Nations' Global Compact, and the Global Reporting Initiative (GRI).[4] The structure and implementation of corporate EHS policies in foreign firms' China operations demonstrate a strong commitment to environmental protection. As firms set up their China operations, company officials with many years of experience in the EHS field work with local management to translate broad EHS principles into particular policies (e.g., no accidental releases) and procedures (e.g., steps to take in case of a release). These policies and procedures cover a variety of EHS issues such as air, water, and waste release, workplace safety, emergency preparedness, and materials transportation. In each of these areas, firms create metrics, checklists, and/or scorecards against which EHS site managers and plant general managers are assessed.

A key pillar of assuring compliance with EHS policies is auditing. There are three main ways in which firms conduct audits. First, the site assesses itself against particular EHS criteria and the data collected at the site get reported up to corporate EHS officers and included in annual reports (most global firms produce a specific EHS or sustainable development report). Firms also conduct external audits of their foreign sites. Typically an audit involves approximately five individuals with experience in EHS who inspect a site for approximately a two-week period for performance in a number of EHS issues. Auditors are internal to the company, but external to the site and often from a different business unit. The frequency of auditing differs across firms, but ranges between two and five years. Sites that have had compliance problems in the past are audited more frequently than those that have been determined "green." Some firms also conduct unannounced spot audits. Finally, many firms open their sites to third-party certification, typically through ISO 14000. With the exception of one firm, all firms interviewed stated that their China operations either were currently ISO certified or in the process of becoming certified.

Foreign-firm representatives clearly feel the pressure of trying to meet the expectations of stringent corporate standards in a context not always favorable to compliance. One representative noted the challenges of meeting his firm's corporate standard, which requires 100 percent compliance with local environmental regulations. Like many other firm representatives, he stated it is common for environmental officials in Beijing to pass a new regulation that local environmental protection bureaus (EPBs) have no way to implement. For instance, with regard to pollution discharges, the local government typically licenses a small number of agencies or laboratories as qualified to sample for emissions and certify that firms meet a regulatory requirement. This foreign-firm representative noted that his company frequently finds these labs have no idea how to monitor a particular pollutant and/or that they themselves are unaware of or unclear about a new regulation. Officials in local EPBs often lack the equipment or know-how to sample and analyze particular emissions (e.g., dioxin). Given this inability to have their discharges monitored and certified, foreign firms cannot comply with China's discharge permit system, which requires enterprises to register with EPBs and apply for pollution permits.[5]

Others were frank that their China operations have encountered problems in the area of environmental and safety protection, especially acquired sites (as opposed to new, greenfield investments). One firm representative stated that it took the company three years to get one acquired site up to full compliance.[6] Another EHS manager, who has overseen the construction and commissioning of a new investment, admitted that there is a "huge gap" between safety and environmental culture, stating: "We're about two years behind in creating an environmental culture comparable with our safety culture; we have a pretty good safety culture now; we don't have a great environmental culture."[7] This acknowledged lag between safety and environmental performance was common. Another firm representative expressed a similar idea, stating: "We're finding the opportunity to sell, to convince people on safety is moving forward very quickly; we still have to work a little bit on the environment."[8] Several firms admitted that it took (or is taking) them longer than anticipated to get their China operations on par with operations in other countries in terms of EHS performance, which is a euphemistic way of stating that Chinese operations perform more poorly than the home-country firm. One manager offered an example of some of the problems his firm encountered in transportation. He noted that HQ insisted on installing high-tech, stainless-steel coupling devices to transfer raw chemicals from the suppliers' trucks to the factory's storage container. When supplier trucks showed up with only a rubber hose to transfer chemicals, the coupling devices were useless and they were forced to create an on-the-spot solution that the manager admitted was extremely dangerous.[9]

If audits are the first pillar of assuring compliance in China operations, training is the second. The extent and variety of this training again points to the seriousness with which large MNCs take EHS in their China operations. Firms provide their employees with a significant amount of both introductory and refresher courses that, for large investments, will total tens of thousands of hours. GE, for instance, provides training to employees in auditing, job safety analysis, and hazard awareness. Business leaders, including plant managers, get extra training such as a two-day seminar on EHS (Gelb and Hulme 2002). In greenfield investments, many of which involve millions of man-hours for construction and commissioning, a firm will train tens of thousands of workers. One project, for instance, conducted basic "site training" for 50,000 workers while another 2,700 workers received instruction in specialized topics such as rigging and lifting, confined space entry, EHS leadership, and gas detection.[10]

In order to keep EHS issues on the forefront of employees' minds, firms also conduct a number of activities that, while not formal training, are nonetheless designed to sharpen employees' EHS awareness. One firm, for instance, routinely performed "side-by-side" walk-through activities in which one foreign manager and one local manager conducted a safety observation of the site.[11] In a similar vein, a manager from a different company reported that every time he visits a site, he randomly selects a local manager/foreman to walk through the site with him to make sure that they are seeing the same things in terms of hazard identification.[12] Other examples of similar awareness-enhancing activities held within companies include daily briefings on EHS issues with managers or foremen, ceremonies designed to stress the importance of commitment to EHS, zero-tolerance policies for EHS violations, and "just in time" training, in which employees are given refresher training immediately prior to commencing a high-risk activity (e.g., rigging or working at heights). Types of training differ across firms, but all the interviewed firms conducted a significant amount of EHS training for employees.[13]

Of course, one would not expect representatives of multinational companies to admit noncompliance, which raises questions about the validity of the above depiction of MNC behavior. There is also the issue of what exactly constitutes compliance. Those familiar with the Chinese regulatory environment will point out that compliance may mean adhering to discharge standards or it may mean paying the fine for violating a discharge standard in a timely manner—two outcomes very different in terms of the impact on the natural environment.[14] To the extent possible, the information presented here was cross-checked with local officials and experts with experience in China's environmental protection. These sources largely supported the idea that MNCs do not operate below China's environmental regulatory standards.[15] In the context of a conversation about large chemical and energy firms, one senior SEPA official stated: "Even though China lacks a comprehensive environmental protection system, multinational companies have good environmental behavior. It is not the case that all have good environmental behavior, but the vast majority do, especially the well-known firms that care a great deal about their reputation like Dupont, BASF, etc."[16] A recently published study looking at corporate environmental behavior in the chemical industry also quotes a senior SEPA official, who compares domestic and foreign-firm behavior, stating: "I am not aware of any MNC engaging in environmental pollution activities in China. It is hard to pick on our own SOEs [state-owned enterprises]; as you know, they have their own problems. We need to be patient with them otherwise there will be major social unrest" (Child and Tsai 2005, 112–13). Another environmental official whom I interviewed, whose responsibility includes oversight of new investment in one of the China's largest chemical industrial parks, indicated that during the environmental impact assessment process that is required by Chinese law for all new investments, it is common for environmental authorities and firms to negotiate over pollution discharge levels. However, he said this is rarely the case for foreign firms because in his estimation, it is not difficult for foreign firms to meet Chinese discharge regulations.[17] This sentiment that foreign firms comply with environmental regulations in their China operations was emphasized by various other local experts, including an environmental lawyer and a UNDP official working in Beijing.[18]

This description of foreign-firm EHS practices does not mean that MNCs are always compliant with China's environmental law. As discussed in Chapter 1, starting in late 2006, a Chinese NGO called the Institute of Public and Environmental Affairs (IPEA) released a list of approximately 2,700 companies accused of violating China's water laws. This list was not only put on the IPEA website, but also released to *Southern Weekend*, an influential investigative newspaper, and picked up by the broader Chinese media (Ma and Xu 2006; Zhang 2006). On the original list were 33 foreign companies including well-known MNCs such as Nestlé, Pepsi, 3M, and Panasonic. The report accused these firms, some of which have signed public declarations of corporate social responsibility for their operations in China, of "relaxing environmental standards." Accusations leveled at the MNCs were based on government reports, which themselves were not made available to the public. The charges included failing to operate water treatment facilities, exceeding discharge standards, and initiating operations prior to installing pollution abatement equipment.

While these accusations must certainly be taken seriously, they also reveal the extent to which foreign firms do *not* violate China's environmental law. Ma Jun, the founder of IPEA, indicated that foreign firms did a better job on environmental protection than domestic firms, pointing out that the 33 foreign firms on the list paled in comparison to the more than 2,600 domestic firms on the list (Zhang 2006). In other words, foreign firms represented less than 1 percent of violations. *Southern Weekend*, offering a view common among Chinese environmentalists, argues that the higher portion of domestic firms, while unfortunate, is understandable, as Chinese enterprises are weaker than their foreign counterparts. Chinese companies, it asserts, are unable to comply, whereas foreign firms are simply unwilling (Ma and Xu 2006). The soundness of this assertion is debatable, but the underlying empirical reality is clear: MNCs may run afoul of China's environmental law—they simply do so with far less frequency than domestic firms.

It should also be pointed out that the positive portrayal of MNCs given in this chapter does not indicate that MNCs' environmental practices are as strong in China as they are in their home country or in their foreign operations in developed countries.[19] As already noted, firms point out there are significant obstacles to implementing corporate EHS standards and occasionally admit that they have not brought China operations up to corporate standards. Moreover, many firms are satisfied with complying with Chinese environmental regulations even though it means leaving a heavier ecological footprint than would be the case if they were producing in their own, more environmentally stringent country. One regulator, focusing on foreign-invested coal companies, noted that foreign firms generally only meet the legal minimum obligation for EHS and that China's most advanced domestic firms exhibit better environmental behavior (Pottinger et al. 2004).

One common example of how foreign firms are content to comply with the law of the land is in the area of wastewater discharges. In many areas,

Chinese regulations presently only require factories to control the concentration of pollutants in wastewater discharges.[20] In other words, restrictions on discharged pollutants are based on the amount of pollutant per unit volume of water. This has long been recognized as a weakness in Chinese regulation because it provides little incentive for factories to control the total amount of pollutants as would a system based on both concentration and mass flowrate of pollutants. Under the current Chinese system, if a factory's discharges exceed the maximum permitted concentration for a particular pollutant, the managers can simply add more water to lower the concentration. Thus, the concentration-based system does not necessarily lower the amount of pollutants being discharged into the water, and it encourages factories to use more water. Some foreign factories operating in China admitted that, because Chinese regulators do not implement a mass-based system, they do not control for total volume of pollutants. One manager of a foreign-owned factory stated that because it is a requirement in his home country, his factory could control for total volume if it needed to, but it presently does not. He expects that as the regulatory regime strengthens over the next few years he will have to start controlling for volume, but he says this will not be a problem for his operation because it is already capable of complying with a more stringent mass-based system.[21]

However, it should be reiterated that the focus of this research is not simply a comparative study of the ecological impact of MNCs' home-country and foreign operations, but rather is an exploration of the impact of firms on China's environmental regulation. The previous paragraphs are only designed to provide a more complete, realistic look at foreign firms' EHS practices. This first section has begun the process of examining foreign firms' influence on environmental governance by exploring the extent to which firms comply with environmental regulations in their China operations. As discussed in the opening chapters, many have argued that firms adopt an exploitative strategy and seek to shirk environmental regulation. The above shows that, when focusing on the China operations of leading MNCs from developed countries, the preponderance of evidence points to the conclusion that this does not occur. Firms comply with local regulation and in some cases have EHS policies that are more stringent than local regulation. Attention can now turn to how foreign firms influence the social and regulatory environment in which they operate.

Foreign Firms Exercising Private Authority

That large MNCs from economically developed, strict-regulation countries comply with environmental regulation in their China manufacturing sites is not entirely surprising. As noted in previous chapters, several econometric studies have shown that environmental performance is positively correlated with firm size, and several studies have shown that MNCs tend to use a single set of corporate environmental practices across global operations. This chapter's look at the process of implementing EHS in China confirms much of what these other studies have revealed. More interesting perhaps is the fact that foreign firms are exercising private authority in China's environmental governance. Moreover, they are employing this authority in a manner that is creating an upward push on the process of implementing environmental regulation. This is evidenced in firms' relations with joint venture (JV) partners, domestic suppliers and service providers, and government regulators. After a brief explanation of the choice of the term "private authority," this section explores the sources of and manner in which firms are utilizing their authority.

Firms are referred to as exercising "private authority," as opposed to "power" or "influence," because authority implies an element of legitimacy. As Cutler, Haufler, and Porter state in the introduction to their work on private authority: "Authority exists when an individual or organization has decision-making power over a particular issue area and is regarded as exercising that power legitimately. . . . Authority does not necessarily have to be associated with government institutions" (1999, 5). Their volume, and others that followed, point out a number of sources of private authority including expertise, historical practice, and delegation by the state (implicit and explicit) (Buthe 2003; Hall and Biersteker 2004). As will become clear in the following discussion, much of foreign firms' private authority stems first from the fact that China's weak environmental governance leaves a space that firms, in a self-interested desire to protect their reputation, partially fill. MNC authority rests on the firm's own expertise coupled with an acceptance by many government regulators and domestic firms that "foreign" equals "advanced," which in turns equals "worthy of emulation." The net result is that what we see in China is an example of the subnational exercise of global private authority in a manner that strengthens China's environmental regulation.

Private Authority in Joint Ventures:
Disputes over Corporate Environmental Policies

One of the areas in which MNCs exercise private authority in a manner that enhances China's environmental regulation is with their joint venture partners. Establishing EHS standards in joint ventures is often a significant part of the investment process and can be one of the more contentious elements of the joint venture negotiations. Whether EHS becomes an area of conflict depends on a number of factors, such as the foreign firm's EHS approach and negotiating strategy, the domestic partner's extant EHS policies, the size and visibility of the investment, and—perhaps most importantly—the ownership structure. In discussions with foreign firms and local experts, the degree of foreign control was repeatedly cited as a critical factor influencing the extent of contention and the project's overall EHS approach. The reasons are straightforward. Most foreign firms have predetermined ownership-based policies guiding EHS in joint venture projects. For instance, one firm representative noted that, if a JV project is more than 40 percent owned by his firm, it is corporate policy that the project will operate to the same EHS standards as a wholly owned operation.[22] MNCs typically set the standard at 50 percent, but all had clear corporate policies in this area. When foreign ownership is well above the 50 percent threshold, there is typically less difficulty reaching agreement on EHS practices, for the simple reason that the foreign firm controls the purse strings.

In cases of an acquisition, obtaining the desired level for EHS practices can be thorny, although EHS issues are typically not a major part of the negotiation process itself. Prior to the agreement the foreign firm will conduct a "gap analysis" of the proposed site as part of a due diligence process. This gap analysis, in essence, is a risk assessment that looks at a variety of environmental aspects such as soil and groundwater conditions, manufacturing facilities, and the overall environmental management practices and regulatory history of the existent plant (e.g., permits and penalties). Once the gap analysis is complete, firms will work to get the required EHS improvements written into the JV agreement. Often, the gaps are significant, as one firm representative stated:

> There are a lot of challenges if you are talking about acquisitions of a local industry; obviously the standard both in terms of engineering and employees' awareness is far below your company's standards. . . . For our own designed

plants, it is easy because we have our own standards with which we must comply, so for instance, we must discharge effluents to the local acceptable standards and we have our own effluent treatment . . . but if it's a new acquisition then we have a lot of work to do.[23]

Another representative put it more simply, saying that if the project is an acquisition, "there will be struggle."[24]

The biggest challenge comes when foreign firms are minority partners or the project is a 50-50 joint venture. In this situation, firms lack the financial leverage necessary to impose standards and can be obliged to engage in extended, occasionally heated negotiations if they seek to assure the project meets corporate standards. Yet even in this situation, firms are able to exercise a degree of authority. Perhaps no case represents this better than Shell's involvement in the West-East pipeline (WEP) project.

West-East Pipeline Project   The $8.5 billion WEP project is a 4,000 kilometer pipeline with a capacity to transport 12 billion cubic meters of natural gas a year.[25] The pipeline originates in Xinjiang on China's northwestern border and traverses the entire width of China, traveling through eight provinces before reaching its final destination in Shanghai. The project is part of China's decision to reduce its reliance on coal and is designed to provide natural gas to both central and eastern China. The pipeline became fully operational in January 2005 and is currently 95 percent owned by PetroChina, while Sinopec controls the remaining 5 percent. The project dates back to the 1990s, but starting in 2001 PetroChina opened the project for foreign investment as a joint venture project. From 2001 to 2004, Shell frequently led negotiations for a consortium of international investors that included Shell and Hong Kong and China Gas (combined 15 percent), Russia's Gazprom (15 percent), and Exxon Mobil and China Light and Power Enterprises (combined 15 percent). Talks over the joint venture framework agreement stalled, and in August 2004, PetroChina terminated the arrangement and decided to forge ahead alone. Both sides cited a failure to find common ground, and analysts attributed the breakdown to a variety of disagreements over commercial considerations including division of shares in upstream gas investments, guaranteed return on investment, and division of output (Browne et al. 2004; Energy Compass 2003).[26]

Though financial concerns were the principal area of discord and ultimate source of the joint venture's demise, EHS was a major area of discussion as well. At the same time Shell was negotiating the commercial aspects of the joint venture agreement, it was pushing for greater attention to environmental and social issues. Shell was never legally a financial partner in the agreement during the negotiations, which were occurring at the same time PetroChina was moving forward with the construction. This fact curtailed Shell's bargaining power on EHS issues. As one individual closely involved in the project stated, "there was absolutely no reason why PetroChina should cooperate at all because Shell was not part of the project at the time; nor was there any reason why they should implement its findings since Shell had not bought into the project."[27] Despite its limited options, a combination of Shell's reputational power and carrot-and-stick strategy allowed it to exert considerable influence over the environmental and health practices of the WEP project. This section first outlines the details of the negotiations before drawing some general conclusions about the Shell case.

In February 2001, PetroChina invited foreign firms to participate in the pipeline project. Several large multinational companies began to bid, including consortiums led by BP, Gazprom, Exxon Mobil, and Shell. By the time foreign investors were invited, the project had already received approval from central-level government and the various EIAs were either completed and approved or underway. Construction was scheduled to begin in September 2001, which gave Shell and all other international bidders a very short time frame in which to review the pipeline design and construction plans, conduct due diligence, and take the numerous other steps that typically precede participation in a major foreign-investment project. Shell did not have access to the EIAs or detailed design plans until shortly before being selected as a partner, so much of the foreign investors' initial negotiation was conducted with less than full information. For instance, during much of the bidding process the only map of the pipeline route provided to the international companies was on a scale of 1:50,000, which for all practical purposes meant that they did not know the detailed route of the pipeline.[28]

Nonetheless, according to Shell officials and others involved in the project, even at this early stage Shell made clear that its participation depended on being able to construct and operate the pipeline to standards consistent with those it used elsewhere in the world and with Chinese standards. Because the project was one of the four major infrastructure projects of the Tenth Five-year Plan (2001–2005),[29] there was a tremendous amount of political pressure on PetroChina to maintain the construction schedule. Therefore, PetroChina was understandably resistant to any major changes in EHS policies that could potentially slow construction. One person involved in the project described the initial attitude of PetroChina as: "The design is done, it meets Chinese standards, do you want to participate or not?"[30] In the early stages of the bidding process, Shell worked with other interested firms to try to remove EHS standards from the bidding process. At one point, Shell officials sat down with other firms tendering offers to table a motion for all parties to adopt a set of common EHS standards. This would allow all bidders to approach the domestic partners with a united front and eliminate EHS considerations from the selection process. However, for various reasons stemming from the different approaches of competing firms, no agreement was reached.

In September 2001, Shell was selected as the preferred partner for further negotiation and began working toward a joint venture framework agreement. Around the same time, Shell officials began the process of translating and examining the EIAs. An EIA had been completed by PetroChina for each of the provinces through which the pipeline passes, and each had been approved by the provincial environmental protection bureaus (EPBs), as well as the State Environmental Protection Administration. Yet it was clear to Shell that there were some significant gaps in the EIAs and that it would be difficult to participate in the project with its current EHS approach.

One of the principal deficiencies in the EIAs was that, although they had been approved at the national level by SEPA, some had not been formally accepted by some local-level EPBs or reviewed by other relevant government agencies.[31] For instance, the original design for the pipeline crossed the Great Wall over a dozen times. In the process of conducting its due diligence, Shell discovered that local officials in the Ministry of Culture had not been consulted on how to conduct the crossings without impairing the wall. The EIAs addressed cultural-relic issues, but EIAs were approved by SEPA, and SEPA did not have authority or responsibility for cultural relics, which belonged to the Ministry of Culture. An additional problem was that in some cases certain aspects of the EIAs were incomplete. For instance, Shell discovered that the pipeline traversed two nature reserves, which were not included in the original EIAs.[32] The biodiversity assessments of the EIAs, according to one person involved in this area, tended to be a superficial "species list." They would simply state that "these are the species that exist in such and such province" and there was no geo-referencing or analysis of the project's biodiversity impact or plans for mitigation.[33] It should be noted, however, that assessing the impact on biodiversity is not an explicit part of China's EIA law. The interviewee was quick to point out that PetroChina was "not below the national bar" in its biodiversity assessment.

Another area in which Shell sought to enhance the environmental and social aspects of the project was compensation and resettlement. The project required the resettlement of approximately 3,000 people and another 230,000 were compensated for short-term impacts on their income (e.g., construction interfering with a farmer's harvest). Shell agreed with PetroChina on a series of joint audits of compensation and resettlement processes, which brought in independent private consultants, local authorities, and the land bureaus. Some of the audits conducted by Shell and Petrochina revealed problems with project-impacted persons (PIP). The audit teams found that many impacted persons were living with relatives and were unclear when they could expect funds for new housing. (The very fact that a transition was necessary was a problem since according to World Bank standards, which Shell sought to use as a basis for dealing with PIP, new domiciles should be complete prior to the destruction of the old ones.) The situation was better in the eastern regions, but according to one person involved in the audits, in the less developed west "the people simply have no expectations and they would accept whatever was provided for them." The representative estimated that in the western regions approximately 50 percent of the people had problems along these lines.[34]

As it was discovering these issues with EIAs, Shell continued to make the case for beyond-compliance EHS standards. Shell asked for additional, enhanced environmental and social impact assessments (ESIAs) and that construction be postponed, which was no small request given that Shell was not formally a financial partner and that construction was set to begin on the eastern portion. In December 2001, Shell and its partners agreed to a standards document of roughly forty pages, which outlined the intended approach to sustainable development, including issues such as ESIA, stakeholder engagement, and social performance.[35] Participating firms agreed on a set of minimum criteria on issues such as construction at cultural relic sites and nature reserves, health and safety issues, and audits and inspections (Seymour 2004).

Also part of the December agreement was a decision that construction would be phased. Construction would go forward, but only in areas in which enhanced ESIAs had been completed and environmental management plans had been drawn up.[36] The goal in the phased construction was to allow time for the extra ESIAs desired by Shell and its partners without excessively affecting the construction schedule. Teams of Shell officials, PetroChina employees, and environmental consultants from Environmental Resources Management (ERM) would go out to particularly sensitive areas (e.g., nature reserves) or to areas where construction was started and conduct what was referred to as "rapid assessment" management plans. These rapid assessments typically involved working not only in conjunction with PetroChina, who as the only investor was in a position to serve as a gatekeeper to all construction sites, but also with local authorities and reserve managers, as well as several local institutes, such as Beijing University's College of Environmental Sciences, Arid Lands and Desert Research Institute, and the Chinese Academy of Sciences. Once ERM and Shell officials created or amended environmental management plans, they would then discuss their findings with PetroChina and if necessary work to persuade PetroChina to accept the findings and pass them on to contractors.

Construction on the first of these "vetted areas" began in early 2002 and full construction did not begin until a complete set of minimum standards had been reached and formally included in the Framework Agreement, which was signed in July 2002. This agreement to conduct additional environmental assessments had a variety of impacts. For instance, PetroChina made an $18 million decision to reroute the pipeline in order to avoid the core and buffer protection zones of the Arjin Shan Lop Nor Wild Camel Reserve (Seymour 2004).

While it was enhancing the EIAs and negotiating a basic EHS approach with PetroChina, Shell also sponsored an additional social impact assessment. This was one of the knottier issues during the negotiations between PetroChina and international investors. Although stakeholder consultation is an explicit part of Chinese EIA law requirements, consultation clauses have rarely been enforced and there is relatively little guidance about how they should be implemented. Not surprisingly, Chinese firms are unaccustomed to addressing the social side of major public works projects, and it had never been done before for a state development project. Knowing that international business standards increasingly require an exploration of social impact, PetroChina had in fact conducted its own social survey prior to Shell's involvement. However, according to those involved the scope was limited—it interviewed only a small handful of residents per province—and did not meet international standards. Thus, Shell began to discuss with PetroChina the possibility of a wider social impact survey (as agreed in the standards document). The wider survey would address issues for affected parties, including farmers who had to lose a year of planting due to construction or rural residents who had to be resettled. In October 2001, PetroChina raised a legal challenge around the fact that Shell was not yet a financial partner in the project and that Chinese law does not authorize foreign entities to conduct private surveys. During this time, the social impact survey could not go forward.[37]

Shell's domestic partners also pointed out that according to Chinese law the Chinese National Bureau of Statistics (NBS) must first review and vet the questionnaire and proposed design (i.e., sample population), and later review the results. However, for foreign companies operating in China to allow the Chinese government to prescreen its survey would be perceived as a threat to the credibility of the findings and leave Shell open to a host of criticisms from organizations in the West. The potentially large impact of the WEP project, combined with its high visibility, made the option of a prescreened survey unacceptable and thus negotiations were at an impasse. The issue was eventually resolved by bringing in the United Nations Development Programme (UNDP). The UNDP had previously worked in China's western provinces, which was one of the most problematic issues in the survey (because of the sensitivity of engaging the Uighur population). The UNDP also had a host of connections and a stronger legal standing for conducting the operation, so the issue was resolved. The social survey went forward and eventually interviewed over 10,000 residents. The final report made available on the UN website was vetted by NBS, but the survey itself was not. In the wake of this effort, the UNDP has received other inquiries from firms interested in doing their own social impact surveys. For instance, the UNDP received inquiries about conducting an ESIA on a plantation in Guangxi for Stora Enso, a Finnish paper company.[38]

In the end, how much influence did Shell have? To what extent was it able to push the project beyond compliance with China's environmental laws? In terms of tangible effects on the WEP itself, there was modest success. As one representative put it, "It was a step forward, not a great stride, but a step."[39] Accomplishments include the decision to reroute the pipeline away from a nature reserve, the "rapid assessments" and enhanced environmental management plans, and the additional ESIA work and social impact survey. There was also success in the protection of cultural relics. Part of the enhanced ESIAs to which PetroChina and other international investors agreed included additional discussions with local Ministry of Culture officials. The joint venture framework agreement included clauses that barred construction of Great Wall crossings without prior regulatory authorization. This meant obtaining approval for crossing designs from the Ministry of Culture at both the local and central government levels. There were also subsequent field visits to assure construction followed the original design plans (Seymour et al. 2005). During the construction of the pipeline, Shell also helped prepare a wide variety of EHS guidelines (e.g., hazard management) as well as providing support in training and monitoring activities for construction crews on the project.

A less tangible, but nonetheless equally important, result of Shell's participation in the project was a transfer of skills and learning process. In the course of conducting the various audits, EIAs, and ESIAs, Shell and Petro-China worked with a dizzying array of local organizations, including the Institute of Environment and Development, Institute of Rural Development of CASS (the Chinese Academy of Social Sciences), China International Center for Economic and Technology Exchanges (CICETE), and many others. Some of this work was a first of a kind for China, such as the aforementioned social audit conducted by the UNDP (which itself was conducted in conjunction with CICETE and six other domestic research institutes). The Chinese Academy of Sciences was also engaged by PetroChina to assist in the crafting of a Green Action Plan, which addresses environmental management along the entire pipeline and covers a variety of issues, such as landscape and ecosystem restoration, soil erosion, pollution control, and cultural heritage production.

Though Shell is no longer part of the project and it would not be accurate to say PetroChina created the Green Action Plan or took other similar steps solely because of Shell, eighteen months of pushing for greater attention to environmental and social issues is likely to have played some role in PetroChina's decision. Many of those who worked on the project provide a similar description of a change in mind-set of their PetroChina counterparts from initial reluctance to gradual acceptance to (in some cases) genuine understanding. One participant who oversaw environmental and social audits stated that at first colleagues in PetroChina "had no idea why we did this" and that much of the work consisted of daily conversations designed to explain the logic and benefits of social audits. As Shell began sharing the results of information gathered in the field visits and making the case that preventative measures could minimize risk and improve management, PetroChina began to gain experience and understanding. The representative said the work was akin to "preaching" and that PetroChina counterparts' learning curve was "flat, flat, flat, and then became very steep."[40] Another participant, who worked in one of the firms hired by Shell to assist with the environmental audits, stated that PetroChina started out "extremely reluctant to even talk to us and finished off actually quite positive about what we'd done."[41]

Why was Shell able to exert authority, especially given that it was never legally a financial partner and was in the unenviable position of attempting to push for more stringent EHS policies in the context of often tense negotiations over the commercial facets of the joint venture agreement? A good part of Shell's influence came from its authority, both material and normative, as a global leader in the energy industry. For instance, Shell was able to provide a significant amount of expertise to the project. At the peak of Shell's involvement, there were roughly forty individuals working full-time on EHS issues. This included a team of twelve to fifteen employees in Beijing, an eight-person EHS team, a five-person team working on compensation and land acquisition issues, and three 4-person field teams that would spend six-week periods in the field overseeing various aspects of construction, environmental management, and quality assurance. Many of these employees and all the team leaders had many years of international experience in environmental and/or social audits and management. ERM, a global leader in environmental consulting and the principal consultant contracted by Shell for the WEP project, provided another fifteen to sixteen experts.

Aside from expertise, Shell, as a global multinational in China, commands a high degree of normative authority in China. Domestic firms, particularly those with aspirations for global MNC status, demonstrate a strong desire to learn international best practices. The policies and practices of foreign MNCs, in the minds of many Chinese managers, are the most advanced and therefore considered worthy of emulation. As one individual involved in the WEP project summarized it: "In many companies in China, in fact most companies in China there is an eagerness to learn. . . . The growth of this country has been absolutely phenomenal even in the last five years and people are always learning new things. China is developing its capacity as fast as it can and this applies to PetroChina as much as any company."[42] Thus, Shell's expertise combined with PetroChina's overarching readiness to acquire international best practices contributed to Shell's authority and ability to bargain from a position of weakness. Moreover, Shell was willing to wield its authority. As one person familiar with the project stated, a key reason for the success was "Shell, using the big stick, saying if you don't do this we'll pull out."[43] Finally, engaging in more robust EHS practices, though costly, did bring discernible material benefits to PetroChina and international partners.[44]

To what extent can one generalize from the Shell case and draw broader conclusions about the impact of multinational firms on joint ventures? In many ways, the Shell case is singular. The project's visibility, for one, made it difficult for Shell to accept anything less than the highest possible EHS standards. In interviews, Shell officials were highly cognizant of the fact that pipeline projects are frequent targets of activist campaigns and were clearly concerned with guarding against detrimental impacts to Shell's reputation. In fact, they were quite proud of the fact that unlike almost every other major pipeline project in the world, the WEP project attracted virtually no negative press coverage. Given its image concerns, Shell felt forced to push harder for international standards than it might have on a smaller project. At the same time, the political importance of finishing the project by the completion of the Tenth Five-year Plan and avoiding delay of construction put tremendous pressure on PetroChina and so undoubtedly stiffened its resistance to Shell's request for additional ESIA surveys and enhanced environmental management plans. As noted earlier, Chinese firms with aspirations for global MNC status tend to be more open to learning international best practices from foreign firms. But in this particular case, other political pressures limited PetroChina's readiness to negotiate on the EHS front. The project's visibility and pressure on PetroChina essentially were external factors that served to make EHS negotiations more contentious than may be the case in other joint venture projects.

The Shell case, however, is not entirely unique. In response to my question about whether EHS is often a bone of contention in JV negotiations, one environmental consultant with many years of experience in China replied somewhat incredulously, "Oh lord yes, very, very common." He further stated that as an environmental consulting firm, they would get "caught between the cogs on JVs as a regular occasion."[45] Another firm representative described his own work on a joint venture in a fashion that very much resembles the Shell case:

> It's made incredibly more difficult by having a joint venture that is a 50-50 joint venture. . . . Every idea you have, every plan you want to take forward requires engagement, involvement, and influence, so it's a lot of extra hard work in doing it here. . . . In [our home country] you get an idea and you do it . . . here you get an idea and you think about how am I going to influence people to do it, and that represents about 80 percent of the work.[46]

Other foreign-firm representatives with joint venture operations in China, though loath to state that their own firm had to push its domestic partners on EHS issues, were nonetheless able to provide examples and stories similar to those described above. It should also be pointed out that other scholars have uncovered similar examples of MNCs working with Chinese partners in a manner beneficial to environmental regulation. For instance, Elizabeth Economy describes several such instances, including one in which South Africa–based Manganese Metal Company worked with Chinese officials and companies to conduct EIAs and host symposia in order to change the toxic process through which most Chinese companies produce manganese (2006, 182).

The presentation of the Shell case does not seek to imply that all joint venture negotiations involve heated discussions over EHS with foreign firms ceaselessly pushing for higher standards. As long as their partner is not engaging in excessively risky environmental behavior that represents an unacceptable liability, many foreign firms are content to comply with the law of the land. More importantly, as mentioned, domestic firms that seek out or are engaged in joint venture projects tend to be have international aspirations and be open to learning and willing to adopt foreign EHS practices. In these cases, which likely represent the majority, there may be contention over EHS, but it is more over the particulars of how stricter standards will be implemented (and paid for) rather than whether such standards are necessary. There may be friction along the way, but both sides tend to be committed to enhancing EHS practices. But the point remains, the Shell case and other examples cited in this chapter show the significance of MNCs' private authority in creating an upward pressure on environmental regulation through their interaction with joint venture partners.

MNCs and Domestic Service Providers:
Building a Green Supply Chain

Another area in which foreign firms exercise private authority is through their relations with domestic service providers and vendors. All foreign firms interviewed had in place some version of a supply chain policy to screen, monitor, and inspect the EHS standards of domestic firms with whom they have commercial relations—a policy which is typically referred to as "greening the supply chain." This includes all types of domestic firms, from raw material suppliers to transportation companies to construction contractors and waste vendors. Furthermore, often in conjunction with government bodies,

MNCs engage in a variety of teaching activities, such as holding seminars and providing training for domestic firms (including competitors). The combination of these teaching and screening activities creates an upward pressure on environmental regulation.

As is the case for firms' on-site environmental practices and their relations with joint venture partners, much of foreign firms' impetus for implementing green supply chain policies comes from a set of standard operating policies designed to minimize risk and damage to reputation. The difference in the case of exerting authority over domestic service providers is that MNCs are not concerned simply with protecting the reputation of their own firm, but with guarding the image of the industry as a whole.

In the wake of Bhopal and other industrial accidents, the reputation of the chemical and energy industries is quite low.[47] As others have documented, and as industry executives readily admit, the driving motivation behind the creation of Responsible Care was to burnish the image of the chemical industry, which in the United States today is still rsecond only to tobacco as the least trusted industry. One of the ways in which firms seek to enhance the image of the chemical industry is through their supply chain and product stewardship policies. Through these policies, which have become a normative part of doing business for large MNCs, firms attempt to encourage and influence commercial partners' environmental practices. This is reflected, for instance, in the ten guiding principles of Responsible Care, one of which reads: "To work with customers, carriers, suppliers, distributors, and contractors to foster the safe use, transport and disposal of chemicals" (ACC 2006). Other voluntary environmental codes have similar clauses. ISO 14000 certification, for instance, requires that a firm assure that its suppliers are certified by a third party (e.g., an ISO certifying agency), a second party (the purchasing firm itself), or provide purchasers with a "declaration of conformity" with environmental standards. Principles such as these typically get incorporated into firms' individual corporate environmental management programs, where they are referred to as "ethical" or "green" supply chain policies or, in the case of downstream users, "product stewardship." In other words, they are part of the firm's normative framework.

In the China operations of large MNCs, green supply chain and product stewardship policies translate into specific procedures for pre-screening and auditing domestic partner firms. For instance, when selecting a raw material supplier, most firms have a similar pre-screening process.[48] The purchasing department identifies potential suppliers and then begins a technical review process for each supplier. The technical review process involves having the potential supplier fill out a questionnaire, which is then reviewed and followed by a visit to the supplier's facilities. The questionnaire and on-site inspection encompass a variety of issues, including financial history, labor practices, quality assurance, and EHS practices.[49] In the area of EHS, firms will look at a variety of criteria, including penalty history, regulatory permits and inspection records, maintenance records, pollution discharges, waste-water treatment facilities, and solid waste disposal practices.

Based on the results of the on-site inspection, suppliers are rejected, accepted, or placed in an "approval pool." Firms in violation of environmental regulation are immediately rejected. Firms placed in the "approval pool" are those with outstanding issues that represent an unnecessary liability for the foreign firm (e.g., sloppy solid waste disposal), but are not egregious enough to warrant immediate rejection. These firms are given a set time in which to resolve outstanding issues and then are subject to follow-up inspections. Most MNCs interviewed stated that a small number of firms are rejected outright. Interviewees could typically relate two or three examples. For instance, one foreign company was preparing to hire a domestic firm to provide a raw material feedstock when its pre-screening process revealed that the domestic firm was openly dumping a solid chemical pollutant. The local environmental protection bureau investigated and determined the pollutant did not qualify as a hazardous waste, so the supplier was not violating any Chinese law. The foreign firm still requested that the supplier build a closed waste-disposal container; the supplier declined and the foreign firm went elsewhere.[50] More common than outright rejection is to place the potential domestic partner in a contingent status of the applicant pool. Estimates about the number of domestic firms that receive contingent status ranged from around 5 to 15 percent. This is not a small number given that an MNC can supply from dozens of firms in a given site and from hundreds over the entirety of its China operations. Once a supplier is chosen, compliance with local environmental law is written into the contract and the foreign firm will conduct annual follow-up activities to assure suppliers have maintained standards.

It should be noted that there is a great variance in the robustness with which foreign firms conduct follow-up activities. Most MNCs are content to have suppliers fill out forms/checklists attesting to the fact that their environmental practices are in compliance with local regulations. The thoroughness of pre-screen also depends to a large extent on the service the domestic vendor provides. There is, in one EHS manager's words, "a hierarchy of risk management."[51] Suppliers of products or services that are more dangerous or that represent a higher reputational liability are more carefully monitored. Domestic firms that tend to generate the most attention include waste vendors, transportation companies, and suppliers of dangerous raw material inputs. For example, in the area of transportation, foreign companies pre-screen domestic contractors for their safety record and check that all drivers have dangerous goods licenses and that there are two licensed drivers per shipment. They inspect the quality of trucks, looking for documents demonstrating regular maintenance as well as making sure the vehicle is equipped with protection articles for emergencies (e.g., goggles, gloves, lights, light reflection panels, transportation emergency card) (Wang Liqun 2005). Firms also often conduct evaluations of a truck as it enters (e.g., inspect the cooling system) and exits the facility (e.g., check for overloading). During transportation, MNCs monitor various indicators such as a temperature tracking chart, warning system, and the refrigeration system. In some cases, a firm even requires the drivers to stay only in certain hotels which their firm has pre-certified. Foreign companies may also provide or support additional training for drivers in partner companies. In addition to transportation companies, construction contractors, because they work on the MNC's own site, also are subject to careful scrutiny and may be given additional training.

In recent years, as green supply chain policies have become more common, NGOs have sprung up to help MNCs implement them. For instance, Shanghai General Motors collaborated with the World Environment Center (WEC), an international nonprofit organization based in Washington DC that works with forty-six MNCs. WEC originally helped train staff in eight domestic suppliers of Shanghai GM; in 2008, the program was expanded to include forty suppliers. MNCs not only screen suppliers and work with NGOs, but also conduct a variety of EHS training and awareness-raising activities for domestic companies, including competitors. MNCs, for instance, provide basic emergency response training for customers and distributors; all provide distributors with Material Safety Data Sheets (MSDSs).[52] One firm trains distributors and local farmers on how to use and dispose of pesticide products. These activities occur "several times a year and with several customers a year" and, recognizing that larger Chinese companies are increasingly serious about EHS, this MNC tends to train customers that are medium-sized domestic enterprises.[53] As well as providing basic training for customers, MNCs also sponsor or organize seminars on EHS issues. Increasingly, the seminars are held in conjunction with the government agency, the China Petroleum and Chemical Industry Association, which works with foreign companies and foreign industry associations to host about a dozen events a year, most of which involve either technology or environmental issues.[54]

These seminars, which are aimed principally at domestic firms, are best described as part training and part inculcation. Foreign firms seek both to offer "how to" advice on EHS and to lay the foundations for a mind-set more favorable to environmental protection. The practical advice offered varies. For instance, much of a two-day Responsible Care conference, which was held in Beijing in June 2005 and attended by over five hundred persons, focused on the nuts and bolts of creating and implementing a Responsible Care policy. Foreign-company representatives conducted most of the approximately thirty-five presentations and provided a wide array of "how to" guidance in areas such as incident prevention, increasing resource productivity, pollution prevention, and conducting internal self-audits. Sometimes the "how to" advice includes recommendations to search for partnerships with foreign firms. For instance, in the Responsible Care conference, a representative from Formosa Plastics (Taiwan) specifically urged Chinese firms to follow its own experience and seek out foreign firms to provide guidance in establishing environmental management systems. He noted that when Formosa Plastics began to address Responsible Care it sought out experts through the American and European Chambers of Commerce to conduct research and "emulation seminars" (Michael Lin 2005). Also, Formosa Plastics set up a buddy system with Dupont.[55] This involved several training activities conducted over the course of one year, which targeted department managers and relevant Responsible Care implementation staff. The Formosa Plastics representative encouraged Chinese firms to seek out similar opportunities, stating that under the buddy system "the coaching firm not only inspires the willpower but also the motivation of the coached company."

Before going too far and making it sound as if MNCs have replaced government regulators as the principal enforcers and disseminators of Chinese environmental regulation, a couple of caveats are in order. First, foreign MNCs are not benevolent champions of the environment valiantly striving against indifferent domestic firms and intransigent government authorities to enhance environmental regulation. As the discussion of the Shell case has made clear, MNCs are motivated by the bottom line, which means protecting the firm from legal liability and loss of reputation by avoiding egregious violations of Chinese environmental standards. Because of image and liability concerns, Shell could not be part of a pipeline project that potentially damaged the Great Wall. A desire to protect the environment, although clearly evident among those who work within EHS departments, was a lesser concern than public image. It is the same with the implementation of green supply chain policies. When foreign companies pick a supplier or any other domestic commercial partner, quality and price are and likely always will be the most important selection criteria. The Chinese supplier's EHS record, so long as it does not glaringly violate local regulations, is typically a secondary concern. For many suppliers, such as providers of mechanical spare parts, foreign firms will conduct only a superficial or pro forma review of EHS. Referring to his company's follow-up review of supplier EHS practices, one representative stated: "Speaking quite frankly, they [the purchasing department] don't do it that seriously; they know that the Chinese supplier will just go down the list and check ok, ok, ok . . ."[56] This appears to be common in other countries as well. Ruud, who focuses on MNCs in India, found that 38 percent of the MNCs screen the environmental performance of suppliers, but this involved self-reporting, and few MNCs made an active effort to follow up or monitor suppliers (2002, 109). In the few cases in which MNCs did take aggressive steps to monitor suppliers' environmental practices, it tended to involve companies that posed a risk to the MNCs' own employees or products. In China, even if follow-up monitoring is less than robust, the mere possibility of foreign-firm inspection may still have an impact. However, for a large portion of domestic companies, foreign commercial partners' green supply chain policies are likely not a tangible concern. Chinese-company representatives were typically aware that foreign companies make environmental demands, but few indicated they felt a great deal of pressure from foreign companies.[57]

Second, an MNC's ability to influence domestic-firm behavior is constrained by several factors. Most notably, there is the attitude of the domestic firm's management. As one might imagine, there is a range of domestic-firm reactions to an MNC's request for verification of EHS practices. As mentioned in previous sections, some are eager to learn international best practices and often not only want foreign firms to point out red flags, but also provide instructions and oversee the process of filling in the gaps, which foreign firms are inclined to avoid for reasons of legal liability. In other instances, domestic firms are interested so long as they can see some kind of immediate material benefit, which means that the size of the current contract and the perceived impact of EHS improvement on the potential for future contracts are both highly important. Not surprisingly, then, several enterprises noted that when suppliers are plentiful or the needed feedstock can be imported, MNC influence is greater. For the same reason, the influence of recognized global leaders with significant investments in China is also more substantial than that of smaller foreign firms. Domestic companies recognize that landing a contract with one well-known foreign firm can enhance their standing with others and so are more willing to meet the requests of industry leaders.

Even so, some businesses are simply beyond the reach of MNCs (and in many cases beyond the reach of the law). One representative stated that certain domestic companies are impossible to convince because they "benefit from noncompliance and think their practice is okay."[58] Another MNC official summed it up by saying: "The good ones are the good ones; the lousy ones are the lousy ones."[59] There is also very little that can be done about surreptitious subcontracting (Harvey 2008). This is particularly a problem in transportation, where for longer trips transportation companies are prone to subcontract out after they cross a provincial border. Two interviewees told stories of transportation firms showing up with a new truck and/or qualified driver and then switching later to a less qualified driver or older truck. Again, this points to the limited ability of MNCs to assure the EHS practices of service providers.

Nonetheless, there are several instances in which MNCs have positively affected domestic firms' environmental behavior via supply chain and product stewardship policies. Sometimes these improvements are easy and result in clear material benefits. For instance, one MNC noticed a supplier was stacking large waste containers without any support structure. Like books stacked on one another, after a certain number the probability of collapse and/or spill increases significantly. The MNC requested that the vendor install a storage structure equivalent to a bookshelf. A relatively low-cost item, the domestic firm agreed and found that after the installation of the "bookshelf," it was much easier to locate and move storage containers and so produced an efficiency benefit. This representative stated that many of the changes recommended to suppliers are equally unproblematic, such as requests to provide employees personal protection equipment. Another example of how supply chain policies produce an upward push on domestic-firm behavior occurred after one foreign firm's home country environmental administration announced that a chemical used in the firm's manufacturing process was an endocrine disrupter in fish.[60] Corporate headquarters decided to discontinue its use in the manufacturing process of all operations—domestic and global. The company's China operation subsequently discovered that one of its suppliers was using the chemical in its own manufacturing process. They requested that the supplier cease using the chemical, which after some back and forth it eventually did.[61]

There is also the less tangible impact on domestic firms' mind-set. The influence of the training seminars and conferences described above, while hard to measure, should not be underestimated. Between sessions during a conference on Responsible Care, one domestic firm representative, candidly admitting that she attended principally to make connections with foreign companies and clearly disappointed to discover I was a researcher and not a corporate representative, stated: "Today is the first time I have ever heard of Responsible Care." While she may not be a die-hard advocate, her statement provides a small example of how conferences spread ideas and potentially plant seeds.

In other cases, foreign firms are continuing to push, but still face serious challenges. Waste disposal is one area in which foreign firms still struggle. All manufacturers in China are required to send waste to government-certified waste disposal companies. As one multinational was expanding its operations into China several years ago, its EHS manager, along with the head of corporate EHS, personally visited all the government-approved waste-management vendors and discovered a host of problems. None of them could meet legal requirements (e.g., secondary containment is required for liquid waste). They found cases of untreated liquid waste going into sewers, soil, and even rivers. There were also many instances in which wastes were not separated or labeled, containers had no roof to prevent mixing with rainwater and runoff, and treatment equipment (e.g., incinerator) was inadequate. These waste-management sites could not meet their own government regulations, and in the EHS manager's words, "We didn't feel comfortable with government approved vendors." The MNC began to communicate with government and push vendors to "clean up their act." In the end, the MNC had minimal success. As of late 2005, it had certified only two of forty waste-treatment vendors in Shanghai and three nationally. The company sometimes stored waste on-site and occasionally had to ship waste hundreds of miles to the approved vendor rather than use a local one.[62]

In sum, as is the case with joint ventures, the risk management strategies and reputation concerns of foreign firms has led to corporate policies designed to enhance domestic company environmental compliance. While MNCs are limited in their influence by a number of factors, they nonetheless possess sufficient private authority to supplement the efforts of public authorities seeking to strengthen China's environmental governance.

MNCs' Government Relations: Lobbying for Transparency

MNCs not only exercise private authority in their interaction with domestic firms, but also in relations with government officials. While it would be inaccurate to say that foreign companies and industry associations have a potent ability to lobby government officials, they nonetheless have developed channels to influence the implementation of environmental policy. As is the case with foreign companies' influence on joint venture partners and domestic service providers, the source of MNC authority is expertise combined with a government that is anxious to adopt international practices.

To say that foreign firms exercise private authority in the environmental governance process, or that they have authority in their relations with government regulators, is not meant to imply that the state has been captured by foreign firms or that there has been a retreat of the state in advance of foreign interests. As Kennedy (2007) has shown, multinationals are constrained in their lobbying by a number of factors, the most important of which is the CCP's overarching control on political activity. Other checks on foreign-firm influence include the nationalism of Chinese officials, the limited autonomy of industry associations, the opaque nature of policy making, and the sheer number of actors that exert influence during the legislative process, which means even if an MNC forges strong ties with one official, there is no guarantee that its preferences are translated into policy. The result, as Kennedy points out, is that much of MNC lobbying is conducted "one-on-one or in informal groups" and the "great majority of such interaction at the national level does not involve patron-client ties" (184–85).[63]

Kennedy's argument holds true for the issue of environmental protection. Foreign MNCs are not politically inert, but influence is weaker than one might expect given the considerable degree of foreign penetration into the Chinese economy. Almost all MNC representatives expressed doubt about the benefits of lobbying via relevant industry associations, and most preferred to rely on direct relationships with government officials. Firm representatives all indicated that their company had spent many years working directly with government officials in an attempt to build trust and gain influence. Indeed, a common concern expressed by MNC representatives in granting an interview to me was that any information I published might embarrass the government and impinge on the firm's relationship with key officials. The nature of the MNC-government relationship in the environmental arena is neither clientelistic nor adversarial, but rather something closer to symbiotic. Foreign companies, for their part, are intent on protecting their own material interests and leveling the playing field vis-à-vis domestic firms. Often they are successful, but corporate victory does not equal government loss. As firms lobby, they typically advocate for greater transparency, consistency, and flexibility in the implementation of environmental law. The result is that an element of pragmatism is inserted into environmental legislation that, when initially introduced by government agents, is often too broad or vague to implement judiciously. This is best shown by the row over the registration of chemical imports that started in 1994 and was not fully resolved until 2003.

The Dispute over Chemical Registration   Regulations governing the import of chemicals is one representative area in which firms have pursued their interests—and largely succeeded in achieving their goals—while simultaneously helping to introduce a measure of pragmatism into Chinese law. In 1994, the Ministry of Foreign Trade and Economic Cooperation (MOFTEC) and the National Environmental Protection Administration (NEPA) jointly issued a new regulation governing the import and export of chemicals, called "Regulations for Environmental Management on the First Import of Chemicals and the Import and Export of Toxic Chemicals" (NEPA 1994). This law, based in large part on the London Guidelines for the Exchange of Information on Chemicals in International Trade (1987, amended 1989) of the United Nations Environment Programme (UNEP), labeled twenty-seven categories and over one hundred specific types of toxic chemicals as "banned" (*jinzhi*) or "severely restricted" (*yange xianzhi*).[64] Prior to importing or exporting any of these toxic chemicals, all companies in China were to register and apply to MOFTEC. The law also contained a "First Import" clause, which stipulated that foreign businesses importing any chemical that was not registered in China must register the chemical and provide NEPA with toxicity and product information, as well as a sample for testing. NEPA could then investigate the potential environmental impact of the chemical, and if necessary, conduct its own experiments.

It was the "First Import" clause that led to an uproar from foreign-invested enterprises. "First import" chemicals, it quickly became clear, meant that all chemicals and commodities containing chemicals had to be registered, even those that were widely known to pose minimal risk. In the words of one expert, "NaCl had to be tested because China didn't have a regulation for salt."[65] One foreign-firm official called the new law the "most damaging legislation China has ever produced" (Foo 1994). Besides expressing concern over the number of chemicals requiring registration, companies were worried about associated fees, demands about the detail of information required on the application, and timeline of registering. Foreign firms, some of which import hundreds or thousands of chemicals, were initially led to believe there would be a fee of $2,000 on most chemicals and $10,000 on more toxic substances.[66] The 1994 regulation stipulated that once approved, companies would be granted a five-year license to import the chemical. It was unclear whether after five years the firms would have to reapply (and pay a second fee).

Foreign companies were also concerned that the registration process required excessively detailed product information, which was both arduous and potentially compromised intellectual property rights. Dow estimated that five people would have to spend six months gathering information and filling in the required forms (Foo 1994). Furthermore, it was also unclear how long companies would have to register their chemicals, which was especially pertinent given that the regulation did not begin to circulate among foreign firms until July 1994, yet was dated effective May 1994. Finally, foreign companies protested that implementing registration requirements on importers of chemicals, but not on domestic producers, was discriminatory against foreigners. The result was that many firms initially failed to comply and began negotiating with Chinese regulators. Negotiations gained a greater sense of urgency in early 1995 when Chinese officials began seizing import shipments (Business China 1994; *China Business Review* 1995; Choy 1994).

For its part, the Chinese government saw the foreign outcry as an excessive reaction to a loss of unjustifiable privilege. Developed countries monitor and register chemical imports and so, rather than representing an arbitrary tax on foreigners, the new law was just a symbol that China was catching up with international environmental practices. From the government's perspective, foreign grumbling about a possible loss of intellectual property was merely an attempt to keep hidden the chemicals they were importing into China (Yan 1995).

In late 1994, the US-China Business Council formed an ad hoc Chemical Working Group, which consisted of approximately thirty companies and which took the lead in lobbying the Chinese government. The working group met on a monthly basis (and sometimes weekly). It began sending representatives with considerable experience in chemical trade issues to negotiate with Chinese counterparts. In December, the Council held a forum, which was attended by approximately seventy individuals, including Japanese and European firm representatives, and during which foreign-company representatives made their case to government officials. It also lobbied the State Council and wrote an open letter to the Standing Committee of the National People's Conference. Meanwhile, the Council maintained a hard line, recommending for instance that firms avoid disclosing proprietary information and offer only an MSDS during the registration process. Many companies threatened that the combined burden of intellectual property loss and added fees would undermine competitiveness in China operations.

In the end, foreign pressure was enough to induce the Chinese government to make significant amendments in the implementation of the law. Following the December meeting, in February 1995 the government published a follow-up document that clarified the regulation and to a large extent assuaged foreign firms' concerns. With continued foreign input during negotiations on WTO accession, the implementation was subsequently refined and codified in an additional implementation guideline in 2003. In the wake of the issue of the February supplement, an official from Bayer noted that Chinese regulators "have listened to our opinions and have shown that they are willing to compromise" (Michael Roberts 1995). First, the February supplement allowed chemical products like paint, ink, and polymers to register as "product groups," meaning firms could simultaneously register different products with varying concentrations. This allowed companies to avoid the laborious task of registering twenty different colors of lipstick one at a time, which would have been the case in the original 1994 regulation. Other products, about which the potential risks were widely known, such as plastics and rubber, were exempt from registration. In addition, the February supplement also specified that domestic firms importing chemicals had to follow the same procedures. The 2003 document, under the pressure of WTO negotiations to remove discriminatory policies, later extended the requirement to domestic producers as well. The February 1995 guidelines also established a more graduated fee schedule based on the risk and toxicity of the chemical. Foreign firms were required to pay $10,000 to register imported toxic chemicals, and either $2000 or $1500 for nontoxic chemicals and $200 for additives and various chemical reagents (domestic firms importing toxic chemicals were only required to pay 2000 RMB).

One might ask: Given that the dispute over chemical registration is an example of MNC lobbying that led to a meaningful reduction of the government's original legislation, why is it not considered an example of regulatory chill? After all, foreign-firm pressure led China to reduce environmental standards to a less strict level, which appears to confirm the expectations of the regulatory-chill argument. There is no way to address this question without engaging in normative judgments about the social desirability of the regulatory change. As discussed in the opening chapter, the underlying concern in the pollution-haven and race-to-the-bottom debate is with the potentially harmful impact of foreign investment on environmental regulation. But as Revesz (1992, 1997) points out, we can only say relaxing standards is harmful if we assume that the original baseline from which standards were lowered was socially optimal (i.e., that it maximizes social welfare). Swire (1996) makes a similar point, distinguishing between descriptive races to laxity and prescriptive races to undesirability. A race to laxity simply refers to a lowering of standards. From a normative view, laxity is not inherently good or bad. Race to undesirability refers to a lowering of standards that is socially undesirable (i.e., a lowering that is prescriptively bad). Revesz, who focuses principally on the American political system, advances the argument that lowering excessively stringent standards can be beneficial because it removes excessive taxes on capital that stem from overregulation. Strict standards in developed countries may also be undesirable from an international perspective, as environmental and health standards are sometimes set artificially high in order to serve as a form of trade protectionism. An increase of environmental stringency in the developing world, where environmental protection is often given modest public policy emphasis, is typically a positive development in terms of enhancing social welfare. But what the arguments of Revesz and others make clear is that one cannot immediately assume that more stringent standards are inherently more desirable.

In the case of China, it has been common for government authorities to introduce initial legislation that, while admirably strict on paper, is not optimal because it is virtually unenforceable. The lack of enforceability may stem from MEP's insufficient capacity or, just as commonly, from the lack of clarity or practicality of the legislation itself. As one expert, familiar with the chemical registration case and with many years' dealing with regulatory affairs in China, put it, the Chinese government often wants to have "regulation with Chinese characteristics." It adopts almost wholesale a foreign regulation (or set of standards) and then introduces it with minimal advance notice to "test it in the market, see what happens, and then adjust." Foreign firms are often the guinea pigs, as regulators start out by enforcing the rules on foreign companies before turning to domestic firms. Although the situation has changed somewhat in recent years, traditionally the legislative process involved minimal expert testimony or outside input. Moreover, the government introduces the regulation in full knowledge that it cannot enforce the rules. In the case of registering chemical imports, this inability to enforce is evidenced by the fact that SEPA had only three junior officials working to register what was potentially thousands of chemicals for hundreds of firms.[67]

This assertion, that stricter regulation on paper does not inevitably foster better environmental protection on the ground, has been highlighted in other studies of China as well. In his exceptionally thorough investigation of environmental protection in Yunnan, Benjamin van Rooij points out that although national air and water pollution legislation has grown stronger, the laws often have not been designed with implementability in mind (2006b, 364). In fact, during the policy-making process the NPC Legal Committee, which played a commanding part in the creation of many of the policies that van Rooij studied, willfully ignored concerns about implementation raised by other actors. "Regulatory unreasonableness" was a major factor that contributed to the lack of compliance with environmental law (374). Van Rooij argues that "lawmakers preferred strict and specific norms to feasible and adaptable norms, no matter what their influence on actual implementability was, caring more about norms that looked and sounded effective" (101). He goes on to state, "The rationality behind more specific and stricter legislation was one of showing that the problem was addressed in a strong manner, not addressing the problem in a realistic way" (102). The bottom line is that in some cases a reduction of stringency does not impede, and possibly enhances, industrial environmental regulation. Interpretations may differ, but my reading of the chemical registration case is that it is one such example.

It is also fair to ask, How unique was the case of chemical registration? Assuming my interpretation is correct and it is an example of foreign firms lobbying for a more implementable set of environmental standards, it is still possible that it is an outlier. Because the lobbying activities of MNCs tend to take place in a one-on-one, informal setting, one must be cautious in draw-ing conclusions. But my sense is that the chemical registration case is repre-sentative and is not the only area in which firms have exerted influence. As of late 2005, foreign companies were also working with government officials on issues related to transportation, as well as pushing for a set of transparent standards on dangerous-goods driver's licenses and warehouses. The case of chemical transport is quite similar to the chemical registration legislation. In this instance, the Ministry of Transportation used a list of hypo-toxic chemi-cals, which was produced by SEPA for a policy unrelated to transportation issues, and announced a blanket ban on river shipments of any chemical la-beled hypo-toxic. This broad legislation again led to impractical results. Given the dangers of China's highways, and the minimal facilities on China's rail-way system that allow for the safe shipment of chemicals, foreign companies assert that some chemicals, such as acrylonitrile, are better transported by river. In the wake of the ban, for instance, BP stopped importing acrylonitrile to China. The Association of International Chemical Manufacturers (AICM), as well as the European Chamber of Commerce's Petrochemical, Chemical, Oil, and Gas Working Group, worked with Ministry of Transportation of-ficials to develop a more pragmatic, "risk based" policy.[68] The goal was to conduct a risk assessment for each chemical and then decide transportation regulations, rather than just banning all hypo-toxic ones. In a similar situa-tion involving the issuing of dangerous-goods licenses, firms complain that licenses are granted or recognized simply by bureaucratic caprice rather than according to a set of transparent standards, which leads to confusion and considerable geographic variation. In one region, the fact that a person has a dangerous-goods license may be meaningful, while in other areas it may have simply been given out with minimal oversight. Firms worked with govern-ment regulators to develop a common set of standards that will determine how companies and drivers are certified with DG licenses.

   It should also be pointed out that foreign companies influence environ-mental governance not only via lobbying on the environmental law imple-mentation issues, but also by carrying out capacity-building exercises with government agencies. Several foreign firms work with local emergency response bodies (e.g., fire brigades) to conduct joint training exercises or simulations. In late 2005, Shell began a program in which it would conduct workshops with environmental officials about how to perform environmen-tal impact assessments. As part of its joint venture project with the China

National Offshore Oil Corporation (CNOOC) in Nanhai, Shell organized defensive driving programs for 210 project drivers—as well as local police! The European Chamber of Commerce's Petrochemical, Chemical, Oil, and Gas Working Group held workshops with Chinese regulators on how to implement Euro III and IV fuel standards.[69] Dupont had a "traveling training program" in which they ship an ISO container around the world and use it to train local employees about what to do in the case of an accident.[70] They have also held activities in cities like Shenzhen, Guangzhou, and Shanghai, in which local fire bureaus were invited to participate (although sometimes for a fee). Dow initiated a three-year program in which twenty to thirty small and medium Chinese enterprises are selected each year for a series of training activities in developing cleaner production plans. These workshops were run by an environmental consulting firm, and local EPBs participated in the design of the program by selecting the participating firms, as well as by sending officials to attend the training sessions.

The range of government reaction to foreign-firm activity, and therefore the effectiveness of MNC lobbying in the area of environmental governance, varies considerably. In some cases, government officials have been uncomfortable with foreign firms usurping what are nominally government responsibilities. For instance, government officials resisted the idea of foreign firms setting up a private Emergency Care Center (ECC) to respond to customers that have had transportation accidents.[71] However, as is the case with domestic firms, government officials also see foreign companies as experts and so a legitimate form of authority. One environmental lawyer, with many years' experience in China, noted that foreign-firm advocacy is perhaps more successful with MEP than any other government agency. He considers this the flip side to China basing so many of its environmental standards on those of other countries. This borrowing of foreign environmental laws, while often a source of frustration for foreign firms who find Chinese environmental regulation a perplexing hodgepodge, has created a mentality in which government regulators are anxious to learn from foreign experts. He noted that Xie Zhenhua, the former head of SEPA, often met with foreign-firm representatives and that the conversations were usually free-flowing and open. Many bureaus, including environmental agencies, have been told by the State Council they should work to incorporate foreign ideas and learn from foreign experience.[72] This general idea was articulated by others with experience in the regulatory affairs arena too. One member of the European Chamber of

Commerce stated that in recent years he has seen an increase in the receptivity and transparency of national environmental officials, although he qualified his statement, noting that "there is still a ways to go."[73]

My interaction and interviews with government officials largely reinforced this idea that Chinese environmental officials, while not without suspicion of foreign firms' and government's motives, are anxious to absorb practices from the international community. In a two-hour interview with four government officials in a chemical industrial park, we spent only about a quarter of the time talking about the environmental practices of the park. After introducing the park to me and offering cursory responses to my questions, the officials apparently decided it was time to get down to the real business of the day. They pulled out their notebooks and said they would like to ask me questions. Assuming, as Chinese officials are prone to do, that if an American is studying environmental regulation in China he must already be an established authority on environmental regulation in the United States, they peppered me with questions about the practices in U.S. chemical industrial zones. Despite my pleas of ignorance, they continued to ask questions about how their own practices differed from those abroad. This spontaneous role reversal from interviewer to interviewee, though rarely as exhausting as in the described incident, happened on multiple occasions. It is only a small example, but it shows how the mere fact of being foreign can confer on MNCs a great deal of legitimacy and hence authority as expert. Unlike me when explaining the practices of American chemical parks, foreign firms often genuinely are experts and can therefore reinforce this perception and in the process enhance their authority.

As this chapter's examples demonstrate, while not able to dictate policy to the Chinese government, foreign companies and the industry associations that represent them exert some degree of authority in environmental governance, particularly in how regulations are implemented and enforced. This influence has not served to undermine China's industrial environmental regulation and in some cases appears to have strengthened it by making it more practical and enforceable. This is not to say that firm-government interaction is without antagonism or that multinationals in China are driven by a selfless notion of public service. In government advocacy, altruism plays a small role, as foreign firms lobby principally for reasons of self-interest. As the case of chemical import registration demonstrates, firm motivation was entirely based on concern about material loss and competitive disadvantage vis-à-vis domestic competitors. Likewise, MNC capacity-building activities are driven by the same concerns as noted in the above sections—risk management, protection of industry image and firm reputation, and competitive disadvantage vis-à-vis domestic firms. My argument is not that MNCs are eco-warriors gallantly fighting to protect China's environment, but that a combination of self-interest and corporate norms serves to steer MNC behavior in a direction that at the very least does not undermine environmental regulation and in some cases enhances it. Returning to the terminology of the first chapter, there is little evidence that, when one focuses on the largest MNCs, foreign firms adopt an exploitative environmental strategy or induce a regulatory chill.

Conclusion

This chapter has shown that, when looking at large chemical MNCs from developed countries, there is little evidence of a firm-induced downward pressure on China's environmental governance. In terms of firm strategy and performance, there is virtually no support for the assertion that foreign firms exert a negative influence on industrial environmental regulation. Multinational companies operate at, if not above, the regulatory requirements of Chinese environmental law. They assist and in some cases pressure domestic partners to improve their own environmental record, and they work with government regulators in a manner that introduces an element of practicality into the implementation of environmental regulation.

Why do MNCs engage in this kind of behavior? Running throughout this chapter is the idea that there is a strong normative element underlying the environmental policies of MNCs. Whether it is keeping an incident register, conducting an EHS audit, or implementing a green supply chain policy, much of foreign-firm behavior is driven by norms and standard operating procedures.[74] MNCs do not decide to invest in China and then select an environmental strategy based on location. Rather, their environmental practices are largely dictated by standard corporate policies. Setting up an EHS department, with all the requisite training and policies, is a taken-for-granted element of establishing a new manufacturing operation whether in the United States or in China. It is hardly different from establishing a finance or marketing department; it is just part of doing business. In this sense, then, the behavior of MNCs in China is largely a function of their policies at home.

However, as studies of corporate environmentalism in the developed world have documented, these standard operating procedures have been developed for strategic reasons and are not the simple result of an acute concern with business ethics, the environment, or philanthropy. EHS managers in multinationals recognize that they "do good" and are proud of the work they perform. But from the perspective of the firm as a whole, policies in the environmental realm are little different than in other areas—they were developed strategically with a strong element of risk management. The EHS policies, with which MNCs comply and push other firms to adopt, have been created to protect the firm's own reputation and the image of the industry as a whole. In some cases, such as lobbying efforts, foreign-firm behavior is also driven by a desire to assure a level playing field and protect material interests vis-à-vis domestic competitors.

In essence, this shows that there is a certain element of historical learning evident in MNC behavior. In the West, inattention to EHS by chemical companies up to and through the 1980s led to a series of accidents and polluting activities that became costly legal liabilities and stained the image of the entire chemical industry. Firms in the West felt (and perhaps still feel) they were losing their "license to operate" and hence were wary of repeating the same mistake in their foreign operations. As one interviewee mentioned in reference to American firms, even in their China operations, U.S. firms can feel eager American lawyers looking over their shoulders waiting for an opportunity to pounce.[75] As mentioned in the Shell case, even though they may not have an office in China, western NGOs serve a kind of remote watchdog function over foreign firms. In short, the legacy of Bhopal casts a long shadow over multinational companies in China.

To say that the environmental behavior of MNCs' China operations is driven by norms and standard procedures, which themselves are the result of strategic decisions designed to protect the firm, is not to argue that MNCs' China operations have the same environmental impact as those in their home country. Various aspects of the Chinese institutional environment, as well as firms' willingness to merely comply with the law of the land, means that the ecological footprint of firms in China is likely larger than it would be in the West (although this is not the case for large-scale, relatively recent investments). Many MNCs operating in China appear perfectly willing to tolerate a gap between local and home-country environmental performance. In that sense, Chinese analysts' accusation of MNC "double standards," although perhaps oversimplified given that a lack of existing environmental infrastructure is often a major impediment to better corporate environmental performance, holds some truth.

From a comparative perspective, the findings presented here stand in contrast to those who have found that foreign firms in the developing world are an obstacle to stronger environmental regulation (e.g., Dauvergne 2005). Rather, this chapter bolsters the argument of scholars who have found MNCs make considerable efforts to avoid noncompliance and are prone toward "beyond compliance" (e.g., Prakash 2000), generally outperform their domestic competitors in the developing world (e.g., Fowler 1995, 13), and can enhance environmental governance in the developing world (e.g., Garcia-Johnson 2000).[76] This chapter is particularly relevant for those who argue that transnational linkages and trade liberalization broadly, and foreign investment specifically, constitute critical mechanisms for diffusing environmental standards from developed to developing countries.[77] The arguments presented here complement, and to a certain extent, extend this scholarship. They complement the literature in that they affirm the basic assertion of many scholars that openness to foreign investment offers the potential for stronger environmental regulation in a developing country. They extend the literature by drawing attention to a relatively understudied mechanism—the interaction between foreign MNCs and key domestic actors within its institutional environment. Much of the focus of the existing literature is on how foreign investment transfers clean production technology (Wheeler 2001), which facilitates compliance and contributes to stronger environmental regulation in developing countries. Another popular topic of scholarly discussion is a phenomenon commonly known as the California effect. This refers to the idea that, as exporters from low-standard countries seek access to the markets of higher-standard countries, they are forced to meet the more stringent environmental standards of their trading partners.[78] These firms can then become a source of political pressure for stronger regulation as they seek to make sure their nonexporting domestic competitors must meet the same environmental standards. Economic openness, therefore, initiates a process that leads to enhanced corporate environmental behavior and stricter regulation. Topics such as technology transfer and the California effect are undoubtedly important. Less frequently studied, however, is how the MNCs operating in developing countries are themselves a mechanism for diffusing norms of corporate environmentalism. A notable exception is Garcia-Johnson's *Exporting Environmentalism* (2000), which argues that U.S. multinationals operating in Brazil and Mexico have helped promote international standards of corporate environmentalism. The basic finding offered here is similar to Garcia-Johnson's—MNCs help the cause of environmental regulation. However, Garcia-Johnson's primary focus is on MNC influence on government. MNCs, as she tells the story, help developing-country governments establish Responsible Care programs, which in turn potentially affect the environmental behavior of firms. Like Garcia-Johnson, I have argued that MNC interaction with the government has generally contributed to environmental regulation by making it more practical and enforceable. However, much of MNC power is exercised privately via their influence on domestic competitors and suppliers through green supply chain policies and capacity-building activities. In that sense, the exporting environmentalism phenomenon is broader than originally documented by Garcia-Johnson. It applies as much to domestic firms as it does to government actors.

Even if one accepts the general assertion that MNCs contribute positively to China's environmental regulation, there is one key question unaddressed in this chapter: How applicable are findings derived from a small sample of elite multinationals to the broader population of foreign-invested enterprises in China? To what extent can we generalize about the environmental practices of a Hong Kong manufacturer of textiles that employs fifty people based on a study of global behemoths like Royal Dutch Shell? Answering this question is the task of the subsequent chapter, where attention turns to a wider variety of foreign-invested companies, including those coming from a less stringent home environment, and the picture becomes more clouded.

6 Beyond Multinationals:
The Environmental Behavior of
Foreign Firms in China

Chapter 5 argued that when one restricts the focus to large multinational corporations (MNCs) from the developed world in the chemical and energy industries, there is little evidence of a corporate exploitation that is turning China into a pollution haven. Quite the reverse, MNCs help diminish China's enforcement gap and narrow the gulf between environmental regulation as it exists on paper and its enforcement on the ground. Yet even if one accepts the argument of the previous chapter, there are questions about generalizability. As noted, the arguments are based principally on interviews with sixteen of the forty largest chemical and energy firms in China. This clearly represents a small fraction of all foreign firms in China, so one can question whether the findings of the previous chapter are applicable beyond this small sample. MNCs may go beyond compliance in their own operations, but do all foreign-invested enterprises display such environmental behavior? Furthermore, how extensive is the purported influence of MNCs on domestic firms? I argued that MNCs exert a positive influence on their domestic partners' environmental behavior, but based on interviews alone it is difficult to get a sense of the extent of this supposed effect. In this chapter I address the issue of generalizability by looking at a wider sample of firms. I base my analysis predominantly on the results of a survey conducted in Jiangsu Province during the fall of 2005, as well as various articles in the Chinese media and academic literature.

The argument put forward in this chapter is that foreign-invested enterprises, particularly those that are foreign-controlled, display better environmental behavior than domestic firms and are often "beyond compliance" in their environmental behavior. However, their impact on domestic commercial partners via green supply chain policies is small; there is no evidence that Chinese firms with sales connections to foreign-invested enterprises exhibit environmental behavior different from other firms. Moreover, not all foreign-invested firms are the same. Companies from industrialized countries outperform firms from developing countries in terms of environmental practices. Firms from developing countries are, in some cases, worse than domestic enterprises.

One of the primary reasons for this difference is that industrialized countries have a history of more stringent environmental governance, which has created habits of corporate environmentalism among firms. Companies from developing countries, by contrast, have developed their approach to environmental protection in a setting in which economic growth is privileged above all else. In other words, much as in the case of MNCs presented in the previous chapter, environmental norms developed in the home country carry over to operations abroad. The fact that firms from developing countries display poor environmental behavior suggests the existence of a pollution-haven phenomenon, but one with a limited scope. This argument is developed both through the survey evidence and via a presentation of a case study involving Asia Pulp and Paper.

Survey Overview

The previous chapter claimed that in their China operations, MNCs comply or exhibit "beyond compliance" environmental behavior. This is consistent with findings of several other scholars who have explored the behavior of MNCs (e.g., Garcia-Johnson 2000). I also asserted that MNCs exert a private authority over domestic commercial partners in a manner that enhances those partners' environmental performance. The question for this chapter is whether these outcomes are manifest at a broader level. Stated formally as hypotheses, the assertions can be posed as:

> Hypothesis 1—Foreign Ownership: Foreign-invested firms in China exhibit better environmental compliance than non-foreign-invested firms.
> Hypothesis 2—Green Supply Chains: Chinese firms that sell to foreign-invested enterprises in China exhibit better environmental compliance than other domestic firms.

To test these hypotheses, I conducted a survey of firms in Jiangsu Province from August to October 2005. The survey is based on the China Green Watch program (*qiye huanjing xinxi gongkai*). Green Watch was developed by SEPA (now MEP) in conjunction with researchers from the World Bank. It is a public disclosure program designed to put pressure on manufacturing firms by ranking them according to their environmental behavior and making the results available to the general public. The program was first launched in 1999 as a pilot program in Zhenjiang (Jiangsu) and Hohhot (Inner Mongolia). In late 2005, when the survey was conducted, Green Watch was being implemented in each of the thirteen provincial-level cities in Jiangsu, as well as in cities in a host of other provinces. The intention is for the program to be implemented nationally, although it has hit several snags (most notably a reluctance of officials to release information to the general public) and it may be several years before that goal is reached.

For scholars interested in corporate environmental behavior, Green Watch represents a significant research opportunity. The principal reason is that it provides information about firm environmental behavior that is readily comparable across firms. In developing countries, and perhaps particularly in China, information about company environmental practices is often extremely difficult to obtain in great detail. Firms with poor environmental behavior are virtually inaccessible for researchers. Under Green Watch, company environmental behavior is ranked on a five-point color scale—green, blue, yellow, red, and black. The EPB limits its rankings to manufacturing firms and aims to include within the program firms that account for 80 percent of local pollution discharges. Green firms, as one might expect, are the most environmentally friendly, while black are the least. A variety of criteria is used to determine the color rankings, including: compliance with various discharge standards and hazardous waste disposal requirements; recent history of accidents, administrative penalties, or public complaints; and aspects of internal environmental management system, such as ISO certification.

Companies that are green or blue have no incidents of violations, although a firm can have public complaints against it and still be ranked as blue. Green firms are separated from blue firms in their internal management, which is usually demonstrated by ISO certification. Firms that have been subject to administrative penalties, such as fines for exceeding wastewater concentration standards, are yellow so long as these penalties are below a certain level (typically less than 50,000 RMB). Those with more serious violations are red or black (Wang Hua et al. 2004). In short, yellow firms are basically compli-

TABLE 6.1 Background information on the three cities included in the Green Watch survey

	Nanjing	Changzhou	Taizhou	Provincial average
GDP/capita (RMB)	29,381	31,920	25,886	27,198
Population (10,000)	490	213	62	161
Foreign firms' gross industrial output (% all output)	27.8%	21.6%	58.5%	36.5%
Government revenue (per capita)	6,584	5,327	4,479	4,532
Foreign industrial firms from Hong Kong, Taiwan, and Macau (% all firms)	12.5%	8.1%	6.3%	7.3%
Foreign industrial firms excluding Hong Kong, Taiwan, and Macau (% all firms)	12.2%	7.8%	6.0%	8.8%
Foreign industrial firms (% all firms)	24.6%	15.9%	12.2%	16.1%

Data from Jiangsu Statistical Bureau (2004).

ant, blue and green are above average, while red and black are poor in terms of environmental compliance.

Green Watch rankings were pooled from three cities in Jiangsu Province—Taizhou, Changzhou, and Nanjing. The three cities were chosen because in initial efforts to gather the relevant Green Watch data, which included the rankings themselves as well as detailed descriptions of the implementation process, the EPBs in these three cities were the most forthcoming and transparent. Several cities were still in the process of producing the rankings. Others were unwilling to share rankings or only willing to provide the list of green firms, which is ironic given Green Watch is a disclosure program. Others were unwilling to describe in detail how they produced the ranks. Though the Green Watch program is being introduced in multiple provinces, because of inter-provincial differences in implementation, the focus was limited to Jiangsu.

Basic demographic data on each of the cities is provided in Table 6.1. Taizhou is the poorest of the three cities in terms of per capita GDP and is slightly below the provincial average. However, it is still well above the national average. All three cities attract a significant amount of foreign investment, which is important given this project's focus on foreign enterprises. Nanjing has the greatest concentration of foreign direct investment in terms of number of foreign firms. Almost a quarter of enterprises in Nanjing are foreign-invested. Of the three cities, Taizhou derives the largest portion of its economic output from foreign firms. As seen in Table 6.1, over half of economic output for Taizhou comes from FIEs, which indicates a high reliance on foreign investment for economic growth.

Given some of the differences across these cities, it is fair to question whether the Green Watch program has been implemented identically across locations. Is a blue firm in Changzhou equivalent to a blue firm in Nanjing? Interviews with two professors who worked closely on the project revealed that there have been some difficulties with implementation. As one might expect in China, there has occurred some measure of bargaining between certain firms and local EPB officials in charge of ranking the firms. According to one official, firms that are important to the local economy exert some influence over their final rank. These firms are large state-owned enterprises (SOEs), which if heavily fined or closed could create employment problems and perhaps even social unrest (because many SOE employees still receive all social welfare, from schooling to health care, from their companies). In all likelihood, some firms in the survey received a higher ranking than they deserved, but it is less likely that there are systematic differences across cities. While the differences in Table 6.1 are clear, the cities are similar in that by national standards all are wealthy and have a significant amount of foreign investment. Moreover, that Jiangsu province was chosen as the first province to implement Green Watch speaks to the fact that its local EPBs have a measure of capacity. In other words, the cities' similarities are more striking than their differences. This fact, plus the common set of criteria used for Green Watch rankings, leads one to conclude that rankings are comparable across cities.

Because the cities included in the survey are wealthier than average, the findings may be somewhat less relevant to China's poorer inland provinces, where a lack of economic development places significant restrictions on the capacity of local environmental protection bureaus to monitor firm behavior. But measured by GDP per capita, the development of the cities included in the survey is quite similar to the provincial averages of China's other more industrialized provinces, such as Shandong, Zhejiang, Fujian, and Guangdong. Though only four provinces, this group represents a population barely less than that of the United States and a physical area equivalent to the east coast

TABLE 6.2 Firm ranking—population
sample versus Green Watch survey sample

Rank	Overall population (%)	Survey sample (%)
Green	5.2	11.0
Blue	53.1	37.7
Yellow	32.3	40.4
Red	8.0	8.8
Black	1.4	2.2

of the United States from Virginia to Florida. So while one should not over-extend the sample and argue that the findings can be generalized for all firms in China, the cities included in the sample are representative of a large and important segment of China.

In total, 228 firms were interviewed, with a response rate of 42.5 percent (i.e., 535 firms were contacted). Based on the results of a 40-firm pilot survey, it was decided that interviews should be conducted by phone. Some calls were made by me, but most were performed by graduate students from local universities in Shanghai. All interviews were conducted in my presence to assure quality and consistency. Interviewees, all of whom were promised anonymity, were typically the head of the general office (*bangongshi*) or the production department (*shengchan bu*) or, in the case of smaller firms, the director (*zhuren*) of the company.

As one might imagine, the pilot study revealed that firms with better environmental behavior tend to be more willing to accept an interview. Therefore, I did not use a random sampling method in selecting firms to interview. Random sampling would have resulted in a sample population with a disproportionately large number of green and blue firms and underrepresentation of yellow, red, and black firms. In order to assure that the population sample accurately reflected the overall population, firms were randomly selected within the color categories. More firms were selected from the black, red, and yellow categories to account for the lower response rate within these colors. As seen in Table 6.2, the sample and overall population samples are largely similar, although the sample population does have a smaller number of blue and greater number of green and yellow firms than the overall population.

Variables

The dependent variable is firm Green Watch rank. The variable was coded: 1 = green, 2 = blue, 3 = yellow, 4 = red, and 5 = black. There were three independent variables designed to test the hypotheses listed in the previous section: "foreign-invested," "foreign-controlled," and "FIE from OECD country." All are dummy variables. "Foreign-controlled" was defined as more than 50 percent foreign-invested. Of course, it is possible that a firm can be foreign-controlled with less than 50 percent investment if there are more than two partners. Fifty percent was chosen because, as mentioned in the previous chapter, a foreign company's typical policy is to demand adherence to home-country corporate practices in enterprises in which it has a 50 percent stake.

In addition to the independent variables, information was gathered on a number of control variables. These control variables were taken from the small literature on firm environmental behavior (Christmann and Taylor 2001; Decker and Jalbert 2003; Halkos and Konstantinos 2002; Hartman et al. 1997; Hettige et al. 2004; Kennelly and Lewis 2005; Wang and Jin 2002). The first set of control variables included company age (measured in years) and whether the company had undergone a renovation since establishment, which was coded as a dichotomous variable. All things equal, one would expect a newer company to have a better environmental management system. Also, a key tenet of China's environmental regulation is the "three simultaneous." This principle, which is repeated throughout China's major environmental laws, requires that an enterprise constructing or expanding a manufacturing operation implement pollution control measures at the same time that the operation is designed, constructed, and operated. This leads one to expect firms that have undergone a renovation or expansion to have better compliance behavior.

Other control variables include SOE (dummy), size, industry type, and profitability. Some have argued that state-owned firms, because of a closer connection to government authorities, have increased bargaining power vis-à-vis environmental regulators and so are able to get away with poor environmental practices (Hartman et al. 1997; Wang Hua et al. 2002). Larger firms, because of reputation concerns and efficiencies resulting from economies of scale, typically exhibit better environmental behavior. This variable was measured by the number of employees (logged). While the number of employees is certainly reflective of firm size, in the context of China it is not an ideal measure, since SOEs tend to be bloated with many redundant employees. For SOEs, the number of employees may not accurately reflect the amount of production or sales, which are other possible indicators of size. However, the pilot study revealed that company managers were reluctant to provide hard numbers about sales, so the number of employees was selected as the indicator for size. SOEs represented less than 9 percent of the sample, so it is likely that there were few distortions in the variable. Because government and customer pressure for corporate environmental regulation can vary across sectors, industry dummy variables were included for sectors with the largest number of firms in the sample. Finally, profitability was coded dichotomously. For each of the control variables, companies were asked about their results in 2003, the year before the rankings were conducted. This is designed to account for the fact that there is a lag effect between the variable and the outcome (i.e., firm environmental behavior). Pairwise correlation was used to make sure there was no multicollinearity between the independent variables.[1]

Finally, it is worth pointing out that because the goal is to determine whether foreign investment and/or green supply chain policies lead to *change* in firm environmental behavior, in an ideal world one would use time-series data rather than the cross-sectional data presented here. In the case of China, a lack of data precludes this possibility. The survey employed here can only provide a snapshot rather than offer a dynamic view of change over time. Still, a snapshot can be revealing. If, for example, partnering with foreign companies changes firm environmental practice, one would expect internationally oriented Chinese firms to display environmental behavior that is different from more domestically oriented companies. A lack of difference calls into question one of the purported beneficial effects of globalization on environmental protection. In order to supplement the snapshot provided by the statistical data, in the summer and fall of 2005 I conducted semistructured interviews with managers in twenty Chinese firms in Changzhou (Jiangsu Province). During these interviews, managers were asked to describe the extent and manner in which foreign firms and markets influenced environmental practices. The interviewed firms were included in the Green Watch program, but not included in the statistical survey and comprised a mix of yellow, blue, and green firms.

Results: Not All Foreign Firms Are the Same

The Impact of Foreign Ownership

With regard to the first hypothesis about the relationship between foreign ownership and environmental behavior, there are two principal findings stemming from the Green Watch survey. First, in contrast to the expectations of the pollution-haven argument and as expected based on the argument of the previous chapter, the survey results provide modest evidence that foreign ownership is associated with better environmental behavior. Although foreign-invested firms overall do not display significantly better environmental behavior than other types of firms, companies that are foreign-controlled do exhibit higher environmental rankings than other firms. The indication is that it is only when a foreign entity controls (and is liable for) a company's environmental protection policies that there is a resulting influence on environmental practices.

Second, there is preliminary evidence that among foreign companies there are important differences depending on the company's country of origin. Though the number of observations is small and the data should be treated with caution, there is evidence suggesting that foreign firms from countries with stronger environmental governance exhibit environmental compliance behavior that is better than that of other firms. Foreign-invested enterprises from countries with weaker environmental governance, by contrast, display environmental compliance behavior that is significantly worse than foreign firms from the developed world. More specifically, FIEs from Asia are most likely to contravene Chinese environmental law, which gives support to the pollution-haven argument—albeit within a limited scope. This section will first provide the evidence that supports these two conclusions before the subsequent section offers explanations for the findings.

Table 6.3 provides the first piece of evidence that foreign firms from developed countries exhibit above-average environmental behavior. Table 6.3 presents the results of three ordered probit models run for all firms included in the sample population. An ordered probit model was used because the dependent variable is ranked ordinal (i.e., green to black coded as "1" to "5"). In Model 1, the variable "foreign-invested" has a negative coefficient (−0.19), but is not statistically significant. Because the dependent variable was coded from "1" for green to "5" for black, a negative coefficient is associated with better environmental behavior. However, the fact that the variable is statistically

TABLE 6.3 Oprobit estimates for the effect of foreign ownership on firm environmental behavior

Variables	Model 1		Model 2		Model 3	
	Coefficient	Standard error	Coefficient	Standard error	Coefficient	Standard error
Independent variable						
Foreign-invested	−0.19	0.22	—	—	—	—
Foreign-controlled	—	—	−1.07***	0.34	—	—
FIE from OECD	—	—	—	—	−0.90***	
Control variables						
Age	−0.005	0.01	−0.007	0.01	−0.01	0.01
Renovation	−0.09	0.19	−0.14	0.20	−0.13	0.24
Size (# of employees)	−0.16**	0.08	−0.14**	0.08	−0.15*	0.09
Profit	−0.30	0.21	−0.34	0.22	−0.25	0.25
SOE	0.10	0.30	0.06	0.30	−0.04	0.34
Chemical	0.37*	0.19	0.42**	0.20	0.36*	0.23
Electronic	−0.96	0.44	−0.73	0.48	−0.92**	0.71
Food	0.51	0.40	0.39	0.47	0.38	0.48
Textile	0.35	0.32	0.35	0.32	0.27	0.34
N	168		158		168	
Wald test	27.63		36.13		36.91	
p-value	0.002		0.0001		0.0001	
Pseudo R2	0.065		0.093		0.087	

$^*p < .1, ^{**}p < .05, ^{***}p < .01.$

insignificant indicates that one cannot say with a reasonable amount of confidence that there is a relationship between foreign ownership and a company's environmental ranking.[2]

Model 2 in the middle column of Table 6.3 provides further details about the relevance of foreign investment in explaining firm environmental practice. Model 2 evaluates the impact not just of foreign investment, but of foreign control on environmental conduct. As discussed in the previous chapter, representatives from foreign firms tend to stress the idea that enhancing the EHS practices of domestic acquisitions and joint ventures is significantly more difficult than in wholly foreign-owned greenfield investments. According to EHS officers in MNCs, the process of changing an entrenched mind-set and company culture inimical to environmental protection can represent one of the biggest challenges of a joint venture project. As one might expect, without control of the purse strings, the foreign partner is less in a position to induce change.

Model 2 in Table 6.3 lends support to this idea, as it shows that foreign ownership is quite strongly associated with positive environmental behavior ($\beta = -1.07$). Over 84 percent (n = 16) of majority-owned foreign firms are either green or blue. By contrast, among FIEs in which the foreign partner controls less than 50 percent of the investment, over half the firms are either yellow or red. This latter figure is roughly equivalent to that of domestic firms, of which 56 percent scored yellow or worse. Put simply, unless an FIE is majority foreign-owned, its environmental performance is indistinguishable from a domestic firm's. Foreign ownership is associated with better environmental behavior, but only when the foreign partner has financial control over the firm.

Because the coefficients of an ordered probit model are not readily interpretable, Figure 6.1 presents the results of Model 2 as "quantities of interest."[3] Figure 6.1 displays the probability of each possible Green Watch rank for both foreign-controlled and non-foreign-controlled firms. All other variables (such as size and profit) are held constant at their means. In this figure, the striking impact of foreign control is apparent. For instance, from the black columns of Figure 6.1 it is evident that if a firm is foreign-controlled, there is roughly a 36 percent chance it is green, a 47 percent chance it is blue, and a 16 percent chance it is yellow. For non-foreign-controlled firms the figures are, respectively, 8, 41, and 45 percent. Put another way, a firm in China that is foreign-controlled is four times more likely to be green than other firms. At the same time, it is only 33 percent as likely to be yellow as other firms. Again, this points to the importance of foreign control in explaining firm environmental behavior.

The survey results also provide interesting information about variations in the environmental behavior of firms from different countries or jurisdictions. First, OECD companies, particularly those from Europe and Japan, exhibit extremely good environmental behavior. Table 6.3 shows that the variable "FIE from OECD" is statistically significant and negative, which in-

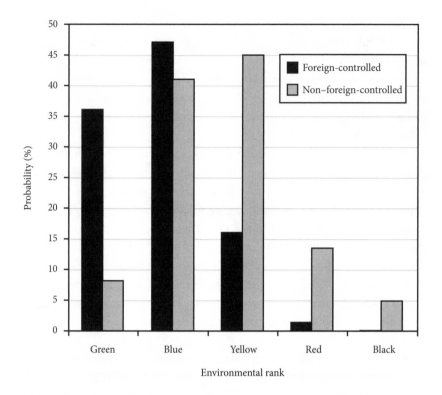

FIGURE 6.1 Impact of foreign control on environmental performance of companies in pollution-intensive sectors.

dicates that companies from OECD nations consistently display better environmental performance. The difference between firms from OECD countries and other nations is further illustrated in Figures 6.2 and 6.3, which show the environmental ranking of FIEs from each of the countries/regions for which there were multiple (more than five) observations in the sample. The survey population is small (only 55 FIEs were surveyed), and the data should therefore be treated with caution. Nonetheless, there are several aspects of these figures worth noting. First, as noted, Japanese and European firms appear to favor strong environmental practices. Figure 6.2 shows that 69 percent of European firms in the sample are green. Half of Japanese firms are green and the other half are blue. In Figure 6.3, one can see that while European firms represent only about a quarter of the foreign firms in the sample, they account for more than half of all foreign firms that have achieved a green status.

Japanese firms are similarly overrepresented in the green and blue rankings. The implication is that European and Japanese firms clearly go "beyond compliance" in their China operations.

Second, American firms display unexpectedly poor environmental behavior—significantly worse than European and Japanese firms. This is evident in Figure 6.2, which shows that 50 percent of American firms are yellow versus 15 percent for European enterprises and none among Japanese. In fact, American firms perform only slightly better than domestic firms. American firms are 13 percent green versus 8 percent for domestic firms. There are no

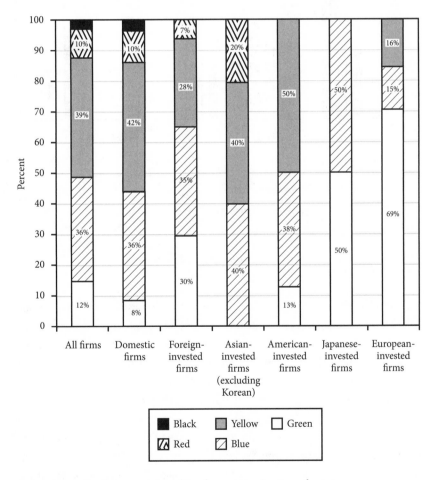

FIGURE 6.2 Environmental ranking by country/region of origin.

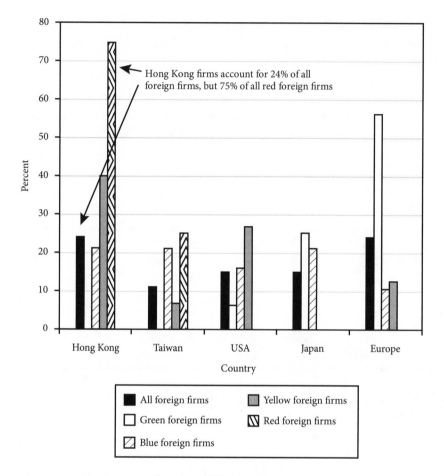

Hong Kong firms account for 24% of all foreign firms, but 75% of all red foreign firms

FIGURE 6.3 Environmental ranking of foreign firms.

red or black American firms, while 14 percent of domestic firms fall into one of these two categories. The indication is that, while U.S. firms do not appear to violate Chinese environmental law, they also do not go "beyond compliance" as often as their European or Japanese counterparts. This "American anomaly" is addressed in the next section.

Finally, Figures 6.2 and 6.3 demonstrate that companies with investment from Asian countries display environmental behavior that is virtually the same as domestic firms—and in some cases worse. This includes firms from Hong Kong, Taiwan, and Malaysia. As evident in Figure 6.2, the percent of blue and yellow firms is similar between Asian FIEs and domestic firms. Further, Asian FIEs have a smaller percentage of green firms and higher percentage of red ones. Hong Kong–invested enterprises, in particular, have substandard environmental practices. As seen in Figure 6.3, Hong Kong firms accounted for almost a quarter of the foreign firms in the sample, but comprised three quarters of the foreign firms with a red ranking. Although not evident in the figures, no enterprise from Hong Kong achieved a green ranking, while almost a quarter of all Hong Kong firms are red. By comparison, as evident in Figure 6.2 among domestic firms, 8 percent are green while only 10 percent are red (4 percent are black). This indicates that, at least when focusing on firms from Hong Kong, there is evidence for the pollution-haven hypothesis.[4]

It should be reiterated that the data in Figures 6.2 and 6.3 are based on a small survey population. The data should be seen more as suggesting a trend rather than firmly substantiating one. Yet they are potentially important given both the value of FDI to China's economic growth and the prevalence of Hong Kong firms in China. Over the course of the 1990s, FDI represented about 15 percent of all fixed investment in China. Even in the western areas of China where FDI figures are relatively low (compared with the east), according to some scholars FDI still accounts for about 10 percent of GDP. This 10 percent figure is roughly the same as in North America (Huang Yasheng 2003b). Through the 1990s more than half of China's substantial FDI inflow came from China's diaspora in Taiwan, Hong Kong, or Macau, with the brunt coming from Hong Kong. Though the percent of FDI inflow coming from overseas Chinese has lessened since the 1990s, it still represents a substantial portion of overall FDI. In 2005, for instance, Hong Kong accounted for 30 percent of China's $60 billion in inward FDI (Reuters 2006a). Over the course of the entire reform period, almost 30 percent of FDI into China has come from Hong Kong (Morrison 2006, table 3). Thus, the poor environmental behavior of Hong Kong firms is a cause for serious concern for those interested in protecting China's environment.

The Impact of Foreign Enterprises on Domestic Firms

The results discussed thus far have shown that, although it depends on the extent of ownership and the company's country of origin, there is a demonstrated impact of foreign ownership on company environmental behavior. However, there is little evidence that FIEs are a significant influence on domestic firms (hypothesis 2). MNCs' green supply chain and product stewardship policies, described in the previous chapter, may influence some Chinese companies to improve their pollution management practices, but the impact is not widespread. In none of the models run on domestic firms was the vari-

able "sell to FIEs" statistically significant, and inclusion of the variable generally resulted in less robust models. The lack of statistical significance of the
variable "sell to FIEs" indicates that domestic firms possessing commercial
relations with foreign firms in China do not display environmental behavior
any different from other domestic firms.

The reasons that green supply chains fail to exhibit a noticeable effect on
Chinese firms' environmental behavior awaits further research. A prima fa-
cie explanation is that there are simply too few foreign companies in China
utilizing green supply chain policies toward too few domestic firms. As discussed in the previous chapters, even the largest MNCs with the most pro-
active environmental stewardship policies tend to operate according to a
"hierarchy of risk management." They scrutinize the environmental, health,
and safety practices of the few domestic suppliers that can harm the reputation of the MNC itself. The environmental record of a Chinese company contracted to transport dangerous chemicals out of a foreign-owned facility gets
far more attention from an MNC than a supplier of mechanical spare parts.
Ultimately, however, this represents a relatively small drop in a large sea of
Chinese companies.

The idea that only a select few Chinese firms garner MNC attention and
adapt their environmental practices as a result of interaction with MNCs is
illustrated in Figure 6.4. As seen in Figure 6.4, domestic companies that sell
to foreign firms in China display a higher rate of green rankings. Roughly
14 percent of Chinese companies that have a sales relationship with foreign
firms attained a green rank, which is more than double the percentage among
Chinese firms that sell only to other domestic firms. Chinese enterprises with
commercial relations with foreign companies likewise displayed a slightly
higher percentage of blue firms and lower percentages of yellow and red firms.
This lends modest support to the idea that MNCs are selecting domestic partners based in part on EHS criteria and that interaction with foreign enterprises potentially has a positive influence on the environmental practices of
Chinese companies.

Interviews with firm managers in China lend credence to the idea that
some, but ultimately a small minority of, Chinese firms adapt their environmental practices as a result of interaction with foreign enterprises. Virtually
all managers had heard of foreign companies raising the issue of environmental practices with domestic partners. But when asked to discuss the relevance of environmental demands made by foreign firms in China to their

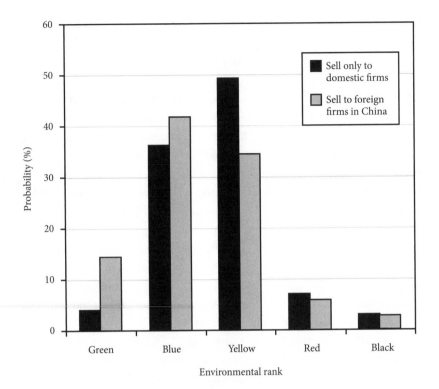

FIGURE 6.4 The manifestation of green supply chain policies? Chinese companies that sell to foreign companies are more likely be green.

own environmental policies, almost all Chinese managers expressed the view that foreign firms were not a significant source of pressure on their pollution management practices. The most common explanation offered by managers was that only a few of the leading MNCs actually seek to enforce specific environmental demands, for example, by including environmental protection stipulations in written contracts. None of the interviewed firms had relations with a Fortune 500 company and none had been directly pressed by a foreign company in China to make specific changes to their EHS policies. A commonly expressed view was that while establishing green credentials such as obtaining ISO certification might increase the odds of establishing commercial relations with a foreign company, the MNCs were often too fastidious and the cost of certification did not justify the possible benefit of greater potential for foreign contracts.

Yet a select number of Chinese managers indicated that there were clear commercial benefits to greening the firm. Each of the interviewed managers in a domestic firm that was green, or that was blue but seeking ISO certification (a requirement of obtaining a green rank), stated that one of their principal motivations was to expand market access (*kuoda shichang*). When asked to discuss how environmental practices expand market access, it was more common for managers to talk about the need to overcome export barriers to European markets than to talk about contracts with foreign firms operating in China. The indication is that, in terms of interaction with the international economy, the more important variable may be whether a firm exports rather than whether it possesses commercial relations with foreign companies operating in the home market.[5] Among the firms citing a desire to go green in order to enhance market access, the only reference to foreign companies in China was the expressed view that MNCs are a valuable source for learning the latest pollution abatement practices. In this vein Chinese firm managers typically expressed frustration that foreign companies are not more willing to act as teachers and share their experience.

In sum, the indication from the survey and interview results is that there is a small segment of domestic companies seeking to go green. Among these firms, commercial considerations are a significant part of the overall calculus, as better environmental practices increase access to overseas markets and increase the likelihood of landing contracts with foreign companies operating in China. For their part, in part due to considerations of environmental protection, some foreign companies are more likely to buy from Chinese companies that have strong environmental records. These are the firms in the far left columns of Figure 6.4, where we see that a higher percentage of Chinese companies that sell to foreign firms obtain a green ranking. But due to the fact that the number of foreign companies implementing robust green supply chain policies is small, foreign investors are not a source of influence on Chinese companies more broadly—hence the insignificant explanatory variable "sell to FIEs."

Discussion: Why Are European Firms Cleaner Than Asian Firms?

While the explanation for the lack of impact of green supply chain policies is relatively clear-cut, interpreting the survey's finding about the relationship between foreign investment and environmental rank requires more elaboration. How can one explain the better environmental behavior of most foreign-controlled firms vis-à-vis domestic firms while still accounting for the significant variation among foreign firms? Why does foreign-firm environmental behavior vary across countries? Put another way, why are Hong Kong firms heavier polluters than European or Japanese firms?

Part of the answer stems from the fact that several aspects of a firm's overseas investment decisions are influenced by its country of origin. One of the biggest impacts of a firm's home country on its overseas operations manifests in decisions about investment stake.[6] As discussed in this chapter, a critical element determining firm environmental behavior is not simply whether the enterprise is foreign-invested, but whether it is foreign-controlled. Enterprises that are foreign-invested, but not foreign-controlled, are indistinguishable from domestic firms in terms of environmental behavior. Therefore, if firms from a given country commonly tend to make small investments and control only a minority stake, that may explain similarities in their environmental behavior. In fact, research has shown that it is not uncommon for companies from the same country to take similar investment stakes in their overseas operations. Pan Yigang's study of joint ventures in China, for example, finds that the greater the cultural distance between the home and host country, the more likely the foreign partner will seek to minimize risk and uncertainty through a higher level of equity ownership (1996, 15).

For the Western firms in the sample, there is a correlation between ownership level and country of origin that influences environmental behavior. Over 80 percent of American firms in the sample are less than 50 percent American-invested. It is among these firms that the yellow American firms are clustered. Those enterprises that are more than 50 percent American-owned are all green. In contrast to American firms, 85 percent of European-invested projects are controlled by the European firm (i.e., more than 50 percent European-owned). The worse-than-expected environmental record of American firms vis-à-vis other developed countries appears to be a function of American firms' tendency to take minority stakes in their Chinese operations.

The above only holds true for Western firms. While Hong Kong firms also tend to take minority stakes in mainland investments, companies that are majority Hong Kong–controlled do not exhibit environmental behavior any different from those in which a Hong Kong firm owns a minority stake. Put another way, even majority-controlled Hong Kong firms exhibit poor environmental behavior. Being from Hong Kong appears to trump being majority foreign-invested. The situation is similar for Japanese-invested firms, which are evenly split between Japanese-controlled and non-Japanese-controlled firms. While Japanese-controlled enterprises tend to have higher rankings than non-Japanese-controlled firms, even non-Japanese-controlled firms display solid environmental behavior (all achieved a blue ranking). The conclusion is that the tendency of firms from the same country to make similar decisions with regard to the equity ownership level in FIEs is one factor that accounts for patterns of firm environmental behavior and helps to explain the "American anomaly."[7]

There are other aspects of a foreign enterprise's country of origin that influence its environmental performance. In particular, the environmental governance system in a firm's home country has a potent impact on the firm's approach to pollution control abroad. Strong environmental governance systems foster norms of corporate environmentalism. These norms of "how business is done" carry over and influence the firm's practices abroad. This was evident in the previous chapter, where it was argued that much of multinational corporations' environmental behavior in China is driven by standard operating procedures that were developed in response to increasingly stringent regulation in the industrialized world. Likewise, firms coming from home countries with weak environmental governance tend to lack these corporate environmental norms; in fact, they may operate under the norm that pollution, so long as it is accompanied by economic expansion, is tolerable. In both cases, the norms and practices generated in the home country carry over to and explain behavior in foreign operations. The next section will develop this idea more fully and present a brief case study of Asia Pulp and Paper. The case study, which in some ways is the exact opposite of the Shell case presented in the previous chapter, is a concrete example of a firm from a developing country that has displayed poor environmental behavior both at home and in China.

One common feature of the firms displaying strong environmental behavior in the survey is the fact that they are overwhelmingly from countries with robust environmental governance. While there are clear differences in the environmental protection regimes of the United States, Europe, and Japan, all have a relatively long history of industrial environmental governance. Among industrialized countries, Japan developed an environmental protection system somewhat later and faced significant pollution issues through the 1970s, but it has since achieved striking success in pollution control. One recent study noted that Japan has about one quarter the OECD average of emissions of sulfur dioxides, particulates, and nitrogen oxides (Rock 2002, 48). As several scholars have shown (and as the previous chapter discussed), the tightening web of environmental regulation in the developed world over the course of the last thirty-plus years has compelled industry to adjust and given rise to norms of corporate environmentalism. To use Andrew Hoffman's (2001) terms, environmental, health, and safety policies have been transformed from "heresy" to "dogma," so that the establishment of an EHS department, the performance of environmental audits and training, the publication of EHS reports, and (for larger firms) the implementation of green supply chain policies have become a taken-for-granted aspect of running a manufacturing operation in the developed world. The evidence in the previous chapter and in the Green Watch survey indicates that these policies and practices developed at home carry over to foreign operations.

By contrast, firms from many of Asia's industrializing countries have developed corporate environmental policies in a very different ideational setting. There is a great deal of variation in the environmental politics of East and Southeast Asian countries, and it is dangerous to paint with too broad a brush. Nevertheless, the Asian countries share certain aspects in their history of industrial environmental governance.[8] First, although they have enjoyed rapid growth over the last three decades, most of these countries got off to a late start and did not get serious about environmental protection until the 1990s. For instance, despite having three factories per square kilometer (about seventy-five times the industrial density of the United States), Taiwan did not create a cabinet-level environmental protection agency until 1987 (Chan 1993). One scholar writing about Taiwan noted that "it is commonly held that environmental protection measures prior to the late 1980s were more for appearance's sake than a real effort to recognize and improve the growing environmental crisis" (Lyons 2005, 185).

Hong Kong took its first step toward better environmental protection in 1978 with the creation of the Environmental Protection Unit (EPU). It was staffed by only five professional officers, and its role was limited to developing policy and conducting environmental monitoring (e.g., measuring air pollution). The EPU had no responsibility for implementing policies, which was left to various other government bodies. It was not until 1986, when the EPU was renamed the Environmental Protection Department, that it was given greater authority and independence (Hills and Barron 1990, 39–40). For much of Hong Kong's recent history, environmental issues have been little more than an afterthought. In 2001, the head of the Environment, Transport, and Works Bureau grumbled that too often, "the environment [is] an empty word" to Hong Kongers. The same official commented that Hong Kongers "enjoy developed-world incomes but labor under a developing-world mentality when it comes to issues like clean air and water" (Clifford 2002).

A second aspect in the recent history of domestic environmental governance shared by newly industrializing Asian countries is a reluctance of political authorities to force industry's compliance with environmental regulation. This both derives from and contributes to an ideational context in which economic growth is privileged above all else. Until the late 1990s, the approach to environmental regulation in most Asian countries can perhaps best be characterized as "pollute first, pay later." Chi summarized Taiwan's environmental dilemma in the mid-1990s, stating: "The main problem rests in the government's insistence on pursuing endless economic growth, which has become an uncontested as well as uncontestable goal. Economic growth is regarded . . . as the source of all virtue for Taiwan" (1994, 36). The same could be said for most other countries in East and Southeast Asia; there is simply an overwhelming desire for and faith in economic growth. One scholar focusing broadly on Asia notes, "Decision makers now largely focus on the financial basis, where the environment is left out of the equation" (Jane Hall et al. 1994, 22). The result is that, as argued in a 1997 World Bank report, investment in environmental protection among East Asian countries lagged behind that of the developed countries when they were at a similar level of development (World Bank 1997).

There are many factors that have contributed to the generation of this norm. The most obvious is that economic growth has lifted millions of Asians out of poverty. In the second half of the twentieth century, the average per capita income in ten East and Southeast Asian countries increased almost ninefold.[9] According to the World Bank, forty million Asians rose above the poverty line in 2003 alone. Many in Asia's middle and upper class have first-hand experience with poverty. It is hardly surprising that the changes they have witnessed in their societies and own lives have created a strong faith in the benefits of economic growth and a corresponding coolness toward the idea that material sacrifices are needed to protect the environment (Jane Hall et al. 1994, 11).

But there are also political economy reasons for the heavy emphasis on producing growth. Notably, in most industrializing Asian countries there is a close connection between business and government elite. Again there is a great deal of variance across countries, which should not be overlooked, but to the extent that there is an Asian model of development it is characterized by a strong government role in industrial policy. In different ways, many Asian governments are active in guiding savings and investment, promoting export industries, and directing trade. All these activities, of course, are for the purpose of promoting growth, and within government bureaucracies economic interests have traditionally been better represented and often privileged above environmental ones. The need to generate growth and the corresponding lesser emphasis on environmental interests have been accentuated by the fact that for much of their history, Asian governments have been authoritarian and in need of shoring up their political legitimacy.[10] One scholar focusing on South Korea and Taiwan states: "The environmental movement was viewed as a nuisance by the developmental state. . . . The developmental state, in close collusion with the big business conglomerates . . . was primarily concerned with maintaining high economic growth rates and, therefore, ignored and suppressed the environmental movement" (Kim 2000, 289). Moreover, in many Asian countries through the 1980s and 1990s it was not uncommon for the government to be the direct owners of industry. Commenting on the lack of pollution controls in many Asian companies, one economist noted that "the beneficiaries often are the powerful local interests connected to the political world" (Jane Hall et al. 1994, 17). In Taiwan, for instance, as of the 1990s about 20 percent of industry was owned by local government or GMD (Guomindang) elite. This figure represents a significant decline from the previous decade, but is still sizable.

The bottom line is that for much of East and Southeast Asia's recent history, de facto decision making over the use of land and natural resources has been in the hands of a business and political elite that favors growth above all else (Pasong and Lebel 2000). This is not a milieu conducive to the construction of robust environmental protection bureaus or to the vigorous enforcement of existing environmental regulation. For instance, through the 1990s the Hong Kong government continued to treat EIAs as confidential and not open to public debate or review. Hong Kong's airport (completed in 1998), as well as many residential projects and other major development proposals, managed to avoid significant public scrutiny. Despite an increased consensus about the need to tackle air pollution problems, in 1996 business groups representing the transportation industry were able to squash plans to move away from the use of diesel fuel (Granitsas 1999). A program to lessen the one million tons of sewage being dumped untreated every day into Victoria Harbor was postponed in 1990 for several years due to a lack of resources and then became mired down in squabbles between the British and Chinese governments in the run-up to the 1997 handover (Henry 1992; Lague 2001).

The situation is similar in Taiwan—a weak environmental protection regime contributed to poor corporate environmental protection practices. In 1990, EPA operations in Taiwan revealed that 21 percent of firms violated emission regulations, 70 percent of firms violated wastewater discharge standards, and 20 percent of firms engaged in construction projects that violated EIA requirements (Chan 1993). Taiwan's EPA became a cabinet-level organization in 1987, but through the 1990s had a staff of just over three hundred, which was simply inadequate to monitor the activities of the thousands of small- and medium-sized enterprises scattered across an island slightly larger than the state of Maryland.[11] The Maryland Department of the Environment employs about nine hundred officials, and this figure does not include employees of the federal-level EPA.[12] Chi, writing in the early 1990s, notes that during the 1980s only ten factories were closed for violating pollution laws and argues: "The EPA is incapable of dealing with the scale and speed of environmental degradation in Taiwan. . . . The various environmental laws that have been passed remain largely unimplemented" (1994, 39).[13]

In the absence of a sustained government push, firms are highly unlikely to improve their environmental behavior. One Chinese scholar of Japanese environmental politics noted that even though Japan became serious about environmental protection in the 1970s, it was not until 1990 that Japanese firms could be said to emphasize environmental protection (Jiang Taiping 2000). This twenty-year lag is roughly the same time frame Hoffman uses to trace the transformation of American corporations' approach to environmental regulation (Hoffman 2001). In the absence of stringent government enforcement, many firms in industrializing Asian countries have lacked the motivation to make the significant investment of capital and human resources necessary to build strong environmental management systems.

The third element that many industrializing Asian countries share with regard to environmental governance is that they are undergoing a process that can be referred to as "environmentalizing." That is, over the last decade a combination of political liberalization and readily visible environmental problems has spurred more genuine attempts at industrial environmental governance.[14] Taiwan's environmental movement did not begin in earnest until the political liberalization in the late 1980s and 1990s. In that early period, one of the defining characteristics was the rise of environmental protests and NIMBY (not-in-my-backyard) politics. From 1980 to 1987 there was an average of 13.5 environmental protests per year. Between 1988 and 1991 that average increased to over thirty-three a year before leveling off and eventually decreasing in subsequent years. The goal behind much of this early environmentalism was to gain monetary compensation from polluting factories. Lacking environmental organizations, which were restricted prior to the lifting of martial law in 1987, it was difficult to organize and mobilize local residents. Leaders used the promise of monetary gain from settlements with polluters as a motivation (Tang and Tang 1997, 284–86). The rise of NIMBY movements, combined with a flurry of environmental lawmaking in the late 1990s, has placed increased pressure on manufacturing firms and made the siting of manufacturing facilities a major issue. One of the most famous incidents in Taiwan's environmental movement was the "Lukang Rebellion," in which protestors in the late 1980s blocked Dupont's plan to build a titanium dioxide plant that at the time would have been the largest foreign-investment project in Taiwan's history (Reardon-Anderson 1992).

Although Hong Kong has traditionally lagged in environmental protection relative to its level of economic development, as is the case in Taiwan, over the last decade there have been several key changes in Hong Kong's approach to the environment. First, it is widely acknowledged that the end of the uncertainty characterizing the years leading up to Hong Kong's 1997 return to Chinese control served to make both local leaders and ordinary citizens more invested in environmental protection. Second, and perhaps more importantly, starting in the late 1990s many business and political leaders began to worry that pollution was undermining Hong Kong's competitiveness as a business and financial center. One Hong Kong official stated, "People react to what they see, and many tourists and business visitors are going away with an impression of Hong Kong as a dirty, polluted city" (Granitsas 1999, 40). A poll in 2000 ranked "the quality of the environment" as the second most unsatisfactory aspect of doing business in Hong Kong. This led to joint initiatives between business leaders, civil society organizations, and government, as well as greater government spending and a general increased receptiveness to en-

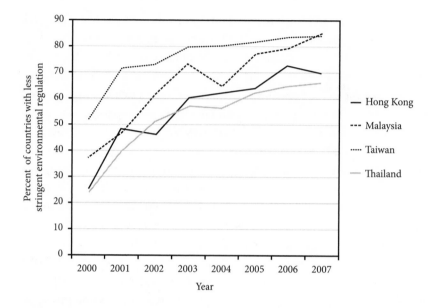

FIGURE 6.5 Environmentalizing East Asia. Data from World Economic Forum 2000–2007. See Chapter 3, "China in Comparative Perspective" section, for a complete description of the data.

vironmental protection (Chung 1999; Pence 2001). Recent years have also seen some victories for environmentalists in Hong Kong. In 1999, for instance, environmental groups and sympathetic members of the media were able to block a proposed plan to build a railroad connecting Hong Kong to Shenzhen. The railway would have gone through a valley serving as a sanctuary to 210 different species of birds—some of which are endangered (Yoon 2001).

The enhancement of environmental regulation in Taiwan and Hong Kong is evident in the World Economic Forum's survey of business executives introduced in Chapter 3 ("China in Comparative Perspective" section).[15] As seen in Figure 6.5, executive perceptions of the stringency of environmental regulation in several East Asian nations have changed rapidly in recent years. In 2000, executives ranked Hong Kong in the 25th percentile globally. Almost three-quarters of the 59 nations included in the sample were deemed to possess stronger environmental regulation. By 2007, Hong Kong's ranking shot up to the 70th percentile, as Hong Kong was ranked 39th out of 131 sampled nations. Taiwan experienced a rapid increase in stringency as well—from the 52nd percentile in 2000 to the 85th in 2007.

While the strengthening of environmental regimes in East Asia is certainly beneficial to the domestic population and local ecology, in the short term it may be complicating the challenge of environmental protection in China. This is particularly true for Hong Kong and Taiwan, where the strengthening of environmental regulation, combined with the relative ease and low transaction costs of investing in China, is contributing to industrial flight. As defined in Chapter 1, industrial flight refers to the migration of pollution-intensive industry from high-standard to low-standard countries, where pollution abatement costs are lower. Some have noted that the pressure of stricter standards is pushing Taiwanese firms, particularly small and medium-sized enterprises in pollution-intensive industries for whom meeting stricter standards is especially demanding, to choose an exit strategy and shift production to China. One survey of Taiwanese enterprises shows that 22 percent of firms stated that additional regulations would leave no choice but to seek out an alternative location where such costs could be reduced, and 66 percent of enterprises stated that they on occasion are forced to violate environmental regulations (Lyons 2005). A recent study of more than 2,800 equity joint ventures established in the mid-1990s found that as a whole the environmental stringency of a Chinese province did not affect the location choice of the JV. However, for pollution-intensive ventures from Taiwan, Hong Kong, and Macau, low environmental levies were a source of attraction (Dean and Lovely 2005). Di (2004) also found evidence that the effective pollution levy influenced patterns of investment, with pollution-intensive sectors attracted to low levies, although she did not distinguish the investment based on country of origin.

There is also ample anecdotal evidence that the tightening of environmental regulation in Taiwan has contributed to the shift of industry to the mainland. Chi documents that in the early 1990s Formosa Plastics, at the time one of Taiwan's largest companies and most notorious polluters, threatened to shift its production to the mainland (1994, 42). Chinese scholars also occasionally discuss the industrial shift of pollution-intensive firms from both Taiwan and Hong Kong. For instance, one article from *China Population, Resources, and Environment* states: "Many Taiwanese and Hong Kong firms have moved production of ozone-depleting substances that are restricted under international treaties to China. In the areas around Hong Kong, most of the pollution in the 1980s and 1990s is from enterprises that have already fallen into disuse [in their home country] and been moved to China. These enterprises produce chemicals, electroplates, prints and dyes, leather shoes, paper, and pesticides" (Peng and Zhang 2004). Another article makes a similar claim, stating, "Since the reform period, almost all of Hong Kong and Macau's heaviest polluters in the textile, dyeing, electroplating, and leather-making industries have shifted operations to China" (Li Zhiping 2000). Others have argued that in Hong Kong, initial pollution reduction, and more recently increases in air pollution, are the result of Hong Kong firms shifting production to the less-regulated Guangzhou (Chung 1999; Henry 1992).

More recently, the Hong Kong press has noted the tendency of Hong Kong firms to shift production out of the more developed parts of mainland China to rural areas. This migration has at least in part been driven by a desire for lax environmental standards. The *South China Morning Post* states that in 2003 Qingyuan, a rural area in northern Guangdong Province, attracted 736 foreign companies, of which 80 percent were from Hong Kong. These firms tended to be pollution-intensive industries such as electronic appliances, ceramics, shoes, and leather. According to the report, a manager of a Hong Kong–listed audio equipment manufacturer "admitted the company had expanded from its base in Dongguan in part because of the lax environmental standards in Qingyuan" (Ying 2004). In 2006, it was announced that 2,000 of approximately 70,000 Hong Kong firms in the Pearl River Delta region were facing closure or relocation orders because they posed an undue environmental hazard (Cheung 2006).

The Green Watch survey also offers some credence to the anecdotes indicating that this localized industrial flight is occurring with regard to Hong Kong firms, although there is little evidence for Taiwanese firms. Within the entire sample (including domestic firms), just over one-third of all firms are categorized as "dirty." The dirty industry category included the iron and steel, chemical, cement, and pulp and paper industries (Mani and Wheeler 1997). For American, Taiwanese, and Japanese firms, the figure is virtually the same. Hong Kong firms, by contrast, have a greater tendency to invest in pollution-intensive industries. Forty-six percent of Hong Kong firms fall within the dirty category, which may in part explain their poorer environmental behavior. European firms, which exhibit the best environmental behavior, are only 15 percent dirty.

In conclusion, over the last quarter of a century, firms in several Asian countries have developed corporate practices in a very different setting than those in the industrialized world. Operating in a milieu in which pollution is tolerated and growth is privileged, until very recently there has been minimal pressure on Asian firms from their domestic governments and general public, which has resulted in weaker corporate environmental policies. Current attempts by Asian governments to protect the environment should eventually lead to better corporate practices, but inevitably there is a lag between government pressure and corporate response. In the meantime, some firms seem to be choosing an exit strategy and investing in China. Whether or not firms' investment in China has been motivated by a desire to escape regulation at home, the fact remains that many Asian companies continue to place minimal stress on environmental protection when compared with firms from other parts of the world. The survey results presented in the previous section indicate that, as is the case with firms from the industrialized world, environmental practices developed in Asian firms' home countries carry over to Chinese operations. This idea is also evident in the case of Asia Pulp and Paper (APP).

Asia Pulp and Paper and the Controversy in Yunnan's Forests

The case of Asia Pulp and Paper (APP) is a specific manifestation of the ideas presented in the Green Watch survey results and is an example of how intra-developing-country investment poses a considerable hazard to environmental protection. It involves a foreign firm from a developing country engaging in behavior detrimental to the environment in China. Furthermore, APP is a firm whose behavior in China is not dissimilar to that displayed in its home country and whose practices in China are largely a function of convention. In essence, the APP case is a classic example of a pollution-haven scenario, in which the actions of a foreign firm desirous of avoiding scrutiny from environmental regulators, combined with domestic government officials eager to promote growth, serves to undermine environmental regulation.

Asia Pulp & Paper (*Jinguang Gongsi*) is an Indonesian company, the largest manufacturer of paper products in Asia, and one of the ten largest in the world. It produces about two million tons of pulp and five million tons of paper and packaging materials a year, selling its products in over sixty countries.[16] It is a unit of the Indonesian Sinar Mas group, which is an organization with a history of financial trouble and, as of early 2006, over $6 billion in debt. In the wake of the Asian financial crisis, APP itself encountered a debt crisis and in the spring of 2001 defaulted on $14 billion in debt. This set off a series of negotiations with international creditors, and a group of bondholders sued for $353 million. In 2005, a New York appeals court ruled in favor of APP.

Despite this debt crisis, APP expanded rapidly in China after it first invested in the mid-1990s. Indeed, the rapid spread of APP in China, much of which was financed by Chinese banks, is part of what initially created misgivings within the Chinese media. By late 2005, APP had thirteen operations and twenty subsidiaries in China, with a total investment of $5.5 billion (Qiu et al. 2005). In both Hainan and Yunnan provinces, APP runs vertically integrated forest, pulp, and paper operations. This includes large-scale tree farms, principally comprised of fast-growth eucalyptus, as well as manufacturing operations for the production of pulp and finished paper products. Most of APP's operations are overseen by APP China. The relationship between APP Indonesia and APP China is not entirely clear. APP Indonesia purportedly owns less than one percent of APP China, but both companies have the same chairman, and the CEO of APP China serves on the board of APP Indonesia.

The APP case began with the publication of two investigative articles in the mainstream Chinese media. The first was published in *Caijing Magazine* in November 2003 and the second in *China Newsweek* in July 2004; both periodicals have wide circulation in China.[17] Each article was a lengthy investigation (roughly 10,000 Chinese characters) that accused APP of a number of illegal and quasi-legal deeds in Yunnan and Hainan provinces. The principal allegations were that APP illicitly obtained forest land and engaged in unlicensed logging. On November 16, the Beijing and Hong Kong offices of Greenpeace held a press conference and issued a report further denouncing APP's logging activities (Greenpeace 2004).[18] Greenpeace's claims were based on the already published articles as well as their own investigations in Yunnan and Hainan in the summer and fall of 2004. Greenpeace's account also drew heavily on Forestry Bureau reports that to my knowledge were not made available to the general public.

In the wake of Greenpeace's press conference and continued effort to draw attention to APP's activities, there was a widespread media outcry. Concern was not only with illegal logging and encirclement of land, but also with the ecological impact of nonnative eucalyptus on the natural environment of Yunnan, which is one of the most biodiverse areas on the planet (Liu Shixin 2005; Qiu et al. 2005). *Southern Weekend* published its own 10,000 character report in December (Xiang 2004). By early 2005 articles began appearing in most of China's main newspapers. APP did not respond formally until January 6, when it published in English a brief rejoinder on an industry website (Asia Pulp & Paper 2005). As the issue gained public interest, college students led by Greenpeace began boycotting APP goods (Jiang and Qin 2005). The Zhejiang Hotel Association announced its one-hundred-plus members would boycott APP and published a list of APP products on its website (Zhejiang Fandian Ye Xiehui [Zhejiang Hotel Association] 2005).

In what can only be described as a bizarre decision, APP then announced it was suing the Zhejiang Hotel Association for defamation of character. Around the same time (early January 2005), the State Forestry Administration (SFA) in Beijing made the first official government comments on the issue (Qiu et al. 2005). It announced it was launching an investigation, the results of which would be released two months later. When the two-month deadline came and went, the media became impatient and began to call for publication of the results. APP dropped its suit against the Zhejiang Hotel Association (the day before the first scheduled hearing), but at almost the same time there occurred another curious incident. The SFA published the findings of its investigation, but the report was dated January 7, 2005 (SFA 2005). This indicates that the investigation was conducted and completed prior to the government's January announcement in which it had indicated it was beginning an investigation and would announce the results in two months.

The SFA report condemned APP's behavior and indicated that APP had engaged in illegal logging, but not to the extent claimed by Greenpeace and others. It made a number of demands on the Yunnan provincial government to rectify the situation and indicated that another investigation was still ongoing. However, as several in the Chinese media pointed out, despite the finding of culpability and the large scale of forest destruction, the APP case was not listed on the SFA's publication of the ten largest incidents of forest destruction for 2004 (Wang Zhongyu 2005).

At the same time, in yet another unusual development, the Yunnan provincial government issued findings from its own investigation that directly rebutted the SFA and completely exonerated APP. The Yunnan government had previously struck back at Greenpeace, stating, "The harsh and unreasonable criticism of Greenpeace toward the pulp and paper industry of Yunnan and APP is due to the fact that Greenpeace does not understand the concrete aspects of work in Yunnan" (Wang Zhongyu 2005). According to the report of the Yunnan provincial government, all illegal logging had been conducted by local villagers or contractors that had no relationship with APP. This announcement met with an incredulous response in the Chinese media (Liu Shixin 2005; Xiao Nanzi 2005).

In late May, Greenpeace reiterated its claims in another press conference, which was held in conjunction with APP and grew heated.[19] The issue died down in the summer of 2005 as all sides waited for the subsequent SFA report. Finally in August 2005, the SFA issued its second report, which again claimed that APP had engaged in illegal felling of forests, but deemed the illegal behavior "accidental." This rather apparent dodge seems to have closed the case and, despite the numerous claims made against it, it appears that no charges or fines will be brought against APP.

What precisely did APP do and how does it fit with the argument presented in the previous sections? Given that the case has not made it to a courtroom, as well as the salmagundi of claims and competing counterclaims appearing in the Chinese media, it is difficult to know exactly what occurred in Yunnan and Hainan provinces. Nonetheless, there is an extremely high level of detail in the investigative articles published in the Chinese media. These articles rely heavily on discussions with unnamed Forestry Bureau officials and other industry insiders, as well as unpublished government documents. Combined, they provide a strong suggestion that there was some degree of illicit behavior.[20] Because government reports only focused on activities in Yunnan, events in Hainan, which are even murkier, are not addressed here. Suffice it to say that according to both the investigative media and Greenpeace, the illegal behavior described below in Yunnan took place on a similar scale in Hainan province as well.

According to the SFA report issued in early 2005, APP engaged in illegal logging of natural forests in Yunnan.[21] Though the details are complex, APP's project in Yunnan was essentially both a manufacturing and an afforestation project. According to the agreement between APP and the Yunnan government, APP was to plant fast-growth eucalyptus on land designated as "barren areas" or "wasteland" (*huang shan huang di*), which refers to sparse growth areas or regions in which the soil is too low yielding for agriculture. These areas serve as a raw material base for the pulp and paper manufacturing operations.[22] According to Greenpeace, APP contracted 1.8 million hectares in Yunnan, but only 17 percent of that was designated by the government as land suitable for afforestation; 43 percent of the land was already forested. Greenpeace therefore argued that APP planned to clear out existing natural forest, using the felled trees as raw material, and then to replant the land with eucalyptus as part of its future raw material base. Both Greenpeace and *China Newsweek* reporters claimed to have witnessed such illegal logging of existing forest. The SFA investigation substantiated these claims, but on a smaller scale, as it determined that in Yunnan's Lancang County, APP contractors logged approximately 642 hectares and afforested another 105 hectares that was land not designated as forestable land. Other counties discussed in the investigative journals were not mentioned in the SFA report.

The SFA also concluded that APP's project was designed with the intention of logging Yunnan's natural forest. It did so by expressing skepticism about the calculations concerning the amount of land available for eucalyptus farms. These figures were used by the Yunnan government when it signed its letter of agreement with APP. The SFA noted that many county governments have not conducted land classification surveys in recent years, or in one case since the founding of the PRC, and simply did not possess sufficient data on the extent and type of forest cover in their area. Put another way, like Greenpeace, the SFA cast doubt on APP's claim that the entire afforestation project was designed to occur on wasteland. The SFA stated: "According to our investigation, the suitable barren land area of Simao City and Wenshan prefecture is simply incapable of satisfying the demands for the construction of raw material in APP's 'agreement.'" The SFA reached a similar conclusion to that of Greenpeace and the media, stating that the lack of open area for the planting of eucalyptus meant the APP project "must make up the deficiency from existing forests. Therefore, if the 'agreement' were completely implemented, it would inevitably lead to the felling of a large quantity of existing forest" (SFA 2005).

There was also compelling evidence of improprieties in the transfer of land rights and evidence that with the aid of government authorities APP obtained the land for its raw material base at artificially low prices. In Yunnan, each *mu* (0.167 hectare) of land was given to APP at a price of 40 RMB (roughly $5) for fifty years, which comes out to 0.8 RMB/year.[23] This led one State Forestry Administration official to respond, "Such a low price is absolutely unimaginable; even a mu of desert in Inner Mongolia is still one RMB per year" (Xiang 2004). Though again only focusing on a limited area, the SFA concluded:

> With respect to the turnover of the collective forests, villagers' common reaction was that the contract money was too low and the unified established price not in accordance with market patterns; at the same time, while villagers were either unaware or unwilling, the village committees and APP agreed on the contracts [for the handover of land use rights]. With respect to the turnover of state-owned forest, there occurred a situation in which state-owned land

was delineated and handed over to APP for the construction of raw material forests without going through the evaluation process. (SFA 2005)

In other words, the SFA determined that APP obtained land use rights at an artificially low price and with the aid of local governments circumvented the normal regulatory channels.

The APP case is a specific example of the phenomenon shown in the Green Watch survey, which showed that firms from developing countries with a history of weak environmental governance tend to display poorer environmental behavior abroad. Indonesia has been slow to invest in its environmental protection regime (Harrison 2002; Rock 2002). This is particularly true with regard to the protection of forests, which have long been a concern of international environmental groups and multilateral lending agencies. The World Bank notes that only 5 percent of the world's forests are in Asia but that Asia accounts for 25 percent of the world's forest loss. It has created the Forest Law Enforcement and Governance (FLEG) initiative, which is designed to bring together government officials, technical experts, NGOs, and private sector leaders to enhance environmental governance (World Bank 2006). Most of the meetings and initiatives have centered on Indonesia. APP itself has come under heavy scrutiny from INGOs for its activities in Indonesia (e.g., Matthew 2001).[24] In my interview with an APP representative, the role of habit was also clear. The representative, despite declining to discuss each of the allegations in turn, made clear that APP was caught completely off guard by the attack and part of its clumsy initial response (e.g., suing the Zhejiang Hotel Association) was the result of this shock. The interviewee emphasized the economic benefits to Yunnan and indicated that APP's leaders were surprised in part because they felt they were just "doing business in their normal way."[25] APP's behavior in China largely resembles its behavior in Indonesia.

The APP case also reinforces much of what has been presented not only in this chapter, but also in previous chapters. It is an example quite similar to the case of China's chemical parks presented in Chapter 4, in which it was argued that in jurisdictions without competitive advantage, the desire to attract investment often leads to the discounting of environmental regulations. Yunnan, as a landlocked province in China's southwest, has traditionally lacked the capacity to attract large-scale investments in the manner of China's more dynamic coastal provinces. For instance, from 1991 to 1996 Yunnan ranked twenty-ninth out of thirty in its rate of poverty change among China's provinces (Donaldson 2005). Clearly, much of the underlying explanation for the

APP case is the Yunnan government's hunger for investment. This is evident in the Yunnan government's original announcement of the projects, which have a triumphant quality as they discuss the securing of the investment. In announcing the agreement between APP and the government for building a commercial forest raw material base in Wenzhou, *Yunnan Daily* stated, "This is Wenzhou's largest ever 'help the poor through opening' project, and presently the two sides are already working hard to quickly start the project." The article goes on to praise the government for landing the project by stating, "This 'huge bird' flying into Wenzhou's nest is the inevitable result of the Wenzhou Party Committee and government heavily emphasizing the establishment of an investment environment, the attraction of big projects, and the implementation of a strong industrial strategy" (Zhang and Liu 2003).

Even Forestry Bureau officials, who have been the strongest critics of APP, make clear the dilemma between the desires to attract investment and to protect the environment. In announcing the investigation into APP, an SFA official stated, "The moment we discover destruction of forests actually has occurred, we will severely punish those responsible according to the relevant laws and regulations." He then followed this statement by noting that "the SFA still warmly welcomes and encourages large investors to invest in China's forestry industry, for example by building tree farms, opening forest, pulp, and paper integrated projects, etc." In fact, this was the standard comment by all forestry officials when addressing the issue publicly (Qiu et al. 2005; Yi and Wang 2005).

Given this enthusiasm for investment, it is not surprising that APP has been strongly supported by local government officials, although there has also been significant intra-governmental infighting. The project has pitted the Yunnan provincial-level branch of the National Development and Reform Commission (NDRC) and a task force set up by the Yunnan Development Research Center, which is an organ of the provincial government, against the Forestry Administration. *Southern Weekend* traces the wrangling as both sides put forth competing estimates about the ideal target capacity for pulp and paper production in Yunnan. The task force and provincial branch of the NDRC favored a two-million-ton-annual-capacity project while forestry officials believed Yunnan could sustain no more than 400,000 tons. The difference in the figures stems from the Task Force's use of what forestry officials believed to be highly exaggerated estimates of Yunnan's forest base. But the provincial government pressed its case by holding meetings in which the Forestry Administration calculations were declared incorrect and in which the government made clear its intentions by making statements such as, "[Yunnan] is the best place in the country for the development of an integrated [forest, pulp, paper] project; it has the conditions to become an important base for the country's production of pulp and paper" (Xiang 2004). Ultimately, forestry officials yielded, indicating that because this is an issue of macroeconomic development planning, it is ultimately the jurisdiction of the provincial NDRC.

Although they ultimately relented, the forestry official made clear the pressure from the upper-level provincial government to push through the APP project. Several articles note the reduced time frame between the signing of the letter of intent and the approval of final agreements (e.g., *Zhongguo Xinwen Zhoukan* [China Newsweek] 2004). One official indicated that in deciding issues like the development of the paper industry, the normal procedure is for the government to give a guiding opinion. Government researchers then decide the relative goals and specific scale and, according to existing natural resources and the ecological situation, put forward several plans for the relevant bureaus to discuss and determine the strengths and weaknesses of each. In the end, the leadership decides by selecting the best among the proposals. In this case, forestry officials indicate that APP's investment project was accepted first, and the macroeconomic plans for Yunnan's development were then written around APP. As the official said, "This decision's procedure has problems; it made a research topic become a 'go through the motions' (*zou guo chang*) process. In a lifetime of scientific research and planning we have never encountered this kind of matter" (Xiang 2004).

In summary, APP is an example of not only how a foreign firm's environmental behavior at home carries over to its operations abroad, but also how the combination of a weak corporate environmentalism combined with a government eager for investment can have a detrimental effect on environmental governance. Together, the survey results, the case of China's chemical parks presented in Chapter 4, and the APP example suggest that the biggest danger to a country's environmental regulation is the combination of a developing-country firm investing in a poor jurisdiction hungry for foreign capital. Where these conditions exist, one will find pockets of pollution havens.

Conclusion

In this chapter I both reaffirmed and extended the argument initiated in previous chapters, which focused specifically on the activities of large multinationals and chemical parks. Utilizing a survey of manufacturing firms in three Chinese cities, I broadened the focus and examined the behavior of foreign-invested enterprises in China. The results of the survey indicate that, from the perspective of firm strategy and practice, there is little evidence for a widespread pollution-haven phenomenon. As discussed in Chapter 1, one mechanism for a country's transformation into a pollution haven is investment by foreign firms that seek to take advantage of weak environmental regulation and adopt an environmentally exploitative strategy. If foreign investment is turning China into a pollution haven in this manner, one would expect to see poor compliance practices among foreign firms.

The results presented in this chapter do not lend support to this idea. On a broad level, foreign firms are indistinguishable from domestic enterprises in terms of their environmental behavior—the results of the survey do not allow one to say with any degree of confidence that foreign ownership in and of itself leads a company to adopt environmental practices that are any better or worse than those of domestic firms. However, foreign-controlled firms typically have stronger environmental practices. This also holds true for firms from industrialized countries such as Japan or the nations of western Europe. Thus, some kinds of foreign ownership are clearly beneficial for environmental protection, which is the opposite of the pollution-haven argument and largely supports the assertions of those who see a positive impact of foreign investment on the environment. This is not to say that the pollution-haven hypothesis can be rejected altogether. As the examples of Asian countries and specifically Hong Kong demonstrate, foreign firms from certain countries exhibit environmental behavior that is in some cases noncompliant with local law. Firms from countries with a short history of environmental governance are more likely to display poor environmental behavior and represent a threat to a developing country's environmental protection. As the cases of chemical parks (Chapter 4) and APP show, the risk is even higher when the foreign firm invests in a less developed region.

This may sound like a particularly narrow set of circumstances that has little applicability beyond Taiwan, Hong Kong, and the PRC. But in the context of globalization, in which barriers to investment are disappearing rapidly, it may have more relevance than initially meets the eye. Although relatively unstudied in the field of environmental politics, the flow of FDI between southern countries has grown swiftly in recent years, and developing countries are increasingly becoming not just a recipient but a source of foreign investment. According to UNCTAD (2004), since the late 1990s FDI between developing countries has grown faster than that from developed to developing countries. According to one report, as much as a third of FDI to developing countries comes from other developing countries. Countries like Malaysia, South Korea, Hong Kong, Chile, South Africa, and India have all positioned themselves as foreign investors.

Perhaps nowhere is the rise of intra-developing-country foreign investment more apparent than in the increase of Chinese firms' activity in overseas markets. China has become a prominent commercial partner with many countries in Southeast Asia, Latin America, and Africa. In 1999, China's trade with Africa was $2 billion; by 2005 it reached almost $40 billion (Taylor 2006, 937). Not only has trade increased dramatically, but in recent years Chinese companies have invested several billions abroad. According to *China Daily*, in 2004 China had $30 billion invested in 160 countries (Xinhua 2004). In the next two years alone China invested several billion dollars just in the oil-rich states of Africa such as Algeria, Sudan, Angola, and Nigeria. Focusing on Chinese overseas investments in Southeast Asia, one study cites an official statistic of $2 billion for the year 2002 and a cumulative total of between $20 and $35 billion, but surmises that the real figures are likely far higher (Frost 2004). Regardless of the actual amounts, it is clear that the figures are rising quickly and that much of this investment is driven by a desire to secure natural resources, which include not only oil, but also timber, iron ore, aluminum, and other basic ingredients of industrialization.

China's expanding role as an investor has grabbed headlines in recent years, with most of the attention on China's willingness to deal with regimes the United States finds unsavory. However, Chinese companies' neglect of workers' rights and environmental protection is also drawing scrutiny. Former president of the World Bank Paul Wolfowitz chided the Chinese for failing to respect environmental protection in their African investments (Callick 2006). In similar fashion, Sierra Leone's ambassador to China made remarks critical of China's activity in Africa, stating: "The Chinese just come and do it. They don't hold meetings about environmental impact assessments, human rights, bad governance or good governance. I'm not saying it's right, just that Chinese investment is succeeding because they don't set high benchmarks" (Taylor 2006, 946). Chinese investment elsewhere in the world has also given rise to environmental concerns. A Chinese mining firm was fined by the Peruvian government in 2002 after an accident resulted in environmental contamination, and in 2005 a blast at a Chinese-operated explosives facility serving a copper mine in Zambia killed forty-six locals and resulted in the worst industrial disaster in Zambian history. Both accidents reportedly stemmed in part from noncompliance with local regulation (Sax 2004; Trofimov 2007).

Not surprisingly, China defends the environmental record of its companies' overseas operations and claims that its investment in Africa is like "sending firewood into snow" (McGregor 2006; Xinhua 2006b). In the absence of more systematic research, it is difficult to ascertain whether accidents such as occurred in Peru and Zambia are indicative of larger trends or are isolated incidents. But the point remains that the environmental impact of foreign investment between developing countries is a topic worthy of greater academic attention.

The implication of the expansion of south-south investment flows is that there are potentially many dyads, or sets of countries, that have the same basic profile vis-à-vis environmental governance and foreign investment as China and Hong Kong or China and Indonesia. For instance, Brazil is similar to China in that it attracts not only a large amount of FDI, but also FDI from developing countries. Roughly a quarter of Brazil's FDI comes from other developing countries and the vast majority comes from other Latin American or Caribbean countries.[26] There may also be historical examples as well, although this would require a dramatically different methodological approach than used in the present chapter. Hall, for instance, suggests that in the 1970s, Japanese firms' overseas investments were driven in large part by a desire to avoid antipollution protests (2002, 22). Others have made similar suggestions that for much of the 1970s and 1980s, Taiwan absorbed (and perhaps welcomed) pollution-intensive investment from other Asian countries. There is ample room for applying and testing the arguments put forward in this chapter in other geographical regions.

7 Conclusion

In the previous chapters I have detailed the role of foreign firms in the process of China's environmental governance. This brief final chapter takes a step back and places earlier chapters' findings in larger theoretical and empirical contexts. I begin with a discussion of the theoretical implications of this research project, looking at how the China case contributes to the academic debate about the relationship between global investment and environmental protection. In the process, I also offer suggestions for further research. Attention then turns to the practical policy implications of this research. This book is not designed expressly with the aim of assessing alternative policies in environmental governance, and the consideration of all relevant policy options is beyond the scope of this chapter. Nonetheless, as touched on in the initial chapter, academic arguments about topics such as races to the bottom have often been closely related to public policy debates, and the issue of foreign-firm influence on environmental governance is one of considerable practical importance. As such, this chapter closes with a discussion of the policy implications of this book's findings for China's environmental governance.

Summary and Extensions

I began with a simple observation—China is heavily foreign-invested and severely polluted. Indeed, one could plausibly argue that an abundance of FDI and industrial pollution are two of the more predominant features of contemporary China, which inevitably raises questions about the relationship between the two. To what extent does China's reliance on foreign investment contribute to—or ameliorate—its pollution problem? As evident in the torrent of "green" initiatives unleashed in recent years, Beijing is intent on strengthening China's environmental protection regime and reining in the industrial pollution that lies at the heart of China's environmental challenge. National environmental officials, increasingly frank in their admission of the severity of China's pollution problem, seem intent on moving beyond the "to get rich is glorious" paradigm and now appear to seek glory in going green. The question is: Does China's reliance on foreign investment help or hurt this cause?

Questions about the impact of foreign investment on environmental regulation are not restricted to China and have a long history in academia and public policy. Not surprisingly, scholars and policymakers express a wide range of views. On the one hand are those who see the increased freedom of global capital as detrimental to developing-country environmental protection, chiefly because it enhances corporate power and weakens regulation. While developing-country governments are increasingly reliant on foreign capital, corporations have a greater number of choices about where to invest. This leads to pressure on governments to weaken environmental standards, a phenomenon referred to as regulatory chill or race to the bottom. The result of reliance on foreign investment is that environmental standards, particularly with regard to foreign enterprises, remain "stuck in the mud" and developing countries are turned into "pollution havens." This situation is potentially exacerbated if developing countries attract firms that adopt an environmentally exploitative strategy, which, as defined in Chapter 1, is characterized by a sacrificing of environmental protection measures for short-term gain.

This perception of global investment as inimical to environmental protection and as liable to turn developing countries into pollution havens, although widely shared among policymakers, scholars, and the NGO community, is nonetheless highly contested. Scholars of political science, international economics, and business studies have pointed out that investment flows even to stringent-standard jurisdictions, which undermines the notion that investors seek to weaken environmental regulation. Focusing primarily on multinationals, they also point out that foreign companies use a common set of standards in their overseas operations, which allows them to comply with environmental laws in developing countries. Moreover, these companies transfer to the developing world norms of corporate environmentalism, as well as advanced environmental management systems and technology. If anything, foreign investors contribute to the process of environmental protection in developing countries.

The empirical evidence presented in the previous chapters indicates that China's integration with the international market has not unleashed a race to the bottom or led to a systemic regulatory chill that has turned China into a pollution haven. Over the course of the reform era, China has absorbed a steadily increasing amount of FDI, but it has also managed to boost the overall stringency of its environmental protection regime, as well as strengthen regulation of the environmental facets of foreign direct investment (Chapter 3). This is a noteworthy accomplishment because it has occurred in a context in which foreign investors have enjoyed a number of legally sanctioned privileges, such as lower tax rates and greater ownership rights. These legal privileges were never extended to the environmental arena, and one could argue that today foreign investors are subject to a more rigorous set of environmental standards than domestic firms. This increasingly stringent set of environmental standards is evident whether one compares China to its own recent past or to other developing countries in Asia. As Chapter 3 demonstrated, surveys of business executives indicate that China has made modest gains vis-à-vis the rest of the world and some of its Asian neighbors in terms of environmental stringency. Chapter 4 indicated that jurisdictions that have attracted a large amount of foreign investment tend to be those that demonstrate more stringent enforcement of environmental regulation. Provinces (and provincial-level cities) that are high in FDI typically score the best on measures of environmental governance such as the percent of wastewater discharges meeting national standards.

With regard to firm strategy, contrary to the concerns of antiglobalizationists, multinational companies from the developed world do not adopt a strategy of low compliance in their China operations. Not only do MNCs frequently go "beyond compliance" in their own manufacturing facilities, but more importantly they adopt green supply chain policies that serve as a source of upward pressure on the environmental practices of domestic commercial partners (Chapter 5). They exert a kind of private authority that helps close the gap between China's environmental legislation and enforcement on the ground. Shell's pressuring of PetroChina in the West-East pipeline project was offered as a prime example. The effect of these green supply chain policies is potentially important, but for the time being restricted. The limits were outlined in the survey results presented in Chapter 6, which showed there is not a clear, statistically significant connection between a domestic firm's links to foreign firms (via sales and supply chains) and its environmental practices.

The general trend in China is one of greater enforcement of environmental regulation, but there have been numerous instances in which foreign firms and government officials' desire to attract external capital has undermined environmental protection. Put another way, China's reliance on foreign investment has generated a weakening influence on China's environmental regulation, but under a particular set of circumstances. In the end, there is no simple answer to the question of whether pollution havens exist, as the impact of foreign investment depends in large part on underlying conditions and the stage of the regulatory process. First, the negative impact of FDI on environmental regulation is more likely to manifest in the implementation phase via poor enforcement rather than the legislative stage via the weakening of standards. This basic insight points to the importance of directing scholarly attention toward implementation and enforcement and broadening beyond the current emphasis on firm investment and government standard-setting. As touched on in Chapter 1, much of the work that has led to a scholarly skepticism about the existence of pollution havens, regulatory chill, and races to the bottom is based on statistical studies of investment patterns (i.e., industrial flight). As Clapp and Dauvergne point out, "The economic literature on pollution havens has dominated the debate" (2005, 168). This economic literature consists of broad econometric studies that seek to prove or disprove the existence of pollution havens by examining the relationship between cross-national investment patterns and outcomes in environmental protection (e.g., industrial emissions, pollution intensity). Many of these econometric studies have shown that high-standard countries are just as likely to attract foreign investment as are low-standard countries, even in pollution-intensive sectors.[1] The main reason is that when compared to other production expenditures, compliance with environmental regulation is not sufficiently costly to influence location decisions. If business does not flee strong environmental regulation or seek out lax standards, there is little need for officials in the developing world to lower standards to entice investment. From this, many scholars infer that lax environmental regulation is an inefficient means of attracting capital and there is no race to the bottom that is turning developing countries into pollution havens.

However, what these empirical studies are illuminating is the impact of regulation on foreign investment, rather than the impact of foreign investment on regulation (see Chapter 1, Figure 1.1). Put another way, they are studies about firm behavior (investment decisions) and not studies of government action (regulatory performance). In that sense, much of the current work on the race-to-the-bottom and regulatory-chill hypotheses does not speak to the central claim of the argument—that the competition for capital affects the process of government regulation. In the scholarship that does place attention on government action rather than firm investment, the focus is typically on standard-setting (see Chapter 1, Appendix). As shown in Chapter 4, an equally important topic for scholars studying the developing world is implementation. When one looks at trends in legislation and the creation of standards, China has made impressive gains and developed a robust set of environmental laws. That China has strengthened environmental law even as it has aggressively pursued foreign investment is an important development that is relevant to the theoretical debate over the impact of foreign investment on environmental regulation. At the same time, however, the case of China's chemical parks described in Chapter 4 indicates that when one turns one's attention to enforcement, the picture looks different. The quest for foreign investment is part of the explanation for chemical parks' neglect of environmental standards. There is a regulatory-chill effect of the pursuit of foreign capital, but it manifests via a lack of enforcement rather than a lowering of standards.[2] It is possible that because scholars have not traditionally focused on implementation, the field has underestimated the frequency of regulatory chill.[3]

The second condition under which the competition for capital leads to weak environmental regulation is related to the type of jurisdiction. Jurisdictions disadvantaged in the competition for attracting capital tend to be more willing to ignore environmental regulation. This is evident in the case of China's chemical parks (Chapter 4). While a rational industrial structure would require China to have only a dozen or so chemical parks, the desire of local governments across China to build a chemical industry based on foreign technology and capital has led to a profusion of parks, many of which have paid little heed to environmental law. This disregard for environmental law has been most problematic in areas unsuited to developing a chemical industry and/or attracting foreign capital, as demonstrated in the case of Shenjia and in Yunnan Province's dealings with Asia Pulp and Paper (Chapters 4 and 6). This is not to say that foreign investment alone caused lax environmental regulation, but clear from these examples is the fact that eagerness for foreign capital is part of the explanation for weak environmental governance in certain areas of China.

This finding also has implications for the study of the pollution-haven phenomenon. What the case of China reveals is that statistical studies that test whether *more* FDI is associated with *less* regulation will potentially overlook or understate the negative impact of competition for investment on enforcement of environmental regulation (e.g., Zeng and Easton 2007). Areas attractive to investors, such as Guangzhou or Shanghai, do not need to weaken regulation to attract investment; and the very features that make them an appealing destination for FDI, such as an educated workforce and good infrastructure, stem from wealth, which itself is associated with strict environmental regulation. It is no surprise that these areas have both large amounts of FDI and strong enforcement. On the flip side, poorer inland cities that hold less appeal to foreign investors have lower amounts of FDI and weak enforcement. Consequently, even controlling for other variables, a statistical study would likely show that, if anything, more FDI is associated with better enforcement (and vice versa). If more FDI is associated with stronger enforcement, the temptation is to conclude that jurisdictions do not weaken regulation to attract capital. But as Chapter 4 showed, this would be a premature conclusion, as areas that are not attractive to foreign investors are quite likely to ignore environmental regulation in their race to set up a development zone for external capital.

What the discussion in the previous paragraph indicates is that one way to test my argument is via a comparative case study examining jurisdictions that are similarly underdeveloped, but which are pursuing different economic growth strategies—one based chiefly on attracting foreign capital, the other on building domestic savings. The expectation of my argument is that both would exhibit relatively low levels of regulation, but the jurisdiction competing for FDI would exhibit worse environmental enforcement. Choosing the correct level of jurisdiction is also important. As the chemical park case demonstrates, much of the neglect of environmental law takes place at the local level. In that sense, comparing large jurisdictions such as nations, provinces, or states may mask much of what lies beneath. Furthermore, statistical studies seeking to explain variance in enforcement across jurisdictions may benefit from finding a way to incorporate "attractiveness to FDI" as an explanatory variable in the model. Put another way, the relevant variable in explaining enforcement stringency may not simply be "FDI amount," but "FDI amount" in interaction with "FDI attractiveness." This is akin to studies of industrial flight that test not whether low-standard jurisdictions receive more investment, but whether low-standard jurisdictions receive more investment from pollution-intensive firms (Dean and Lovely 2005). Just as certain features of a firm determine how it reacts to an investment location's environmental stringency, particular characteristics of the jurisdiction determine whether it is likely to manipulate the level of stringency to attract capital. The wider theoretical implication is that the impact of FDI on implementation of environmental regulation is not universal, but rather dependent on the characteristics of the host jurisdiction.[4]

If the attractiveness of a jurisdiction to foreign capital influences the likelihood that it will relax regulation, this raises the question, How does one define "attractiveness to FDI"? In one sense, it is a subjective issue based on the perceptions of government regulators. What ultimately matters is whether government decision makers feel themselves disadvantaged in the race to attract capital. As Oates (2001) noted: "Irrespective of the actual facts on the location decisions in polluting industries, whether officials use environmental regulations for competitive purposes depends largely on perceptions. If policymakers think that these regulations matter, then they may well craft environmental legislation in the light of their objectives for economic development."[5] Of course, perceptions are hard to measure absent extensive survey research, which is a formidable challenge in the case of China. However, there is a large literature on the determinants of FDI, which grants insight into the characteristics of a jurisdiction that contribute to its ability to secure foreign investment (Chang and Kwan 2000; Chen Chien-Hsun 1996; Head and Reis 1996). These characteristics can differ across industrial sectors. Labor-intensive industries such as textile manufacturing may place more emphasis on the supply and quality of a locale's labor force than capital-intensive sectors such as the chemical industry. This means that any future study will have to account for sectoral characteristics. In China, a number of characteristics have proven appealing to foreign investors. These include a developed transportation infrastructure, an established industrial base, a large local or regional market, and the presence of special economic zones offering preferential policies. There is also evidence that foreign investment is self-reinforcing and that it agglomerates. In other words, FDI begets FDI. The principal reason for agglomeration is that the presence of foreign firms in a region indicates to a potential investor that the area has an ample supply of local partners, potential suppliers, and a well-trained workforce. In this sense, it is understandable that Beijing has encouraged the establishment of chemical industrial parks in areas that have history in the chemical sector and discouraged it in areas that are removed from major transportation routes and that lack experience in the chemical sector.

Finally, firm type is an important explanatory factor in weak regulation, as there are clear differences across foreign investors in terms of environmental strategy. Although as a rule foreign companies display environmental behavior superior to domestic firms and in compliance with China's environmental law, foreign enterprises from developing countries are often an exception and tend toward the "exploitative" end of the spectrum of firm environmental strategy as laid out in Chapter 1. In the case of China, firms from Hong Kong have environmental practices that are worse than domestic companies and often violate environmental regulation, which is precisely what those concerned about the impact of economic globalization on environmental protection frequently fear.

The principal explanation offered for the discrepancy in foreign-firm behavior is the impact of the home country environmental governance system. Firms from countries with a long history of stringent environmental governance have been forced to adjust and develop extensive corporate EHS policies (Chapter 5). The practices established in the home country become the standard operating procedures for foreign operations. Companies from developing Asian countries have forged their approach to environmental protection in a milieu in which economic growth is privileged and the environment is a lesser priority. The result is divergent behavior in the environmental policies of foreign firms' China operations (Chapter 6).

In sum, the desire for foreign investment and the widespread presence of foreign firms is not inimical to enhanced environmental regulation, but foreign investment does not automatically bring cleaner technologies, higher standards, stronger corporate environmental management, and better environmental protection. Put another way, the impact of foreign-firm investment is conditional—a great deal depends on where the investment comes from and where it goes. This research has given a broad sense about the conditions under which foreign investment is likely to undermine environmental regulation and the types of firms that represent the most probable source of downward pressure. These conditions, although presented as findings here, are perhaps best considered hypotheses for future research. The underlying factors that create pollution havens—competition for limited capital and an inflow of firms from countries with weak environmental governance—are by no means unique to China. As discussed in the conclusion to Chapter 6, the growth of trade between developing countries means there are many potential sets of countries in which the ideas presented in this research project could be tested and refined. Although this study has focused on the impact of foreign firms in China, the continued expansion of the Chinese economy means that Chinese firms themselves are becoming foreign investors. As a result, the impact of Chinese firms on environmental governance in other developing countries is a topic of increased importance. For instance, Chinese investments in Indonesia have raised concerns about the impact on Indonesian forests. While American companies' investment in Indonesia is declining, China is expected to invest $30 billion in Indonesia over the next decade. Much of this investment is in infrastructure designed to hasten the flow of Indonesian oil, timber, and other natural resources to China (Perlez 2006). More recently, China's activities in Africa have drawn scrutiny. As one reporter focusing on China's investment in Africa writes: "The Chinese are coming. They are coming for trade, investment and joint ventures, and they are consuming all the energy, minerals and other raw materials that the continent can offer" (Jiang Wenran 2006).

One manner in which the ideas presented in this research project might be tested is via a study of export processing zones (EPZs). Like China's economic development and technology zones and chemical industrial parks, EPZs are set up to promote economic growth and attract capital through the extension of preferential policies to foreign investors. EPZs have become a global phenomenon. As of the mid-1990s, Singapore alone had 22 EPZs employing 217,000 workers (Palan et al. 1996). Vietnam, which competes fiercely with China for FDI, has 115, and according to one source over sixty-seven countries already have or plan to establish EPZs (Gibbons 2004). These zones have long been a focus of those concerned with labor exploitation (e.g., Abell 1999). Exploring what they label a state strategy of "downward mobility," Palan et al. focus on social practices inside EPZs and point out: "Traditionally, the finger of blame has been pointed at the nefarious activities of transnational capitalists seeking to maximize surplus value by exploiting Third World workforces. Increasingly, however, it seems that governments in a number of these countries have been deliberately attracting such capital by using policy instruments to 'trade down' long-term environmental or social goals for a short-term quick economic fix" (Palan et al. 1996, 141). The similarity between the assertion of Palan et al. and the depiction of environmental governance in China's chemical parks presented in Chapter 4 is apparent. Like most researchers, Palan et al. are concerned principally with labor practices. Less understood is the environmental governance of these zones, but as China's chemical parks show, the environmental impact of industrial parks is an important issue.

A comparative study of the environmental governance process in EPZs represents just one possible avenue for future research, and one can easily envision others. One can also imagine a more nuanced discussion of the manner in which a firm's home country influences its environmental practices abroad. In this project, firms were divided roughly between those from the industrialized world and those from Asian developing countries. While this is a relevant comparison, there are certainly clear differences across countries within each category, and more detailed studies might be better able to capture the subtleties. In short, there remains much work to be done with regard to empirical testing and theorizing about the impact of foreign investment (and the attempt to attract it) on environmental regulation.

Implications for China's Environmental Protection and Governance

What does all this mean for the future of environmental protection in China? What measures can regulators adopt to assure that China enjoys the benefits of FDI while limiting the environmental costs? Before answering these questions, the limitations of my argument and evidence should be made clear. I have asserted that, all things equal, one would expect an area that is competing for foreign capital and disadvantaged in the competition to exhibit worse enforcement than jurisdictions that either are not seeking foreign capital or that initially possess qualities that appeal to foreign investors. In essence, I am only making an argument about what happens at time 1. This raises the question: What happens at time 2 and beyond? There are several reasons to think that even if some jurisdictions do initially soften regulation in the quest to attract investment, the general trend is still toward better enforcement. In other words, even though some areas in China are clearly ignoring environmental law in their race to build parks that draw investment, it is likely that over time this phenomenon will decrease in frequency and scope. The chief reason is that, as described in Chapters 3 and 4, the chemical park phenomenon is taking place in a broader context of strengthening environmental law, which is being accompanied by more robust, if still woefully insufficient, enforcement. Another reason to expect the chemical park scenario to dwindle is that a race-to-the-bottom strategy often appears to unleash a number of countervailing forces that serve to undermine it. This was the case in Ireland, where growing popular awareness about the hazards of industrial pollution led the government to abandon its strategy of using weak standards to attract investment (Leonard 1988, 129–30). Similarly, DeSombre (2006) shows that although some states set environmental and labor standards low in order to increase ship registries, they eventually draw the interest of international NGOs and organizations, which pressure them to raise standards. In the case of China, the most important countervailing force may be central government attention, which itself is often the result of increasingly common citizen complaints and protests. Chapter 4 made clear that the problems in China's chemical parks have appeared on the radar of China's national leaders. Indeed, had they not drawn central government interest I would not have had the materials needed to analyze the issue. Some have also argued that China's leaders increasingly see stronger environmental law in China's special economic zones as an impetus for firms to access advanced Western technology (Profaizer 1993), which should contribute to a greater emphasis on enforcement in areas designed for foreign investment. It is not always the case that greater scrutiny from the central government leads to the amelioration of environmental problems, and Beijing's streamlining of the investment approval process through the enhancement of local government authority restrains the ability of national leaders to impose their desire for stronger enforcement (see Chapter 3, "Mid-1990s to 2007" section). Nonetheless, one can expect better enforcement of environmental law if higher-level authorities continue efforts to compel local officials to place greater emphasis on environmental protection.[6]

The market liberal scenario also would expect weak enforcement to be transitory. Jurisdictions may relax implementation to boost foreign investment, but ultimately FDI promotes economic growth, growth leads to increased government capacity, and increased capacity leads to better enforcement (Hartman et al. 1997). This basic argument is supported by the fact that, as was shown in the opening part of Chapter 4 and has been demonstrated more robustly elsewhere (Dean and Lovely 2008; Zeng and Easton 2007), higher levels of FDI are associated with lower pollution intensity. This suggests that even if some locales ignore environmental regulation in order to attract capital and thereby create more pollution than would otherwise occur, the majority do not. Furthermore, other positive benefits of foreign investment, such as the contribution to income growth and the transfer of clean production technology, may overwhelm the impact of poor enforcement in certain jurisdictions, so that the net impact of FDI in a province is one that contributes to better implementation of pollution management standards and ultimately to better environmental quality. Of course, for the citizens living around chemical parks where environmental law is abandoned, the fact that the province as a whole is experiencing better enforcement may matter little.

The fact that FDI has shown a clear tendency to agglomerate in China indicates that once initial success in attracting investment is achieved, it may be less necessary to ignore environmental standards. In fact, this is the flip side of my argument that disadvantaged jurisdictions resort to weak enforcement. Certainly it is common today to hear government leaders in China's wealthiest and most foreign-invested cities comment on the importance of strengthening environmental protection in order to increase investment. For instance, one of the justifications for Guangzhou's pursuit of National Environmental Protection Model City status, which is awarded by Beijing to cities that have met a series of specific environmental quality and development targets, is that "the prestige inherent in this title is expected to attract even more outside investment" (Economy 2006, 179).

Yet if one looks back at the start of China's economic reforms, it is not difficult to find examples of special economic zones that, although today they are praised for the quality of environmental law and enforcement, formerly exhibited a willingness to ignore environmental protection. As Ross and Silk argue: "There is little doubt that environmental protection was far from the minds of China's leaders when they first established the Special Economic Zones . . . to attract foreign investment. . . . Natural ecosystems were bulldozed, the SEZs developed in a manner reminiscent of boom towns, and some operations involving hazardous technology . . . started operations without sufficient preventative measures" (1997, 11–26). In the late 1970s Shenzhen accepted investment from fifteen Hong Kong–based tanneries, which sought refuge from stiffening regulation in Hong Kong. By the mid-1980s, Shenzhen authorities were weighing action against the tanneries because of pollution (Lam 1986, 75). In 1981, Hong Kong–based Kaida concluded a $16 million investment agreement to build a toy factory in the Shekou industrial district that would employ 1,100 people. Shortly after operations began, local residents voiced complaints about noise and air pollution. After refusing local environmental authorities' request to take remedial action, Kaida was sued in Shenzhen Intermediate People's Court. Part of Kaida's defense was that it bore no responsibility because the original investment agreement signed with Shenzhen authorities did not contain environmental protection provisions. That there was no mention of possible environmental impact or required pollution control in the original contract speaks to the lack of concern for environmental protection on the part of Shenzhen authorities. The court acknowledged this fact, as well as the fact that specific industry discharge standards had not been issued at the time of the agreement (or the court case), but it did not exempt Kaida from broader state standards. Eventually, Kaida was ordered to cease operations until it could comply with relevant standards and to pay a HK$20,000 fine as well as government investigation and court costs (Ross and Silk 1997). Although this case, settled in 1984, is generally highlighted as the turning point that marks Shenzhen's more rigorous approach to environmental protection, it also demonstrates that even the special economic zones that are today considered models of environmental protection were willing to forgo pollution control in their initial quest to attract investment. These lines of reasoning suggest that, although some jurisdictions may lag behind those with high standards and stricter enforcement, assuming they continue to develop, eventually they will move in the direction of stronger environmental policies. Low-standard jurisdictions should converge at a higher level of environmental protection implementation.

That concept notwithstanding, the problem of weak enforcement stemming from the pursuit of foreign capital will likely persist for many years. Beijing became aware of environmental problems in China's special economic zones almost immediately after the launch of the reform policies in the late 1970s. A constant theme in policy documents through the 1980s and 1990s is Beijing's concern that local governments were ignoring environmental regulation in zones designed to attract overseas capital. Anecdotes from the 1980s and early 1990s of special economic zone officials granting foreign investors land-use rights without first gauging the pollution impact, welcoming pollution-intensive projects rejected by areas with stronger standards, or approving investments prior to completion of the environmental impact assessment are commonplace (e.g., Lo and Yip 1999, 367; Profaizer 1993, 343; Ross and Silk 1997, 11–26). The ongoing problems with environmental regulation in China's chemical parks, which as noted are typically located inside ETDZs, indicate that the problems have persisted into the first part of the twenty-first century. Three-plus decades into the reform era and Beijing still faces considerable challenges in combating the tendency of local governments' eagerness for foreign capital to overwhelm their concerns about environmental protection.

It is also worth pointing out that the extent to which the harmful environmental impact of foreign investment is controlled depends heavily on the quality of foreign investment. The market liberal argument that, ceteris paribus, more FDI leads to more robust regulation and eventually better environmental quality, is based on the assumption that the investment inflow is of high quality in terms of its technology and environmental impact. At the very least, the foreign investment is assumed to be of higher quality than comparable domestic industry. This discounts the possibility that foreign investors adopt the environmentally exploitative strategy described in Chapter 1. But as Chapter 6 demonstrated, a great deal of foreign investment in China is of low quality in terms of the environmental strategy of the investing firm and more broadly in terms of its environmental impact. There is an increasing number of studies that provide evidence that investment in China flows to areas with low pollution-abatement costs (Dean and Lovely 2005, 2008; Di 2004; Ljungwall and Linde-Rahr 2005). For example, Dean and Lovely (2005) examine over 2,800 joint venture projects between 1993 and 1996 and find that low pollution levies are a source of attraction for foreign investment from Hong Kong, Macau, and Taiwan. According to a survey done at National Chengchi University in Taiwan, one of the main reasons Taiwanese businesses invest in China is to avoid strict pollution standards at home (Kellher 2002). Although China's tendency to attract pollution-intensive investment in low-standard areas does not mean that enforcement will remain weak, the large stock of pollution-intensive investment still represents an additional challenge to enhancing environmental regulation. Finding a proper balance between the desire for foreign investment and the need to protect the environment will remain a crucial challenge facing Beijing for many years to come.

Regardless of future trends, for the present it is clear that one of the more dangerous external threats to China's current environmental governance is investment by a firm from a developing country in a jurisdiction that has rarely demonstrated the capacity to attract foreign investment. The policy implication is that, in the MEP's quest to improve the efficiency of implementing environmental law, there is a clear benefit to being able to rank firms and jurisdictions in terms of the risk of violating environmental law. In fact, risk assessment is a key element of environmental governance in several developing countries, for the simple reason that it helps target and utilize scarce resources more effectively. For example, in Brazil, factories are ranked according to size and pollution, health, and welfare risks. In Rio, it was discovered that targeting the 50 largest factories could reduce 60 percent of the state's serious industrial pollution; targeting 410 could reduce risk by 90 percent (Luken and van de Tak 2002).[7] Although China clearly could not pass a law that requires firms from Hong Kong to undergo more stringent approval procedures, MEP could still direct resources and more closely monitor areas that attract foreign investment from certain regions or that are generally low-capacity areas in terms of attracting FDI. This would be relatively feasible, as existent national regulations already require investment projects that are approved at the local level to be reported to higher levels (e.g., an EIA approved by provincial authorities must be reported to MEP in Beijing).

This book's findings also point to the need for increased government expenditure on environmental protection. This is hardly the first study to reach such a conclusion, as it is widely recognized that China's spending on environmental protection is growing but still insufficient. In fact, Chinese spending on environmental protection fell 30 percent short of targets for the Tenth Five-year Plan (2001–2005). The Eleventh FYP calls for spending equivalent to 1.5 percent of GDP, which is about half the level most experts recommend (Agence France-Presse 2005). Nonetheless, the findings here point to a need for increased investment in environmental protection, especially in spheres such as capacity building among local environmental officials and programs designed to green business. As many Chinese scholars point out, the upside of this spending may not only be a cleaner environment, but also better market access for firms selling their products abroad.

China's industrial environmental governance would also benefit from greater oversight from the media and civil society. In the context of the Chinese political system, this clearly is a sensitive issue. At the same time, many Chinese localities are testing novel ways to give the general public greater influence on the behavior of government. Aside from the well-known reforms to allow the election of village committees, roughly a dozen cities have experimented with direct elections of urban residence committees. In Guangdong Province, several counties have allowed greater public scrutiny of budgets and hiring practices, and in Jiangsu Province, residents participated in a referendum in which they listed the worst official in several administrative areas. For instance, taxi drivers voted for the worst traffic police officer (Baum 2005).

The environmental realm has seen perhaps the greatest variety of programs involving public participation. This research project has relied heavily on the Green Watch program and discussed the importance of the public participation component of the EIA Law (Chapters 6 and 3). Chapter 2 also discussed a variety of other new measures, including the expansion of the environmental complaint system, environmental disclosure requirements, and the (now defunct) Green GDP plan. These trial programs show that while one cannot realistically expect vibrant participation of civil society under China's current political system, it is not hopelessly quixotic to call for greater public and media scrutiny in China's environmental governance. And the increased transparency that comes with enhanced civil society involvement is vitally important in strengthening China's industrial environmental governance as well as guarding against pollution-intensive investment projects. The neglect of environmental law associated with pollution havens, almost by definition, takes place behind closed doors; hence the more opaque the governance process, the easier it is for firms and governments to ignore environmental law. Without the investigative reports of the Chinese media (and to a lesser extent Greenpeace), as well as the Green Watch public disclosure program, much of the research presented in the previous six chapters could not have occurred.

There are many ways in which the public could be brought into the environmental governance process. Certainly the continued expansion of Green Watch and the promotion of the public participation clause of the EIA law are warranted. China also needs to foster more NGOs like the Center for Legal Assistance to Pollution Victims. The Center does not exactly serve as a corporate watchdog in the traditional Western sense, but does put some pressure on industry via its legal aid to those harmed by excessive polluters. The creation of a program akin to the U.S. Toxic Release Inventory (TRI) would also enhance outside scrutiny. In the United States, the TRI program makes available to the public information about toxic releases down to the county and firm level, which allows for considerable public scrutiny. Seven countries, including South Korea, have similar programs. There would be many challenges to implementing such a system in China, not the least of which would be gathering information on toxic releases and assuring government officials did not distort data. But under current aspects of China's environmental protection system, such as the pollution discharge system, firms are already required to report emissions of various pollutants to local EPBs. In some provincial statistical yearbooks, environmental data such as the discharge of pollutants or number of environmental accidents is published at the municipal level. Thus, there is an existing foundation on which China could build a TRI system. Such a program could be particularly effective if it released not only data about pollution outputs but also about chemical inputs. As Paoletto and Termorshuizen state in their survey of governance of the chemical industry in Asian countries, this "would shift manufacturers' focus from waste management to process innovation" (2003, 202). China's Measures on Open Environmental Information (Trial), which was described in Chapter 2 and requires local governments to provide to the public information about firms with a history of violations, took effect in mid-2008 and is an encouraging development. In time, it may serve a function similar to that of the U.S. TRI. At the time of writing (a few months after the law took effect) it is too early to tell whether it will be sufficiently and broadly enforced.

Another possible way to increase public oversight within the context of China's current political system would be to make the ISO 14000 certification process more open. ISO does not have a strong public disclosure element (unlike the European Union Eco-management and Audit Scheme [EMAS]). Given the already significant Chinese commitment to ISO, Chinese authorities may consider amending requirements to make the process of firm certification more transparent. As a government official commented in reference to one of China's more famous companies, "I know that Hai'er is ISO certified, but I do not really know much about what it did to become certified."[8] Requiring firms to publish data relevant to their ISO certification process might help assure the integrity of the ISO system in China.

In addition to enhancing the role of the public, the expansion of private sector participation in China's environmental regulation is a relatively low-cost, high-return approach to enhancing China's environmental governance. It essentially means taking advantage of the fact that many Chinese companies seek a "green pass" to access foreign markets, as well as the reality that both Chinese environmental officials and most multinational corporations are interested in closing the gap between environmental regulation on the books and enforcement on the ground. There are numerous ways for Chinese and foreign governments to work together to harness these private sector forces and improve China's environmental governance. For instance, governments can sponsor more forums between MNCs, domestic firms, and NGOs so that business leaders can share best practices in environmental management and ethical supply chain policies.[9] In my interviews, domestic firm representatives repeatedly expressed both a belief that foreign-firm environmental practices are worthy of emulation and a frustration with their inability to access foreign firms. Participation in such forums does not change behavior overnight, but it lays the foundation for stronger corporate environmental norms.

Industrialized-country governments can work with the Chinese government to help small foreign companies find green partners. Small foreign firms typically lack the resources to pursue green supply chain policies on their own. Although some INGOs, such as the World Environment Center, have stepped in to fill the void, there is still a need for agencies that can help foreign firms partner with green Chinese companies. The Foreign Commercial Service (FCS) of the U.S. Embassy presently aids American investors in finding suitable domestic partners and suppliers. In essence, the FCS helps small firms conduct financial due diligence. Performing "environmental due diligence" and providing information about potential partners' environmental practices not only would help small firms choose suppliers based on environmental records, but would offer an additional incentive for domestic firms to devote more resources to pollution control. This could be done in conjunction with MEP through the Green Watch program.

The Chinese government can also look for opportunities to expand the environmental elements in preferential policies designed to attract investment. As discussed in Chapter 3, the Chinese government already grants preferences (e.g., lower tax rates) to investors using the most advanced manufacturing technology or investing in certain sectors, such as air pollution control facilities. Preferential policies could be expanded and offered to investors that supply from environmentally certified domestic firms, offer EHS training activities and educational opportunities to employees or partner firms, or conduct capacity-building activities with environmental regulators. The Chinese government can also provide a more formal mechanism to allow foreign firms and regulators to work together on issues related to environmental standards and their enforcement. As it stands today, most firms rely on ad hoc personal connections or work through industry associations to resolve issues related to environment regulation (Chapter 5). Working to augment the private sector's role in China's environmental protection will not alone solve China's environmental problems. As stated in Chapter 5, the private authority of MNCs can only be a supplement to and never a replacement for govern-ment enforcement. In the end, there is no silver bullet. No single strategy or policy measure will ensure China avoids the environmental pitfalls of attract-ing foreign investment, but the above recommendations offer modest guid-ance and a practical way for China to enhance environmental governance, and more importantly, to improve the lives of Chinese citizens.

Notes

Chapter 1

Portions of this chapter's first section have been previously published in the *Journal of Contemporary China*. See Stalley (2009).

1. Unless otherwise stated, in this book the $ symbol represents U.S. dollars.

2. For a good overview of the full extent of China's environmental damage, see Mitamura (2008); Economy (2004, 2007b); Smil (1993); and World Bank (2007). For a description of the international impact of China's pollution problem, see Diamond and Liu (2005).

3. I take a broad view of the term "industrial environmental regulation." At its basic level, industrial environmental regulation is the process through which the government controls the environmental impact of manufacturing firms. It involves policy making via the creation of environmental laws and standards, government enforcement of existing laws, and firm compliance with environmental standards and pollution abatement programs.

4. There is some empirical support for this argument, as scholars comparing jurisdictions that vary in terms of openness to foreign trade and investment have found that more open economies adopt clean technology faster (Birdsall and Wheeler 1993; Wheeler 2001, 2002).

5. Other studies of firm ownership detect no relation between foreign ownership and environmental performance (Dasgupta et al. 1998; Hartman et al. 1997). One study found that subsidiaries of corporations are more likely to display inferior environmental behavior than other facilities in the same sector (Grant and Jones 2003).

6. In U.S. politics, there is a considerable literature probing the lobbying power of business in the environmental arena. One of the most thorough studies in this area

finds that in roughly 80 percent of the cases, business takes no position regarding proposed environmental legislation (Kamieniecki 2006). When corporations do take a position, and are opposed to the new regulations, often their influence is offset by other interest actors such as citizen groups. The extent to which business wields influence is also contingent on the nature of the legislation, which itself is affected by the administration in the White House.

7. For good literature reviews of the race-to-the-bottom debate, see Clapp and Dauvergne (2005); DeSombre (2006); Frankel (2005); Spar and Yoffie (2000); and Vogel and Kagan (2004). Woods (2006) also provides a good overview of the literature as well as an empirical test that finds support for the race-to-the-bottom hypothesis. Some of the key work in this area includes: Esty (2001); Mabey et al. (2003); Neumayer (2001b, 2001c); Porter (1999); Zarsky (1999); and Zarsky and Gallagher (2003).

8. The environmental race-to-the-bottom concept has a long history of debate, not only in globalization studies, but also in American-politics scholarship, where it is often part of a discussion about "environmental federalism" (e.g., Adler 2003; Crusto 1999; Engel 1997; Esty 1996, 2001; Mock 1998; Oates 2001; Oates and Schwab 1988; Revesz 1992, 1997, 2001; Swire 1996). The race-to-the-bottom debate is also frequently applied to issue areas other than environmental protection, including labor politics (e.g., Mosley and Uno 2007), government spending (e.g., Garrett 2001), and welfare benefits (e.g., Volden 2002).

9. Although the assertion itself is both simple and straightforward, as Esty (1996, 607n134) points out, the fact that one must gather data on events that did not occur, such as the nonstrengthening of environmental standards, and then link nonevents to concerns about competitiveness as an investment location, makes the regulatory-chill phenomenon extremely difficult to observe.

10. It is not uncommon for scholars to use the terms "pollution haven" and "race to the bottom" interchangeably. Some may state, for example, that a state pursues a pollution-haven strategy when it uses weak environmental standards to lure industry (e.g., Neumayer 2001a). Others refer to states engaging in regulatory competition as engaging in a race-to-the-bottom strategy (e.g., Konisky 2007). To the extent possible, throughout the volume I have tried to be consistent and use the terms according to the definitions provided in this opening chapter.

11. Much of China's concern over pollution transfer stems from the issue of the importation of electronic waste, a great deal of which occurs illegally. This issue, although important, is beyond the scope of this volume. See Lin et al. (2002).

12. These articles rarely analyze the extent to which this investment is filling China's development demands. Chemicals, concrete, paint, paper—these are the products needed in the process of industrialization. In that sense, what is relevant is not the amount of investment in pollution-intensive sectors, but the amount of foreign investment that is aimed toward exporting. If China exports pollution-intensive products back to the developed world, it is stronger evidence of a "pollution transfer." See Chai (2002).

13. Another figure commonly cited in the Chinese-language literature that is of-

fered as proof that foreign firms are seeking out China as a pollution haven is the statistic that Japan and the United States have shifted, respectively, 60 and 39 percent of their pollution-intensive industries offshore. Unfortunately, it is rarely clear how scholars define "pollution-intensive." Presumably the figure that 29 percent of FIEs are in pollution-intensive sectors is from the results of the Third Industrial Census, which was completed in 1995 and provides a wealth of statistical information about China's industrial profile.

14. The assertion that local governments sacrifice environmental protection to attract foreign capital is common not only in the Chinese press, but also in English-language academic work. For example, Sitaraman states: "Local government officials are more concerned that draconian steps to remedy the pollution problems will have direct economic consequences in the form of increased unemployment, loss of foreign direct investment, and a decline in economic competitiveness" (2007, 314). In a similar vein, Li Zhiping avers: "To attract more investment, some local governments relax their environment regulations and lower their environmental requirements to encourage businesses to move to their area" (2005, 381).

15. Under the ISO 14000 system, companies have their environmental management program certified as in accordance with international standards by external third parties. This system is discussed more extensively in Chapter 2.

16. There are exceptions, as some scholars of American politics have focused on enforcement: Konisky (2007) and Woods (2006).

17. Among scholars concerned with the impact of foreign investment on environmental regulation, I am not the first to make a call for a wider approach. A few scholars have taken direct issue with the field's traditionally narrow definition of (and emphasis on) pollution havens and argued for a broader line of inquiry. As discussed more extensively in Chapter 4, much of the evidence used to assess the saliency of the race-to-the-bottom and pollution-haven arguments consists of econometric studies that look for correlations between the stringency of environmental standards, on the one hand, and trade or investment patterns, on the other. The basic assertion of these econometric studies is that, if weak standards are used to attract industry, then we should be witnessing a global migration of investment as well as an increase in pollution-intensive exports in low-standard areas. While such evidence is certainly relevant for understanding the influence of foreign investment on environmental regulation, these studies nonetheless narrow the field of inquiry to a study of the most readily quantifiable relationships. Noting this fact, Clapp declares: "It may be time to abandon the narrowly constructed pollution havens debate in favor of a more open-ended analysis of the linkages between global trade and investment and environmental regulation" (2002, 12). She goes on to state: "Instead of searching for statistical proof that pollution havens exist within the current, narrow and economistic framework, a broader, more nuanced approach to the issue should be taken. Key in a broader approach would be an exploration of the incentives, real or perceived, that affect state policy and firm behavior. These incentives are as much political as they are economic" (17). Strohm makes a similar point when she urges scholars not to think in

narrowly defined terms of pollution havens, but rather to consider the notion of an international "transfer of environmental risk" (2002, 31).

18. I am thankful to an anonymous reviewer for prodding me to make this point more explicitly.

19. The work of David Konisky (2007) is exemplary in this fashion. Examining the race-to-the-bottom argument with regard to American states, Konisky aptly demonstrates that there is no simple yes-or-no answer to the race-to-the-bottom question; whether a race to the bottom occurs depends on certain underlying conditions. Konisky finds that regulatory enforcement in one American state influences the stringency of enforcement in competitor states. However, the nature of the influence is not clear. In some cases, states react to strong enforcement in competitor states by enhancing their own regulatory effort. In other cases, states weaken enforcement. Thus, there is marginal support for both a race to the bottom as well as a race to the top. This leads Konisky to speculate that other factors, such as the size of a jurisdiction's economy relative to that of its competitors, as well as the structure of its economy and its reliance on pollution-intensive industries, may impact whether a state pursues a race-to-the-bottom or race-to-the-top strategy.

20. I thank an anonymous reviewer whose memorable phrase "China is not Guatemala or the Gambia" helped me to clarify my own thinking on this particular point.

21. It is also worth pointing out that it is well established in the pollution-haven literature that one is much more likely to see a negative impact of foreign investment on environmental regulation in industrial sectors characterized as pollution-intensive (see Mani and Wheeler 1997). This makes intuitive sense, as one would not expect firms for whom environmental compliance is cheap, such as insurance companies, to flout regulations or press for less rigorous standards. For that reason, this volume focuses primarily on pollution-intensive manufacturing industries—most notably the chemical industry. While this is logical given my interest in the potentially negative influence of foreign investment on environmental regulation, it indicates that the findings are limited to a handful of sectors, albeit sectors that have received a tremendous amount of FDI (see Figure 1.2). Nonetheless, one must be cautious about generalizing too far beyond the empirical foundations.

22. For more on the public-policy implications of the race-to-the-bottom argument, see Bhagwati (1993, 177; 2004); Crusto (1999); and Zarsky (1999). For discussion about the policy implications of environmental races to the bottom between American states, see Engel (1997) and Esty (1996).

23. There is an enormous literature concerning both the relationship between trade and the environment and the impact of rising incomes on the quality of the natural environment. Copeland and Taylor (2004) offer an excellent overview of this issue.

24. For a first-rate work that does look at the issue from the macro-level, see Kevin Gallagher (2004).

Chapter 2

1. Different scholars come up with different numbers. Alex Wang (2002) states that China's legal regime "includes at least six laws addressing pollution prevention and nine laws concerning natural resources protection, 29 sets of environmental protection regulations, more than 70 statutes, and over 900 local regulations." Carter and Mol state that there are 20 laws and 140 executive regulations (2006, 152). Shi and Zhang state that there are over "100 environmental laws and regulations" and "500 environmental standards" (2006, 276). The website of MEP (http://english.mep .gov.cn) provides a comprehensive list of China's environmental laws and regulations. All but the most recent have been translated into English.

2. Aside from the four mentioned, the list includes (1) the PRC Constitution, (2) international agreements, (3) other laws issued by the NPC (National People's Congress) Standing Committee (*falü*), (4) interpretation of the Constitution and basic laws issued by the Standing Committee, State Council, national ministries, and Supreme Court (*lifa jieshi*), (5) regulations issued by local people's congresses (*difang fagui*) and by the executive branch of local people's governments (*difang zhengfu guizhang*), and (6) individual cases decided by the Supreme Court as well as lower courts (Alford and Shen 1998).

3. Because SEPA was only recently promoted to MEP, and most of the government actions described in this volume took place prior to the promotion, I typically refer to MEP as SEPA.

4. For several excellent overviews of China's evolving approach toward environmental governance, see "Environmental Governance" (2006), which offers several articles on China's environmental challenges. CCICED (2006) also provides a solid discussion of the changes and challenges in China's environmental protection efforts.

5. Alex Wang (2007) indicates that CLAPV has participated in approximately seventy cases and achieved a positive result in just under half of them.

6. The Civil Law also touches on environmental protection, as Article 124 states that "any person who pollutes the environment and causes damage to others in violation of state provisions for environmental protection and the prevention of pollution shall bear civil liability in accordance with the law" (NPC 1986a).

7. Other environmental crimes include illegal logging, fishing, or mining, as well as destruction of endangered species (plant and animal). The occupation of cultivated land is also deemed a criminal act. After its release in 1997, there have been four revisions to the Criminal Law, two of which have strengthened provisions related to the environment. In the fourth revision, the Criminal Law was amended to forbid the illegal import of not only solid waste, but liquid and gaseous waste as well.

8. To date, there is minimal evidence that environmental cases involving foreign firms have been a major focus of criminal law. There are a few sources that provide information about cases heard in Chinese courts. Two of the more useful include: *Overview of Important Judgments and Cases in China (Zhongguo Shenpan Anlie Yaolan)* and the *Gazette of the Supreme People's Court of the People's Republic of China (Zhon-*

ghua Renmin Gongheguo Zuigao Renmin Fayuan Gongbao). The former is an annual publication that offers a collection of representative cases collected since 1992. Each volume has different categories of cases. The environmental cases typically fall within the category "jeopardizing the social administrative order" (*fanhai shehui guanli chengxu zui*). The latter of these two sources publishes judicial documents and selected court judgments and cases. Prior to 2000, it was published quarterly; between 2000 and 2004 it was published six times a year; and it is presently issued ten times a year and offers basic statistics about cases heard before the SPC. Going back to 1997, the vast majority of the environmental cases concern illegal logging or the sale or purchase of endangered species. There appear to be no environmental cases involving foreign firms (although there are many cases with foreign firms involving contracts and copyright infringement). Indeed, despite the manifold problems with governing the environmental behavior of firms in China, based on these sources it appears that few environmental cases involve manufacturing companies, foreign or domestic. Apparently, regulators handle issues outside the courtroom (Legal Studies Department of China's People's University 1992–; Supreme Court of the PRC 1997–; Zhu 2005).

9. As of August 2006, China was well behind in its goal to lower energy consumption per unit of GDP. The goal for 2006 was 4 percent, but through the first half of the year actual energy consumption had increased by 0.8 percent (Deutsche Presse-Agentur 2006).

10. Estimates about the number of environmental NGOs vary widely, depending in part on whether one includes government-organized NGOs (GONGOs) and in part on speculations about the number of nonregistered NGOs. Yang (2005) indicates that there were seventy-three ENGOs in China in 2002. According to the All-China Environment Federation, as of 2005 there were approximately three thousand ENGOs.

11. The role of NGOs in environmental litigation was vitally important in the early stages of the U.S. environmental movement (e.g., *Tennessee Valley Authority v. Hill*, *Chevron v. Natural Resources Defense Council*) (Nagle 1996).

12. China has also begun to experiment with an emissions trading scheme for SO_2 and cost pricing for natural resources such as energy and water, the cost of which has increased considerably over the last decade (Economy 2006).

13. Not everyone agrees with Wang and Wheeler about the effectiveness of the levy system. Sitaraman provides a detailed summary of the levy system's inadequacies and concludes: "The evidence suggests that the PCS [pollution control system] system is highly inefficient and has failed to control pollution or assist industries with pollution management techniques" (2007, 313). For a useful overview of the discharge permit system, see Li Zhiping (2005) and Wang Mingyuan (2008).

14. Another weakness of the discharge permit system is that it is common for environmental officials to monitor wastewater discharge standards only with regard to the concentration of pollutants, rather than the total volume or mass load (Sun 2008c). This means that enterprises can comply with the law simply by diluting their discharges. It also results in a situation in which, even if every enterprise in a given area complies with discharge limits, the total amount of a pollutant released into a

watershed can exceed its carrying capacity so that the water source fails to meet overall quality standards. This was the case with the Taihu Lake algae bloom that generated a great deal of press coverage in 2007. Officially, the permit discharge system and pollution levy system are based both on concentration and total volume of pollutants and have been since the late 1980s when the deficiencies of a concentration-based system became clear (Li Zhiping 2005, 376–77).

15. Like China's ISO regime, the eco-label system is overseen by government, but much takes place in the private sector. There are three classes of environmental labels. Class I is very stringent and involves the entire life cycle (from design to production to use to disposal). Class II is less stringent and allows the firm to select for placement on their product label one or more of twelve possible phrases (e.g., "decomposable," "low energy," "long-life product"). Class III labels are more open; firms can promote the environmental aspects of their product, such as "no formaldehyde remnants." In each case, the firm applies to a provincial-level government EPB, who reviews the application, performs on-site investigations, samples a product, and conducts follow-up investigations. Much of the process, such as the on-site investigation and the product sampling, is outsourced to private or quasi-governmental organizations (He 2003; Hu et al. 2005).

16. Interview with manager, Environment and Safety department, domestic electronics firm #1, interview #40, Changzhou, September 5, 2005. For a description of the interview coding method, please see Chapter 5, Note 1.

17. To combat this last problem, on July 31, 2002, the central government authority issued a list of all firms that are certified to inspect and evaluate a company's application for an environmental label (Wu and Pan 2002).

18. "Building materials" refers both to materials used to build large structures, such as cement or flooring materials, and to household goods such as furniture, paint, rugs, wallpaper, and ceramics.

19. VOC refers to a large number of carbon-based compounds, some of which are carcinogenic and most of which contribute to the process of ozone depletion.

20. Other Asian countries are discussed extensively in Chapter 6.

Chapter 3

1. It is not always easy to find English translations of Chinese environmental laws, particularly once one goes beyond the approximately one dozen main environmental laws (e.g., 1989 EPL) and looks for various secondary legal instruments (e.g., "Notice on Strengthening the Environmental Management in the Foreign Investment Construction Projects"). However, for scholars proficient in Mandarin there are many sources for information on China's environmental law. There are several compendia of China's environmental law, such as Pu et al. (2002); SEPA (2004a, 2004b). Most of these are published by the China Environmental Sciences Press (Zhongguo Huanjing Kexue Chubanshe). The *China Environmental Yearbook* is also a good source for de-

velopments in environmental law. There are several online databases, although most require subscriptions. For instance, Beijing University Law School operates the China Law Information website (*Beida Falü Xinxi Wang*) (English: www.lawinfo.china.com, Chinese: www.chinalawinfo.com). Almost all the laws and government cited in this chapter can be found on the China Law Information website. Another database that offers a large number of legal texts in Mandarin even without a subscription is the China Laws website (*Zhongguo Falü Ziyuan Wang*) (www.lawbase.com.cn). Many legal documents can also be found on MEP's website (http://english.mep.gov.cn) or through the Chinese search engine Baidu. For an overview of some of the challenges of conducting research on the Chinese legal system, see Clarke (2003).

2. This estimate is based on searches on the China Laws website. The majority of the legal instruments have been issued by provincial level governments often in response to a central government regulation. There are a number of administrative regulations that deal with aspects of FDI that have little to do with the environment.

3. This law has been revised twice—once in 1989 and again in 2001.

4. One somewhat unusual aspect of translating laws governing industry from Chinese into English is the term "construction." The use of "construction" in this context refers to any project in any sector that involves building or expanding physical facilities. It is not limited to the construction industry alone as the term implies in English. Thus, the building of a new chemical plant, the expansion of a textile mill, or the addition of a new manufacturing line in an automobile factory would all be considered "construction" projects in China. This is worth keeping in mind, as many Chinese laws governing all industry refer to "construction projects."

5. A handful of earlier legal documents reference the environmental impact assessment system, although they provide few concrete details. The 1979 EPL has a one-sentence statement that says enterprises must turn in an environmental report when making new investments or expanding existing facilities. For an overview of the development of China's EIA system, see Niu and Wu (2005).

6. NEPA's name was changed to SEPA (State Environmental Protection Administration) in 1998 when it was promoted to ministerial status.

7. MOFERT (Ministry of Foreign Economic Relations and Trade) was renamed MOFTEC (Ministry of Foreign Trade and Economic Cooperation) in 1993 and then the MOC (Ministry of Commerce) in 2003. NEPA was renamed SEPA in 1998 and then MEP in 2008.

8. The importance of this clause will become clearer in subsequent chapters, which show that the environmental behavior of Hong Kong firms is often worse than domestic firms.

9. This 1993 document was eventually abolished after it was deemed a violation of WTO principles.

10. One exception to this lack of specific information is the growth of detail on the EIA process. During the late 1980s, the central government did offer increasingly precise information concerning the required content of environmental impact reports as well as the EIA approval process. The problem was that the process was so

exceedingly complex and involved such a large number of agents that it was extremely difficult to implement. Issues of corruption, lack of local EPB capacity, NEPA's low bureaucratic status, and the willingness of both firms and regulators to turn a blind eye to the law's requirements all served to undermine the EIA system in this period.

11. The Provisions document has been amended three times (1997, 2002, and 2004) and the Catalogue five times (1997, 1999, 2002, 2004, and 2007). As China initiated government reforms in the late 1990s, the government bodies issuing the amended Provisions and Catalogue changed correspondingly. The 2002 Catalogue was issued by the State Development Planning Commission, the State Economic and Trade Commission, and MOFTEC. The 2004 and 2007 Catalogues were authorized by the National Development and Reform Commission (NDRC) and the Ministry of Commerce (MOC).

12. One example of a tax incentive enjoyed by encouraged industries is reduced tariffs on imported equipment.

13. Investment projects that are encouraged, or not on the Catalogue and so deemed permitted, require approval from the national-level MOC and NDRC when the investment is greater than $100 million. State Council approval is required if the investment is greater than $500 million. Investments lower than $100 million can be approved at the local level. For restricted sectors, the threshold for national-level approval is lowered to $50 million and any restricted project greater than $100 million requires State Council approval (Man et al. 2008).

14. My attempts to gain insight into the question via interviews with SEPA officials in Beijing failed to bear fruit. The respondents were either unable or unwilling to share information about SEPA's influence on the drafting of the Foreign Investment Catalogue.

15. Benzidine is used to manufacture a host of synthetic dyes and so is closely associated with the textile industry. It is suspected of being a carcinogenic.

16. From 1997 to 2004, ion-membrane caustic-soda production was restricted. In 2007, the restriction was widened to include all caustic-soda production. In the 2007 Catalogue, caustic soda is referred to as sodium hydroxide.

17. Although caustic soda is a high energy/pollution product, the most energy efficient means of producing caustic soda is the membrane cell process.

18. For a good overview of the history and application of China's environmental impact assessment program, see Wang Yan et al. (2003). For an analysis of some of the program's early problems, see Lo et al. (1997).

19. The main regulation governing the licensing of EIA service agents includes the 2005 "Administrative Measures for the Certification of Construction Project Environmental Impact Assessments." Originally passed in 1989 under a slightly different Chinese name, it was updated in 1999 and again in 2005 (NEPA 1989; SEPA 1999, 2005).

20. The EIA engineer certification program is in its early stages. It consists of a national exam given once a year. Those seeking certification must first apply and already have either an educational or professional background in the EIA field (e.g.,

MA and three years of experience or PhD and one year of experience). The first exam was given in the spring of 2005. MEP's website (www.zhb.gov.cn or http://english .mep.gov.cn) provides links to numerous documents introducing the system.

21. Huang Yasheng's arguments about the causes and consequences of privileging foreign investment have generated a great deal of controversy, as is evident in the reviews published in the July 2005 issue of *Management & Organization Review* (vol. 1, issue 2). However, the basic fact that foreign investors have traditionally enjoyed a privileged legal status in many areas is not questioned.

22. In 2007, the National People's Congress passed a unified Enterprise Tax Law that reduced tax incentives offered to foreign investment and took a major step toward dismantling the separate legal regime that foreign investors have long enjoyed in China.

23. Huang Yasheng notes that the bias toward foreign firms is particularly acute with regard to private domestic firms and less so when foreign companies are compared to state-owned enterprises (2003a, 409).

24. The use of "new source performance standards," which apply more stringent requirements for new facilities, is common across many countries (Levinson 1996).

25. It is not surprising, then, that econometric studies seeking to test the impact of the stringency of environmental standards on FDI patterns have relied on proxy measures for environmental stringency. Often the proxy for environmental stringency is simply pollution intensity (e.g., Dean and Lovely 2005; Javorcik and Wei 2004), which is defined by the amount of some pollutant or set of pollutants divided by economic output. The disadvantage of this as a measure of regulatory stringency is that pollution intensity can decline as a function of stronger legislation, stricter enforcement, technological upgrading, and/or changes in the composition of the jurisdiction's economy, such as a shift from heavy to light manufacturing. It is difficult to separate out the causal factors. Another common proxy for environmental stringency is pollution-abatement cost, which is determined for either a jurisdiction or a specific sector (e.g., Eskeland and Harrison 2003). The logic is that jurisdictions with strict regulation will have higher abatement costs. A disadvantage to this measure often appears when it is used for comparing stringency across nation-states. Some studies construct their measure by taking U.S. data on abatement costs for a given sector and multiplying it by the value added of individual sectors in the country of interest. In other words, these studies assume that the abatement cost of a chemical firm in the United States is the same as it is in China. Other proxies include a country's participation in international treaties, its environmental sustainability index (ESI) ranking (Javorcik and Wei 2004), and spending by the government on environmental protection (Mani et al. 1997). Although there are a host of indexes ranking U.S. states' environmental stringency (Levinson 1996), there are very few ranking nation-states. Tobey (1990) relies on a 1976 United Nations report ranking approximately fifty countries, while Javorcik and Wei (2004) employ a 1997 European Bank for Reconstruction and Development Report that ranked twenty-five countries, primarily based on whether they had adopted a maximum permissible concentration standard.

26. There is a copious literature tracing the development of China's environmental law, most of which can be found in international law journals. However, there is a surprising dearth of work that places China's environmental law in a comparative perspective. Rock (2002) is one notable exception.

27. Rock's criteria are wide-ranging and include many aspects of the political system, including the cohesiveness and strength of the bureaucracy and the insulation of government from business interests (2002, 13–14).

28. The survey started before 2000, but in its initial years did not include questions about environmental regulation. The 1999 survey asked an environment-related question, but it focused on the transparency and stability of regulations, rather than stringency.

29. According to the World Economic Forum's 2007 Global Competitiveness Report, the survey's overall purpose is to provide data that serve as a "gauge of the current condition of a given country's business climate" (85). The local institutes hired to conduct the survey are instructed to "carefully select companies whose size and scope of activities guarantee that their executives benefit from international exposure and are therefore well positioned to compare the situation in their own economy with the situation prevailing in others" (93). It should be noted that the nature of the sampling method makes the survey data inappropriate for drawing inferences about other firms in China. Rather, the data are intended to help paint a more accurate picture of the business climate in which firms operate. As the Global Competitiveness Report indicates, "the Executive Opinion Survey's main goal is not to form specific inferences about the population of firms in a country. For instance, the sample should not be used to estimate the average firm size in a country. We do, however, aim to construct a sample of firms that is adequately broad and representative to estimate non-firm information about an economy. The survey helps to assess the economic environment within which firms operate by sampling the perspectives of a diversity of executives and managers across many business sectors and firm sizes" (2001, 167).

30. According to the World Bank Quick Reference Tables, in PPP terms the 2007 per capita GDP for the countries are: Russia ($14,400), Malaysia ($13,570), Thailand ($7,880), China ($5,370), Philippines ($3,730), Indonesia ($3,580), India ($2,740), and Vietnam ($2,550).

31. The percentile was generated by the following formula: $1 - $ (country rank/ total no. of countries in the sample).

32. A lack of data makes it difficult to know how China compared to other countries in the 1980s and 1990s. One JV manager, reflecting on his four years' experience in China during an interview in 1990, stated: "China does not have stricter environmental regulations than other developing countries" (Ross et al. 1990).

33. For instance, starting with the first Foreign Investment Catalogue published in 1995, China restricted foreign investment in benzidine (see Note 15). However, controls on the production of benzidine in China go back much further than 1995. According to one report, the first restriction was issued by the Chemical Ministry in the 1970s (Runnalls et al. 2002, 168). In 1984, the State Council prohibited small and rural

enterprises from producing benzidine. Additional legal notices banning the production of benzidine were issued in 1999 and 2004. Foreign firms are required by various foreign-investment laws to abide by all Chinese laws and regulations, so in one sense the 1995 restriction of foreign investment did not represent a new legal development, but more of a clarification and a signal to both investors and authorities charged with approving investment projects to abide by existing laws.

Chapter 4

1. Utilized solid waste refers to solid waste that is recycled, processed, or otherwise treated in a way that allows it to be used as a raw material input. The utilization rate refers to the amount utilized divided by the amount produced.

2. For a more detailed description of the firms interviewed, see Chapter 5.

3. Other studies have made a similar assertion. Klee and Thomas (1997, 39) state that there is often unequal enforcement between domestic and foreign companies: "Because many Chinese officials consider international companies to have more resources and more experience in meeting pollution-control requirements, they often expect them to be in full and immediate compliance with the requirements."

4. This is a simple way of testing the race-to-the-bottom argument. For a more sophisticated application of the argument, see Woods (2006).

5. Utilized FDI refers to foreign direct investment that has already been made. There is often a gulf in Chinese statistics between contracted and utilized FDI.

6. The correlation coefficient for wastewater, SO_2, and the combined measure, respectively, are: 0.43, 0.43, and 0.38. Each of the coefficients is significant (<0.05).

7. In each of the four figures, two provinces (Guangdong and Jiangsu) do not appear on the table. They attracted, respectively, $10.6 and $8.5 billion. Because they have taken in so much more FDI than other provinces, including them would skew the chart and make it difficult to print on a single page. Both provinces follow the trends shown in the figures. Guangdong's percentage of wastewater discharges and SO_2 emissions meeting standards are 84.6 and 69.0 percent. Jiangsu's are 95.3 and 88.3 percent. The overall environmental measures for the two provinces are, respectively, 72.7 and 83.9 percent.

8. The figures presented here should be treated with caution. First, official Chinese statistics are often of questionable accuracy. Second, provinces may be too large a unit of analysis. Intra-provincial differences may be as relevant as inter-provincial variation. Given the strong role of the municipal government in China's environmental protection regime, a more useful comparison might be between cities rather than provinces. The *Jiangsu Province Statistical Yearbook* does provide information about environmental governance measures on a city-by-city basis for each of its thirteen prefecture-level cities between 1997 and 2000. However, my examination of the data led me to conclude that it is not sufficiently reliable. The *China Environmental Statistical Yearbook*, which has been published annually since the late 1990s, improves with

each year, as do most provincial yearbooks. It is possible that such a municipal-based analysis will be possible in the future. The World Bank has conducted a township-based survey of environmental implementation. Arguing that townships do not typically engage in activities to attract FDI (which usually occurs at the municipal level), its survey did not include FDI as a variable (Wang and Di 2002).

9. In distinguishing between effect and outcome, I am drawing on the work of Copeland and Taylor, who make a distinction between the pollution-haven effect and the pollution-haven hypothesis (2004, 9).

10. Zeng and Easton (2007) provide empirical support only for a relationship between the amount of FDI and pollution intensity and not for a link between FDI and government enforcement. The latter relationship is inferred based on theory and used as a possible explanation for the observed empirical relationship. It is possible that the improvements in pollution intensity observed by Zeng and Easton stem from changes in the structure of the economy or production processes rather than from more stringent enforcement. In fact, the measure of enforcement included in their model proves statistically insignificant. This is not to say that Zeng and Easton are necessarily wrong in their assertion that FDI has a positive impact on enforcement and implementation. The point is simply that there is a dearth of studies that fully examine the relationship between FDI and implementation of environmental regulation and that, given the absence of data in the Chinese case, statistical studies are hard pressed to make connections between the two variables.

11. The very fact that there is an abundance of media articles on environmental problems in China's chemical parks is itself a sign of the central government's increased concern not just with environmental problems but with social welfare issues as a whole. Although the publication of critical articles allows for insight into recent problems with environmental governance, because such articles have only recently begun to appear, it is difficult to get a sense of trends or to know how today's problems compare with those in the 1980s or even in a large part of the 1990s.

12. An ethylene cracker is a fundamental element of a country's chemical industry infrastructure. Ethylene is by far the most heavily manufactured chemical product; 40 percent of all organic chemicals produced are based on ethylene. Ethylene-based materials are in almost every product used in daily life, such as containers, adhesives, pharmaceuticals, paints, and gasoline additives (Smiley and Jackson 2002, 119–20). Ethylene is produced in crackers, which are high-pressure devices that add steam to a hydrocarbon (e.g., ethane, propane, naphtha, gas oils). Crackers are highly sophisticated, capital-intensive operations and so are typically owned by major corporations such as BP, Exxon Mobil, Dupont, Shell, and Dow. China in recent years has witnessed significant investment by these corporations seeking to increase China's ethylene capacity.

13. "Greenfield investment" refers to investment in the construction of a new facility, as opposed to purchasing or investing in an existing operation.

14. In Table 4.2, two parks do not have investment percent listed because the park representatives did not provide the information.

15. In addition, numerous regional economic development and technology zones are explicitly attempting to attract chemical firms (by my count there are at least sixteen of these).

16. Interview with president of Chinese consulting firm (for the chemical industry), interview #39, Beijing, March 24, 2005.

17. Interview with director at CPCIA (department not included to preserve anonymity), interview #33, Beijing, March 22, 2005.

18. I conducted two sets of interviews in the park on two separate days, ten days apart. The protests, to my knowledge, received no coverage in the local or international press. After both of my interviews, I made a modest attempt to speak to some of the protestors, but was approached by what I assume were nonuniformed public security officers, who stated the area was closed and asked my business at the park. Recognizing that a foreign presence changes the dynamic and not wishing to endanger the protestors, my host unit in China, or my research, I feigned ignorance of Mandarin and left. The cab drivers who had driven me to the park (and waited outside while I conducted the interviews) were my principal source of information and explained that the farmers' grievance was the enclosure of land by the park and inadequate compensation.

19. The legal documents aimed toward the rectification of problems with China's chemical parks have been published together in a recent volume (Pan Derun 2004). The volume provides a one- or two-page introduction to approximately forty chemical parks and has been published in both English and Chinese. The English version does not contain the legal documents related to the problems of China's chemical parks.

20. Admittedly, Chinese industry journals are not in the business of embarrassing local governments or firms by publishing news of closings. Nevertheless, when the central government orders a crackdown on illegal activity of any kind, whether it is pirating software or polluting rivers, industry and mainstream newspapers tend to report facts and figures lauding the government effort. The absence of such news indicates that the government has been incapable or undesirous of launching action against chemical parks.

21. Although the focus of this chapter is on government rather than firm behavior, one might ask: To what extent have foreign firms taken advantage of park officials' eagerness to attract investment? Have foreign firms sought out parks willing to ignore environmental standards and/or engaged in practices that violate China's environmental laws? Park officials who were interviewed, as one might expect, denied the existence of environmental problems in their parks and declined to speculate about the types of firms that violate environmental regulations in other chemical parks. In Beijing, CPCIA and SEPA officials were no more forthcoming. They acknowledged the existence of environmental problems caused by competition for investment, but (at least publicly) adopted a rather blasé attitude and expressed a faith that the market mechanism will eliminate the inefficient parks, a faith that is somewhat ironic in a nominally communist country. In articles concerning environmental damage in

chemical parks, there occasionally are vague references to developed countries ex-acerbating the problems in chemical parks by shifting pollution-intensive industries to China. The exact meaning of these references is unclear, especially given that, by definition, a foreign investment in a chemical park is an investment by a pollution-intensive industry (Wang Xiaoyang 2004; Xu 2002). None of the media reports I surveyed highlights a specific case involving foreign-firm malfeasance in a chemical park. This absence could be a reflection of reality or a result of the nature of the Chinese media. The tradition in Chinese media coverage of scandalous cases is to avoid the use of proper names (at least until the violator has been specifically deemed by high-level authorities as suitable for use as a negative example). So while foreign firms rarely appear by name in articles describing the problems in chemical parks, there are also few named references to domestic firms, parks, or even locations. Unfortunately, in dealing with China, one typically has to judge the extent of the problem principally by the amount and tone of media coverage rather than compiling the detailed facts of specific cases. This makes it difficult to analyze the extent to which violations of environmental regulation in chemical parks involve foreign versus domestic firms. Chapters 5 and 6, although not focusing specifically on chemical parks, discuss firm environmental behavior extensively.

22. The accomplishments of Shenzhen in tightening its environmental policies have led some to conclude that the race-to-the-bottom hypothesis is not evident in China. Richardson (2004b, 129), for instance, argues that "contrary to the race to the bottom thesis, Chinese authorities have actually expanded and strengthened environmental controls in SEZs and open cities in recent years." While developments in Shenzhen and other well-known special economic zones clearly point to enhanced environmental regulation, Richardson is generalizing from a subset of all jurisdictions that are not necessarily representative of investment zones as a whole. As the case of chemical parks indicates, in some jurisdictions, at least in the short-term, environmental regulation may move in a direction opposite that of Shenzhen.

23. The broader theoretical and methodological implications of this assertion are discussed in greater detail in the final chapter.

24. In Chapter 7, I discuss how this assertion might be tested in other studies.

Chapter 5

1. Several of the representatives were interviewed more than once; for the sake of simplicity all interviews with a particular representative are cited as a single interview. Foreign firms interviewed for this chapter were chosen based on *Chemical Week*'s annual list of the top fifty largest chemical firms. Any of the top fifty without at least one majority-owned JV operation in China was eliminated. I then selected twenty-two firms at random among the remaining forty-plus firms. Eight firms failed to respond, responded but never found a time to meet, or responded curtly saying they would be in touch if they believed this matter warranted further attention. A

few of the firms interviewed were chosen not based on this methodology, but simply based on personal connections made during the research process itself. There is some potential bias in this selection method, as firms with worse environmental behavior are less likely to respond, although in general the response rate is relatively high. The interviewees differed depending on the firm. Those formally interviewed included six corporate directors of EHS who were based in China (3), the West (2), and Asia (1). In addition, there were five middle- or senior-level managers working in the EHS group of the company's China headquarters in Beijing or Shanghai. Each person interviewed had more than two years of experience with EHS in China and most had several years. Other interviewees included those working within the China headquarters of the MNC and charged with quality control, a global product line, external affairs, or manufacturing support / regulatory affairs. Finally, one was the manager of a local chemical facility owned by an MNC. All interviews were conducted in confidentiality. Unless otherwise specified, the names of companies and interviewees are withheld by mutual agreement and both will be referred to only by description and number. I randomly assigned each interviewee a number. Also, each firm has a number based on its country or region of origin (domestic electronics firm #16 refers to the sixteenth Chinese firm, European chemical firm #3 refers to the third European firm, U.S. chemical firm #2 refers to the second American firm, etc.). In one case, I interviewed EHS directors who were from the same parent company based in Europe but worked in different manufacturing facilities. In these citations, I also include a facility number (e.g., European chemical company #1, facility #1).

2. This chapter uses the terms multinational corporation (MNC), foreign-invested enterprise (FIE), and foreign firm interchangeably. This is simply to avoid a tiresome repetition of the term MNC. However, the research in this chapter focuses only on large multinationals in a single sector (chemical industry). The behavior of smaller FIEs in other sectors is considered in subsequent chapters.

3. The subsequent description of corporate EHS policy is not of any one particular firm, but more a compilation of common features shared by many firms.

4. Responsible Care (RC) is implemented by national chemical industry associations in individual countries. RC is a voluntary initiative in which firms pledge to implement a variety of environmental, health, and safety initiatives. National RC committees do not monitor or audit firms' behavior. For more information, see www .americanchemistry.com. The Global Compact is a voluntary initiative in which a firm's CEO sends a letter to the Secretary General of the UN expressing support for the Global Compact's principles of business ethics. In addition, the firm pledges to take certain broad steps such as advocating for the Global Compact and publishing in corporate reports how it is supporting the Global Compact. It is not legally binding and the UN does not monitor or audit firms' behavior (www.unglobalcompact.org). GRI is an independent organization, though it collaborates with the UN Environment Programme (UNEP). It offers guidance for companies to support their sustainability performance and provides a number of indicators against which companies can assess themselves. These indicators encompass many areas, one of which is envi-

ronmental (e.g., total water use, greenhouse gas emissions, incidents of noncompliance). In the 2003 GRI guidelines, there are thirty-five environmental indicators, and many firms use these guidelines to determine which data to report in their annual corporate reports.

5. Interview with EHS director, U.S. chemical company #1, interview #4, Shanghai, May 24, 2005.

6. Interview with manager, Manufacturing Support Center and Regulatory Affairs Committee, European chemical firm #4, interview #13, Shanghai, July 9, 2005.

7. Interview with HSE (Health, Safety, and Environment) director, European chemical company #1, facility #1, interview #1, Shanghai, May 12 and July 15, 2005.

8. Interview with EHS director, U.S. chemical company #4, interview #19, Shanghai, June 30 and July 1, 2005.

9. Interview with director of corporate initiatives, U.S. chemical company #1, interview #3, Shanghai, February 24, 2005.

10. Interview with HSE director, European chemical company #1, facility #1, interview #1, Shanghai, May 12 and July 15, 2005.

11. Ibid.

12. Interview with project manager and director of safety program (for China operations), U.S. construction firm #4, interview #9, Shanghai, July 5, 2005.

13. Further proof of foreign-firm compliance comes from internal company EHS records. On the condition of anonymity, two firms provided an "incident register" for their China operations. The incident register is essentially a spreadsheet in which each accident or near miss has columns for description, cause, recommended action, and status of follow-up. These registers, which typically record several incidents a month and include everything from a scaffold worker who fails to use a safety harness to a compressor that leaks oil into the soil, show the considerable detail with which operations are monitored (interview with EHS director, U.S. chemical company #6, interview #22, Beijing, June 15, 2005).

14. I am thankful to an anonymous reviewer for reminding me of this important point.

15. The information in these interviews was supplemented and (to the extent possible) cross-checked via interviews with the directors and one senior manager of two environmental consulting firms that work with MNCs, an INGO (international non-governmental organization) representative who served a year in an MNC while on secondment, and three environmental lawyers working in Beijing and Shanghai. Although I was not able to interview government officials charged specifically with regulating the MNCs interviewed, I did hold formal interviews with a number of government officials, including the head of a SEPA research center, a representative from both the EIA Office and Waste Management Division in SEPA, three middle and senior officials in the CPCIA, and three environmental officials from two chemical industrial parks. The list above does not include the countless informal discussions that occurred on the sidelines of the various EHS conferences and meetings I attended while in China.

16. Interview with division chief (department not included to preserve anonymity) of SEPA, interview #30, Beijing, June 15, 2005.

17. Interview with Economic and Trade Department official, chemical park #1, interview #31, March 28, 2005.

18. Interview with chief representative and managing partner, Beijing office of international law firm, interview #32, Beijing, June 24, 2005; interview with UNDP official based in Beijing, interview #28, Shanghai, August 10, 2005.

19. This is a common finding. One study of MNCs in the pesticide industry in Thailand found that 25 percent adopted global standards and more than 50 percent admitted that they only adopted local standards (Fowler 1995, 12, 14).

20. Over the years, the pollution levy system has been amended so that, at least according to formal law, firms are required to control for both concentration and volume. My interviews with EHS managers indicated that enforcement is more often based on concentration. See Table 2.2 in Chapter 2 for a more extended description of the pollution levy system.

21. Interview with senior manager, Resources Department, Japanese chemical company #1, interview #17, Shanghai, August 3, 2005.

22. Interview with manager of HSE, European chemical company #1, facility #2, interview #2, Shanghai, April 8, 2005.

23. Interview with manager, Manufacturing Support Center and Regulatory Affairs Committee, European chemical firm #4, interview #13, Shanghai, July 9, 2005.

24. Interview with manager of HSE, European chemical company #1, facility #2, interview #2, Shanghai, April 8, 2005.

25. This case study is based on interviews with a half-dozen current or former Shell employees, or environmental consultants who were intimately involved in the environmental and social elements of the WEP project. One of the interviewees works for an international environmental NGO and was on secondment at Shell during the WEP project. PetroChina did not respond to requests for an interview. Because of the sensitive nature of some of the material presented in this case study, all identifying information of the people interviewed has been removed. Two brief articles published by Shell employees are also cited in the text. The views expressed in this section are those of the author only and do not represent those of Shell or any of the other parties involved in the WEP project.

26. These were the same problems that induced Shell to pull out of the Xihu natural gas project two months later.

27. WEP interviewee #5, interview #25, Shanghai, May 23, 2005.

28. WEP interviewee #3, interview #7, Beijing, March 23, 25, and 29, 2005.

29. The others were a $12 billion investment in electricity transportation, the Qinghai-Tibet Railway and a Beijing-Shanghai high-speed railway, and the North-South Water Diversion Project.

30. WEP interviewee #3, interview #7, Beijing, March 23, 25, and 29, 2005.

31. WEP interviewee #2, interview #6, Beijing, March 22, 2005.

32. Ibid.

33. WEP interviewee #7, interview #27, Shanghai, April 14, 2005.

34. WEP interviewee #4, interview #8, Shanghai, April 13, 2005.

35. WEP interviewee #1, interview #5, Beijing, March 22, 2005.

36. The interim agreement (December 2001) covered a range of issues and was not limited to EHS standards.

37. As many foreign researchers know, Chinese law is murky in the area of survey research—it neither sanctions nor prohibits foreign organizations and individuals from conducting survey work. Typically foreigners have to find domestic partners that will conduct the research on their behalf.

38. Email correspondence with UNDP official based in Beijing, August 10, 2005. Also, see the UNDP China website (www.undp.org.cn) for a copy of the 200-plus-page ESIA they conducted for Stora Enso.

39. WEP interviewee #6, interview #26, Shanghai, April 14, 2005.

40. WEP interviewee #4, interview #8, Shanghai, April 13, 2005.

41. WEP interviewee #6, interview #26, Shanghai, April 14, 2005.

42. WEP interviewee #5, interview #25, Shanghai, May 23, 2005.

43. WEP interviewee #6, interview #26, Shanghai, April 14, 2005.

44. Shell bore the brunt of the costs for the additional ESIAs, which undoubtedly made it easier for PetroChina to receive material benefits.

45. Interviewee #6

46. Interview with HSE director, European chemical company #1, facility #1, interview #1, Shanghai, May 12 and July 15, 2005. The firm's home country name was removed from the quotation.

47. Bhopal refers to an industrial accident that occurred in Bhopal, India, in 1984, which released forty tons of methyl isocyanate into the air, killing thousands and injuring many more.

48. Most firms described similar procedures and the description provided is based on a compilation of interviews rather than reflecting the practice of any single firm.

49. Although the inspection process is essentially an audit, foreign-firm representatives are careful to avoid such words, as they sound overly critical. They tend to say they are reviewing facilities looking for "areas of concern" or "outstanding issues."

50. Interview with director of corporate initiatives, U.S. chemical company #1, interview #3, Shanghai, February 24, 2005.

51. Interview with Asia-Pacific EHS director, U.S. chemical company #5, interview #20, Beijing, June 14, 2005.

52. An MSDS gives a basic overview of a chemical, including its physical properties, stability, toxicology, transportation information, and recommended personal protection equipment.

53. Interview with sustainable development manager, Corporate Communications for Greater China, European chemical firm #3, interview #11, Shanghai, July 12, 2005.

54. Interview with director at CPCIA (department not included to preserve anonymity), interview #33, Beijing, March 22, 2005.

55. In Taiwan, Bayer has also made use of a "buddy system."

56. Joint interview with ISO System Control Department manager and Equipment Department assistant manager, Japanese chemical company #1, interview #18, Shanghai, August 3, 2005.

57. In my interviews, Chinese-company representatives usually stated that regulators and local citizen complaints were the largest source of pressure on their environmental behavior.

58. Interview with EHS director, U.S. chemical company #1, interview #4, Shanghai, May 24, 2005.

59. Interview with sustainable development manager, Corporate Communications for Greater China Department, European chemical firm #3, interview #11, Shanghai, July 12, 2005.

60. Endocrine disrupters inhibit the functioning of the endocrine system, which is a set of glands (e.g., thyroid, pituitary, adrenal). Hormones produced by endocrine glands influence the growth, development, reproduction, and behavior of animals and humans.

61. Interview with senior manager, Resources Department, Japanese chemical company #1, interview #17, Shanghai, August 3, 2005.

62. Interview with EHS director, U.S. chemical company #1, interview #4, Shanghai, May 24, 2005.

63. Kennedy identifies a number of strategies that MNCs utilize to increase their influence. He argues that foreign interests are most likely to prevail when they are shared by local industry. Sanyal and Guvenli (2000) show that MNCs with a longer history in China report better government relations than other firms. However, they report that good government relations allow firms freedom from intrusion by CCP or government officials in the day-to-day operations. Again, this indicates that firms, rather than capturing the state and regulatory process, pursue modest goals in their political activity.

64. The London Guidelines were part of a series of international rules developed in the 1980s and 1990s to govern trade in chemicals. They were a voluntary initiative that provided guidance for countries in the process of informing one another about chemicals that were banned or severely restricted in their territory. They also contained suggestions on chemical management, information exchange, classification, and other topics. The 1989 amendment to the London Convention included a prior informed consent clause, in which countries could inform the UNEP whether they permit the import of a particular chemical. The UNEP would then transmit the information to other countries, and all signatories were required to respect other countries' decisions.

65. Interview with the former president of a U.S. business advocacy organization based in Beijing, interview #34, Shanghai, August 11, 2005.

66. As is typical in Chinese law, the 1994 legislation did not put forward a fee schedule, but simply stated that fees would be "formulated separately" (NEPA 1994, 1995).

67. Interview with former president of an American business advocacy organization based in Beijing, interview #34, Shanghai, August 11, 2005.

68. These are the two most influential industry associations in China's chemical sector. AICM represents forty-three multinational companies that account for $15 billion in foreign investment and 15,000 employees in China. The European Chamber of Commerce's Petrochemical, Chemical, Oil, and Gas Working Group represents twenty-five companies with EUR 15 billion invested.

69. Interview with representative of European Chamber of Commerce, Petrochemical, Chemical, Oil, and Gas Working Group, interview #36, Beijing, June 23, 2005. Euro III and IV standards refer to an increasingly stringent set of emission standards for automobiles sold in Europe. The higher the number, the more stringent the standard. Euro III was introduced in Europe in 2000; Euro IV in 2005. In 2004 China indicated that it would adopt Euro III standards nationally, and in the run-up to the 2008 Olympics, Beijing announced that it would replace many of its older buses with new ones that met the Euro IV standard.

70. An ISO container is used to ship chemicals over both land and sea.

71. Interview with manager of Responsible Care and Quality Management for Greater China Department, European chemical company #3, interview #11, Shanghai, April 19, 2005.

72. Interview with chief representative and managing partner, Beijing office of international law firm, interview #32, Beijing, June 24, 2005.

73. Interview with representative of European Chamber of Commerce, Petrochemical, Chemical, Oil, and Gas Working Group, interview #36, Beijing, June 23, 2005.

74. Early in the process of research, I typically asked interviewees, "Does your firm conduct audits?" I tended to receive blank or disbelieving stares indicating that my question betrayed a naiveté about life in a multinational corporation. I might as well have asked, "Does your firm seek profits?"

75. Interview with project manager, U.S. chemical company #2, interview #10, Shanghai, May 12, 2005.

76. For a good overview of the literature on firm compliance, see Gunningham et al. (2003, ch. 2). As these authors note, there is a split in the "business and environment" literature about just how common it is for firms to go beyond compliance, as well as a general lack of knowledge about the factors that push firms to exceed legal requirements. Some argue that noncompliance is far less common today than in the past and highlight the numerous examples of firms going beyond compliance. Others point out that beyond-compliance behavior is restricted to a small fraction of firms and does not describe the reality on the ground.

77. Perkins (2007) provides a first-rate overview of the various transnational forces that are thought to contribute to convergence between developing- and developed-country environmental standards.

78. See, for example, Falkner (2006); Vogel (1995, 2000); Vogel and Kagan (2004); Alasdair Young (2003).

Chapter 6

Portions of this section have been previously published in the *Journal of Contemporary China*. See Stalley (2009).

1. Among the independent variables, the highest pairwise correlation was 0.25.

2. The variables "size" and "chemical" are significant. As expected, larger companies exhibited better environmental behavior and chemical companies worse, which is not surprising given that it is among the most pollution-intensive sectors. Age and renovation are not significant. The principal reason for the lack of statistical significance of the variables "age" and "renovation" may stem from the fact that few of the firms in the sample are old. The average age of all firms is seventeen years, with 75 percent of firms established after 1980. Also, as one might expect given a country that has averaged 9 percent growth for two decades, a large number (two-thirds) of firms have undergone a renovation or expansion since establishment. In other words, these variables are too rough a measure to have sufficient explanatory power to differentiate between firms that use more advanced, clean production technology and those that do not.

3. All quantities of interest were generated using the CLARIFY program. For more on CLARIFY, see King et al. (2000) and Tomz et al. (2001).

4. In focusing on Hong Kong, one has to consider the possibility that HK investment represents "roundtripping." That is, the "foreign" investment from Hong Kong is actually domestic investment routed through Hong Kong for the purpose of enjoying the privileges accorded to foreign investment in China. Huang Yasheng cites studies that estimate somewhere between 7 and 15 percent of FDI may be from domestic firms (2003b, 38). If this is the case, some of the Hong Kong firms in the sample are actually domestic firms. There is no way to confirm whether this is the case, so the findings must be interpreted with caution.

5. The argument, first put forward by David Vogel, that exporting to high-standard countries can lead to positive changes in firm environmental behavior and ultimately influence a lower-standard country's environmental regulation is often referred to as "trading up." Because the focus in this book is on the influence of foreign firms and investment, the "trading up" argument is not addressed in this volume. However, several studies have tested the idea. For examples of an application of the "trading up" hypothesis to China, see Stalley (2009) and Zeng and Easton (2007).

6. The theoretical basis for exploring relationships between "country of origin" and various aspects of foreign investment is Dunning's eclectic theory of international production. Dunning's eclectic theory is a broad paradigm that offers a holistic explanation for the extent, form, and pattern of foreign investment. One element of Dunning's work posits that patterns of FDI vary in part based on country or jurisdiction of origin. The principal reason is that "country of origin" has an impact on firm-specific endowments. For instance, in a country where there is a large domestic market, firms may tend to be large and so have advantages of economies of scale. When firms invest abroad they choose their investment strategy, which includes choices about location, entry mode, and numerous production-related issues, based on a de-

sire to use firm-specific advantages in conjunction with the location-specific endowments present in the host country. Big firms from countries with a large domestic market are more likely to make bigger investments than firms coming from small markets. The short of it is, because "country of origin" has an impact on firm endowments, and because firm endowments in turn influence foreign investment strategies, one can expect to see similarities in investment patterns among firms from the same country (Dunning 1980, 1988). Several scholars have addressed Dunning's theory and shown that there is a "country of origin" effect on various aspects of foreign investment; the most frequently studied relationship is between country of ownership and entry mode or ownership type (e.g., joint venture versus wholly foreign-owned).

7. There seems to be no major correlation between size and country of origin. European firms are on average the largest, with an average of 894 employees, but Japanese firms, which are almost as environmentally friendly as European firms, are the second smallest, with an average of 391 employees. Taiwanese firms are typically the smallest, with an average of 263 employees, yet they perform as well as or better than American firms, which have an average of 403 employees. Hong Kong firms have the worst environmental behavior but are the second largest, with an average of 429 employees.

8. Because Hong Kong and Taiwanese firms are the heaviest investors in China, most of the examples in this section focus on these two jurisdictions.

9. In real terms, the average went from $1,299 to $11,312 (in 1990 dollars). The countries included in the average, in order of the 1996 per capita GDP, are: Hong Kong, Singapore, Japan, Taiwan, Korea, Malaysia, Thailand, China, Indonesia, and the Philippines (Hernandez 2004, table 1).

10. South Korea, Taiwan, Indonesia, Thailand, and the Philippines each underwent a democratic transition after 1986.

11. Taiwan's area is about 13,900 square miles, while Maryland's is 12,400.

12. Maryland Department of the Environment: www.mde.state.md.us.

13. In the early 1990s, investment in pollution control represented about 2.8 percent of all fixed investment for Taiwanese industry. This figure is approximately 80, 66, and 33 percent for the amount invested, respectively, by Japanese, American, and German industry (Chi 1994, 39).

14. Not all countries have undertaken environmental protection with equal zeal or achieved the same results. Taiwan, Singapore, and Hong Kong have achieved more success than countries like Indonesia, Thailand, and China. For a good overview of the various accomplishments of Asian nations, and the factors that explain cross-national variation, see Rock (2002). Esty and Porter (2001) produce an environmental regulatory regime index that ranks seventy-one countries. The ranking of NE and SE Asian countries is: Singapore (3rd), Japan (17th), Korea (37th), Malaysia (38th), China (44th), Thailand (45th), Indonesia (54th), and the Philippines (59th).

15. Since 2000, the WEF survey has asked executives the same question: How stringent is your country's environmental regulation? Responses range from "1" (lax compared to other countries) to "7" (among the world's most stringent). Responses

are averaged to produce a country score—the higher the score, the more stringent the regulation. The percentile ranking shown for each country in Figure 6.5 represents the proportion of countries that were deemed by business executives as possessing weaker environmental regulation. For example, in 2007 Hong Kong's stringency score was 39th out of 131 countries, which placed Hong Kong in the 70th percentile. This means that executives working in 29 percent of the countries in the sample considered their country's environmental regulation more stringent than executives working in Hong Kong considered Hong Kong's environmental regulation. See Chapter 3, "China in Comparative Perspective" section, for a complete description of the survey.

16. The background information presented in the next two paragraphs is based chiefly on Hoover's Company Records (accessed via Proquest).

17. *Caijing* translates as "Finance and Economics," but the magazine is typically referred to simply as *Caijing. China Newsweek* has occasionally run into problems with censors. It was closed temporarily in March 2003 for publishing an article deemed too critical of outgoing prime minister Zhu Rongji.

18. The Greenpeace reports, to put it frankly, are not of the quality one would expect from a major international NGO. The Beijing office of Greenpeace only opened in 2002 and the reports, which are occasionally sloppy, reflect the fact that they were produced by a young organization with little experience in this kind of campaign. The reports were produced in English and Chinese, although some were in English only. There appears to be no major difference in the two versions. It should also be noted that Greenpeace Beijing declined my request for an interview and indicated that if I desired to learn more about the case I should join the campaign.

19. Interview with APP spokesperson, interview #35, Shanghai, July 18, 2005. The APP spokesperson felt that the Greenpeace members, most of whom were in their twenties, failed to show proper respect to the APP representative, who was much older.

20. Each of the three main investigative articles published focuses on a different aspect of APP's alleged behavior. The *Caijing* article deals primarily with APP's questionable financing in China and whether there has been illegal logging in its Hainan project. The *China Newsweek* article focuses principally on Yunnan and claims that APP has both illegally obtained and logged forest land. The *Southern Weekend* investigation also focuses on Yunnan, but places more attention on the aspect of government relations. It details the intra-provincial struggles over the APP issue and shows how certain government bureaus, such as the provincial Development and Reform Commission, were able to trump experts in various other bureaus, particularly the Forestry Bureau, which was skeptical about the desirability of the APP project.

21. Most of the attention has been on three main areas in Yunnan Province: Simao City, Lincang City, and Wenshan Prefecture, which is often shortened as Wenzhou. Simao and Lincang, respectively, are composed of ten counties (*xian*) or areas (*qu*). Wenzhou is an autonomous area comprised of national minorities. Within Simao City, Lancang County, which is easily confused with Lincang City, has been one of the areas where there has been the most controversy.

22. Under China's property rights system, companies such as APP do not own the land, but rather control the rights for determining how it is used. After the agreement was reached with the Yunnan provincial government, local governments (municipal and county) negotiated on behalf of APP with local farmers in order to transfer the land rights to APP. Farmers and/or contractors then plant the eucalyptus on behalf of APP. Farmers are given a land transfer fee and in some cases are eligible for various subsidies from the national government.

23. This price is for land development rights and does not include the price for the transfer of land, which was 70 RMB per *mu*. *Southern Weekend* maintains that this 70 RMB figure is itself artificially low and the result of the provincial government conspiring with APP. It quotes Forestry Administration officials who argue a reasonable price would have been at least 250–300 RMB.

24. In 2008, the office supply company Staples announced that it was severing its contracts with APP.

25. Interview with APP spokesperson, interview #35, Shanghai, July 18, 2005.

26. The exact percent that comes from other Latin American countries is difficult to determine, since much of Brazil's FDI comes from countries like Bermuda and the Cayman Islands, which may indicate that much of that investment is from firms setting up in offshore tax havens (UNCTAD, FDI Country Profiles, www.unctad.org).

Chapter 7

1. These studies arguing against the existence of industrial flight are quite numerous. Some examples include Bailey (1993); Bhagwati (1993, 2004); Bhagwati and Srinivasan (1996); Birdsall and Wheeler (1993); Dean (1993); Eskeland and Harrison (2003); Grossman and Krueger (1993); Jaffe et al. (1995); Leonard (1984, 1988); Mani et al. (1997); Pearson (1987); Thompson and Strohm (1996); Tobey (1990); Van Beers and Van den Bergh (1997); and Walter (1982). Others have pointed out that there is evidence of a shift of dirty industry to the developing world. Low and Yeats (1992) show that in the period from 1965 to 1988 the share of dirty goods among total exports declined in OECD countries from 20 percent to 16 percent, while rising in developing countries. While this does not necessarily indicate that developed-country firms are physically relocating to lower-standard jurisdictions, it does provide evidence that dirty goods are being produced in areas with weaker regulation. More recently, scholars have corrected for methodological errors of earlier work and found evidence that regulatory stringency influences trade and investment patterns. For example, see Becker and Henderson (2000) and Henderson (1996). Copeland and Taylor (2004) provide an excellent overview of the development of this literature.

2. In this sense, the pursuit of FDI is part of what Weidner and Jänicke refer to as a "convergence of policies, but divergence of outcomes" (2002, 440). They note that environmental policies have converged between northern and southern countries, but capacities for implementation have become more unequal.

3. Some studies (e.g., Zeng and Easton 2007) use pollution intensity (emissions/economic output) or the average pollution abatement costs for firms as a measure of environmental regulatory stringency. Because lower pollution intensity can result from stronger enforcement, these studies can be said to focus indirectly on implementation. However, there are numerous potential problems with using pollution intensity as a proxy for implementation. See Chapter 3, Note 25 and Chapter 4, Note 10.

4. Zeng and Easton (2007) hint at this in the literature review, but curiously do not test it in their empirical model.

5. Likewise, Jaffe et al. report that, based on the statements of legislators and lobbyists, "there appears to be widespread belief that environmental regulations have a significant effect on the siting of new plants in the United States" (1995, 148). Indeed, some of the more interesting work being done on the race-to-the-bottom argument in American politics involves surveys of government officials (Engel 1997; Konisky 2006). As these scholars point out, for a race to the bottom to occur, government officials must think in terms of a race. They should see environmental stringency as potentially detrimental for attracting investment and be aware of the policies of competitor states. Based on a survey of environmental officials, Konisky (2006) finds evidence that government regulators do in fact think in terms of a race to the bottom.

6. Wang and Di (2002) have demonstrated that attention from provincial-level authorities is associated with better environmental performance at the township level.

7. China has already begun to improve firm environmental performance through a ranking system. For example, in 2006 Beijing launched the "Top-1000 Energy Consuming Enterprises Program," which set energy efficiency targets for the included companies. The targets were to be reached by 2010.

8. Interview with director (department withheld to preserve anonymity), SEPA, interview #37, September 16, 2005.

9. For a good overview of some ongoing efforts in this area, see Baldinger and Turner (2002) and Turner (2003).

References

Abell, Hilary. 1999. "Endangering Women's Health for Profit: Health and Safety in Mexico's Maquiladoras." *Development in Practice* 9 (5): 595–600.

ACC (American Chemistry Council). 2006. Distribution Code of Management Practices, Responsible Care Toolkit. www.americanchemistry.com.

Adler, Jonathan H. 2003. "Let Fifty Flowers Bloom: Transforming the States into Laboratories of Environmental Policy." Federalism Project/American Enterprise Institute. www.federalismproject.org.

Agence France-Presse. 2005. "China Falls Short on Environmental Protection Spending." March 30.

Alford, William P., and Yuanyuan Shen. 1998. "Limits of the Law in Addressing China's Environmental Dilemma." In *Energizing China: Reconciling Environmental Protection and Economic Growth*, ed. Michael B. McElroy, Chris P. Nielsen, and Peter Lydon. Cambridge, MA: Harvard University Committee on Environment.

Alford, William P., Robert P. Weller, Leslyn Hall, Karen R. Polenske, Yuanyuan Shen, and David Zweig. 2002. "The Human Dimensions of Pollution Policy Implementation: Air Quality in Rural China." *Journal of Contemporary China* 11 (32): 495–513.

Andonova, Liliana B. 2003. "Openness and the Environment in Central and Eastern Europe: Can Trade and Foreign Investment Stimulate Better Environmental Management in Enterprises?" *Journal of Environment & Development* 12 (2): 177–204.

Asia Pulp & Paper. 2005. "APP Hits Back at Greenpeace's Latest Allegations of Illegal Logging." January 12. Originally posted to www.paperloop.com; currently available at www.chinawood.org/news_e/news/1270.html.

Asian Economic News. 1999. "Experts Differ on Environmental Effect of China in WTO." November 15.

Associated Press. 2006. "Official: China's Songhua River Suffering Near-daily Chemi-cal Spills." September 10.

———. 2007. "Why Is a Barren Chinese Mountain Being Painted Green?" *New York Times*, February 14.

———. 2008. "China Auto Production Sales Climb 20 Percent." MSNBC, January 13. www.msnbc.msn.com/id/22637142.

Bailey, Norman A. 1993. "Foreign Direct Investment and Environmental Protection in the Third World." In *Trade and the Environment: Law, Economics, and Policy*, ed. Durwood Zaelke, Paul Orbuch, and Robert F. Housman. Washington, DC: Island Press.

Baldinger, Pamela, and Jennifer L. Turner. 2002. *Crouching Suspicions, Hidden Potential: United States Environmental and Energy Cooperation with China*. Washington, DC: Woodrow Wilson Center.

Baum, Richard. 2005. "Statement for the Hearing on China's State Control Mechanisms and Methods." U.S.-China Economic and Security Review Commission, April 14.

Beck, Lindsay. 2006. "China Issues Guidelines to Tackle Pollution." Reuters, February 16.

Becker, Randy, and Vernon Henderson. 2000. "Effects of Air Quality Regulations on Polluting Industries." *Journal of Political Economy* 108 (2): 379–421.

Bhagwati, Jagdish. 1993. "Trade and the Environment: The False Conflict?" In *Trade and the Environment: Law, Economics, and Policy*, ed. Durwood Zaelke, Paul Orbuch, and Robert F. Housman. Washington, DC: Island Press.

———. 2004. *In Defense of Globalization*. New York: Oxford University Press.

Bhagwati, Jagdish, and T. N. Srinivasan. 1996. "Trade and the Environment: Does Environmental Diversity Detract from the Case for Free Trade?" In *Fair Trade and Harmonization: Prerequisites for Free Trade, Volume 1, Economic Analysis*, ed. Jagdish Bhagwati and Robert E. Hudic. Cambridge, MA: MIT Press.

Bi, Feng. 2003. "Huagong Yuanqu Bu Shi Qiye de Fanban" [Chemical Parks Are Not Enterprises' Refurbishment]. *Zhongguo Huagong Bao* [China Chemical News], May 17.

Birdsall, N., and David Wheeler. 1993. "Trade Policy and Industrial Pollution in Latin America: Where Are the Pollution Havens?" *Journal of Environment & Development* 2 (1): 137–49.

Boxer, Baruch. 1989. "China's Environmental Prospects." *Asian Survey* 29 (7): 669–86.

Boyce, James K. 2004. "Green and Brown? Globalization and the Environment." *Oxford Review of Economic Policy* 20 (1): 105–28.

Braithwaite, John, and Peter Drahos. 2000. *Global Business Regulation*. Cambridge: Cambridge University Press.

Bremner, Brian. 2006. "What's It Going to Cost to Clean Up China?" *Business Week*, September 27.

Brettell, Anna. 2008. "Chasing the Dragon's Tail: Economic Growth, Citizen Demand, and Environmental Quality in China." Paper presented at the Association of Chinese Political Studies Annual Conference entitled "Greater China in an Era of Globalization," Hong Kong, July 14–15.

Browne, Andrew, Matt Pottinger, and Patrick Barta. 2004. "China Gas Is Fuel for Doubts: Shell, Unocal Withdrawal from Project Highlights Sector Problems." *Wall Street Journal*, October 1.

Business China. 1994. "Chemical Changes." *Economist Intelligence Unit* 19 (20), September 19.

Business Roundtable. 2009. "China: The Environment and Trade." Business Roundtable Trade Resource Center. http://trade.businessroundtable.org (under Trade).

Buthe, Tim. 2003. "Governance Through Private Authority? Non-state Actors in World Politics." *Journal of International Affairs* 57 (1): 245–53.

Caijing Zazhi [Caijing Magazine]. 2003. "Yinni Zhiye Jutou APP Hainan Zhongsheng Diaocha" [Investigation into the Renascence of the Indonesian Paper Industry Tycoon APP]. November 6.

Callick, Rowan. 2006. "Wolfowitz Holds Beijing to Account over Africa." *The Australian*, October 25.

Cao, Hengwu. 2002. "Huagong Yuanqu Gaoceng Yantao Hui: Tansuo Woguo Jingxi Huagong Yuanqu de Fazhan Geju" [Chemical Park High-level Seminar: Exploring the Situation of China's Fine and Specialty Chemical Parks]. *Zhongguo Huagong Bao* [China Chemical News], October 16.

Carter, Neil T., and Arthur P. J. Mol. 2006. "China's Environmental Governance in Transition." *Environmental Politics* 15 (2): 149–70.

CCICED (China Council for International Cooperation on Environment and Development). 2006. Report of the Task Force on Environmental Governance, Third Phase. October 11. www.cciced.net/encciced (under Publications).

Chai, Joseph. 2002. "Trade and Environment: Evidence from China's Manufacturing Sector." *Sustainable Development* 10 (1): 25–35.

Chan, Deborah C. 1993. "The Environmental Dilemma in Taiwan." *Journal of Northeast Asian Studies* 12 (1): 35–56.

Chang, Leonard K., and Yum K. Kwan. 2000. "What Are the Determinants of the Location of Foreign Direct Investment? The Chinese Experience." *Journal of International Economic Law* 51:389–400.

Chen, Chien-Hsun. 1996. "Regional Determinants of Foreign Direct Investment in Mainland China." *Journal of Economic Studies* 23 (2): 18–30.

Chen, Guocheng. 2004. "Guojia Huanbao Chanye Zhengce Yu Huagong Yuanqu" [China's Environmental Protection Industrial Policies and Chemical Industrial Parks]. *Huagong Guanli* [Chemical Management] 2:14–15.

Chen, Hongbo, and Shaogang Zhu. 2003. "Lun Fazhan Zhong Guojia Zai Jingji Quanqiuhua Zhong de Huanjing Anquan Duice" [Environmental Security of Developing Countries in the Process of Economic Globalization]. *Zhongguo Renkou Ziyuan Yu Huanjing* [China Population, Resources, and Environment] 13 (5): 20–23.

Chen, Kent. 1992. "Booming South 'Taking the Lead.'" *South China Morning Post*, November 7.

Chen, Weihua. 2007. "Relocating Pollution Is the Wrong Solution." *China Daily*, July 7.

Chen, Yingqi, and Ke Chen. 2004. "Bie Bei 'Jiankang' 'Lüse' Wu Dao" [Don't Be Misled by "Healthy" or "Green"]." *Guangming Ribao* [Guangming Daily], September 18.

Cheung, Chi-Fai. 2006. "Dirty HK Factories in Delta Face Closure." *South China Morning Post*, May 15.

Chi, Chun-chieh. 1994. "Growth with Pollution: Unsustainable Development in Taiwan and Its Consequences." *Studies in Comparative International Development* 29 (2): 23–47.

Child, John, and Terence Tsai. 2005. "The Dynamic Between Firms' Environmental Strategies and Institutional Constraints in Emerging Economies: Evidence from China and Taiwan." *Journal of Management Studies* 42 (1): 95–125.

China Business Review. 1995. "Taking the Lead on Chemicals." January/February, 13.

China Daily. 2006. "Polluters Feel Impact of Ignoring Assessment." October 13.

———. 2007. "Greener Use of FDI." November 8.

———. 2008. "Curbing Polluters." January 15.

Choy, Linda. 1994. "Caustic Response to Chemical Fees." *South China Morning Post*, December 14.

Christmann, Petra, and Glen Taylor. 2001. "Globalization and the Environment: Determinants of Firm Self-regulation in China." *Journal of International Business Studies* 32 (3): 439–58.

———. 2006. "Firm Self-regulation Through International Certifiable Standards: Determinants of Symbolic Versus Substantive Implementation." *Journal of International Business Studies* 37:863–78.

Chung, Yulanda. 1999. "Now You See It . . . Now You Don't." *Asian Week*, October 1.

Clapp, Jennifer. 2002. "What the Pollution Havens Debate Overlooks." *Global Environmental Politics* 2 (2): 11–19.

Clapp, Jennifer, and Peter Dauvergne. 2005. *Paths to a Green World: The Political Economy of the Global Environment*. Cambridge, MA: MIT Press.

Clarke, Donald. 2003. "Empirical Research in Chinese Law." In *Beyond Common Knowledge: Empirical Approaches to the Rule of Law*, ed. Erik Jensen and Thomas Heller. Stanford, CA: Stanford University Press.

Clifford, Mark. 2002. "Her Dirty Job: Cleaning Up Hong Kong." *Business Week*, December 6. www.businessweek.com.

Copeland, Brian R., and M. Scott Taylor. 2004. "Trade, Growth, and the Environment." *Journal of Economic Literature* XLII (March): 7–71.

CPCIA (China Petroleum and Chemical Industry Association). 2004. Guanyu Woguo Huagong Yuanqu Fazhan De Zhidao Yijian [Guiding Opinion Concerning the Development of China's Chemical Industrial Parks]. March 5. www.cpcia.org.cn.

Crusto, Mitchell F. 1999. "All That Glitters Is Not Gold: A Congressionally-driven Global Environmental Policy." *Georgetown International Environmental Law Review* 11:499.

Cutler, A. Claire, Virginia Haufler, and Tony Porter. 1999. *Private Authority and International Affairs*. Albany: State University of New York Press.

Dasgupta, Susmita, Hemamala Hettige, and David Wheeler. 1998. "What Improves Environmental Performance? Evidence from Mexican Industry." World Bank Working Paper 1877. www.worldbank.org.

Dasgupta, Susmita, Benoit Laplante, Hua Wang, and David Wheeler. 2002. "Confronting the Environmental Kuznets Curve." *Journal of Economic Perspectives* 16 (1): 147–68.

Dasgupta, Susmita, Ashoka Mody, Subhendu Roy, and David Wheeler. 2001. "Environmental Regulation and Development: A Cross-country Empirical Analysis." *Oxford Development Studies* 29 (2): 173–87.

Dauvergne, Peter. 2005. "The Environmental Challenge of Loggers in the Asia-Pacific." In *The Business of Global Environmental Governance*, ed. David L. Levy and Peter J. Newell. Cambridge, MA: MIT Press.

Dean, Judith. 1993. "Trade and Environment: A Survey of Literature." In *International Trade and the Environment*, ed. Patrick Low. Washington, DC: World Bank.

Dean, Judith, and Mary E. Lovely. 2005. "Are Foreign Investors Attracted to Weak Environmental Regulations? Evaluating the Evidence from China." World Bank Working Paper 3505. Available at Social Science Research Network: http://ssrn.com/abstract=659122.

———. 2008. "Trade Growth, Production Fragmentation, and China's Environment." National Bureau of Economic Research Working Paper W13860. Available at Social Science Research Network: http://ssrn.com/abstract=1106586.

Decker, Jeffrey L., and Terrence Jalbert. 2003. "An Empirical Analysis of Where Firms Choose to Emit and Corresponding Firm Performance." *Journal of American Academy of Business* (September): 190–96.

DeSombre, Elizabeth R. 2006. *Flagging Standards: Globalization and Environmental, Safety, and Labor Regulations at Sea*. Cambridge, MA: MIT Press.

Deutsche Presse-Agentur. 2006. "China Consumes More Energy Despite 'Green' Policies." *Monsters and Critics*, August 1. www.monstersandcritics.com.

Di, Wenhua. 2004. "Essays in Environmental Economics and Policy." PhD thesis, Harvard University.

Diamond, Jared, and Jianguo Liu. 2005. "China's Environment in a Globalizing World." *Nature* 435 (June): 1179–86.

Donaldson, John A. 2005. "The Political Economy of Local Poverty Reduction: Economic Growth, Poverty Reduction, and the State in Two Chinese Provinces." PhD thesis, George Washington University.

Drezner, Daniel. 2000. "Bottom Feeders." *Foreign Policy* 2000 (November–December): 64–70.

Dunning, John H. 1980. "Toward an Eclectic Theory of International Production: Some Empirical Tests." *Journal of International Business Studies* 11 (1): 9–31.

———. 1988. "The Eclectic Paradigm of International Production: A Restatement and Some Possible Extensions." *Journal of International Business Studies* 19 (1): 1–31.

Economy, Elizabeth. 2004. *The River Runs Black: The Environmental Challenge to China's Future*. Ithaca, NY: Cornell University Press.

———. 2006. "Environmental Governance: The Emerging Economic Dimension." *Environmental Politics* 15 (2): 171–89.

———. 2007a. "Opinion: Green GDP, Accounting for the Environment in China." PBS. *China from the Inside*. www.pbs.org.

———. 2007b. "The Great Leap Backward?" *Foreign Affairs* 86 (5): 38–59.

Energy Compass. 2003. "Chinese Sign Xihu Gas Deal with Unocal, Shell." August 21.

Engel, Kirsten. 1997. "Environmental Standard-setting: Is There a 'Race' and Is It 'to the Bottom'?" *Hastings Law Journal* 48:271.

"Environmental Governance in China." 2006. Special issue, *Environmental Politics* 15 (2).

Eskeland, G. S., and Ann E. Harrison. 2003. "Moving to Greener Pastures? Multinationals and the Pollution Haven Hypothesis." *Journal of Development Economics* 70 (1): 1–23.

Esty, Daniel C. 1994. *Greening the GATT: Trade, Environment, and the Future*. Washington, DC: International Institute for Economics.

———. 1996. "Revitalizing Environmental Federalism." *Michigan Law Review* 95 (3): 570–653.

———. 2001. "Bridging the Trade-environment Divide." *Journal of Economic Perspectives* 13 (3): 113–30.

Esty, Daniel C., and Michael E. Porter. 2001. "Ranking National Environmental Regulation and Performance: A Leading Indicator of Future Competitiveness?" In *The Global Competitiveness Report 2001–2002*. New York: Oxford University Press.

Europa Chemie. 1997. "China Province Attracts Chemical Industry." No. 22/23. August 12.

Falkner, Robert. 2006. "International Sources of Environmental Policy Change in China: The Case of Genetically Modified Food." *Pacific Review* 19:473–94.

Fergusson, James. 2009. "A Brief History of Air-conditioning." *Prospect* 126 (September).

Ferris, Richard J., and Hongjun Zhang. 2003. "Reaching Out to the Rule of Law: China's Continuing Efforts to Develop an Effective Environmental Law Regime." *William and Mary Bill of Rights Journal* 11:569–602.

———. 2005. "Environmental Law in the People's Republic of China." In *China's Environment and the Challenge of Sustainable Development*, ed. Kristen Day. Armonk, NY: M. E. Sharpe.

Florida, Richard. 1996. "Lean and Green: The Move to Environmentally Conscious Manufacturing." *California Management Review* 39 (1): 80–105.

Floyd, Sigmund. 2002. "Cracking the Chemical Sector." *China Business Review*, March/April, 29–39, 47.

Foo, Choy Peng. 1994. "Foreign Chemical Firms Slam Environment Law." *South China Morning Post*, September 22.

Fowler, Robert. 1995. "International Environmental Standards for Transnational Corporations." *Environmental Law* 25:1–30.

Frankel, Jeffrey A. 2005. "The Environment and Economic Globalization." In *Globalization: What's New?* ed. Michael M. Weinstein. New York: Columbia University Press.

Frankel, Jeffrey A., and Andrew K. Rose. 2005. "Is Trade Good or Bad for the Environment? Sorting Out the Causality." *Review of Economics and Statistics* 87 (1): 85–91.

Friedman, Thomas L. 2006. *The World Is Flat: A Brief History of the Twenty-first Century.* New York: Farrar, Straus and Giroux.

Frost, Stephen. 2004. "Chinese Outward Direct Investment in Southeast Asia: How Big Are the Flows and What Does It Mean for the Region." *Pacific Review* 17(3): 323–40.

Fu, Jihong. 2003. "Huagong Yuanqu Zai Zou Kaifaqu de Laolu?" [Are Chemical Parks Following the Same Road as Economic Zones?]. *Zhongguo Jingji Shibao* [China Economic Times], November 3.

Gallagher, Kelly Sims. 2006. *China Shifts Gears: Automakers, Oil, Pollution, and Development.* Cambridge, MA: MIT Press.

Gallagher, Kevin. 2004. *Free Trade and the Environment: Mexico, NAFTA, and Beyond.* Stanford, CA: Stanford University Press.

Gang, He. 2008. "China's New Ministry of Environmental Protection Begins to Bark, but Still Lacks Bite." *China Dialogue,* July 17.

Garcia-Johnson, Ronie. 2000. *Exporting Environmentalism: U.S. Multinational Chemical Corporations in Brazil and Mexico.* Cambridge, MA: MIT Press.

Garrett, Geoffrey. 2001. "Globalization and Government Spending Around the World." *Studies in Comparative International Development* 35 (4): 3–29.

Gelb, Catherine, and Virginia A. Hulme. 2002. "Ensuring Health and Safety in China Operations." *China Business Review,* January/February, 40–45.

Gibbons, Andrea. 2004. "The Poor LDCs in a Global Trade Era." *UN Chronicle* 41 (3): 35–37.

Glen, Dowell, Stuart Hart, and Bernard Yeung. 2000. "Do Corporate Global Environmental Standards Create or Destroy Market Value?" *Management Science* 46 (8): 1059–74.

Gongyi Shibao [China Philanthropy Times]. 2006. "Huanbao Zongju Yi Zhou Nei Foujue 7 Ge Zhongda Touzi Xiangmu" [SEPA Refuses 7 Large Investment Projects in One Week]. February 7.

Granitsas, Alkman. 1999. "Hard Choices." *Far Eastern Economic Review,* March 11.

Grant, Don, and Andrew W. Jones. 2003. "Are Subsidiaries More Prone to Pollute? New Evidence from the EPA's Toxics Release Inventory." *Social Science Quarterly* 84 (1): 162–73.

Greenpeace. 2004. "Investigative Report on APP's Forest Destruction in Yunnan." November 16. Greenpeace China. www.greenpeace.org/china/en.

Grossman, Gene, and Alan Krueger. 1993. "Environmental Impacts of a North American Free Trade Agreement." In *The Mexico-U.S. Free Trade Agreement,* ed. Peter Garber. Cambridge, MA: MIT Press.

Gu, Lixin, and William R. Sheate. 2004. "Institutional Challenges for EIA Implementation in China: A Case Study of Development Versus Environmental Protection." *Environmental Management* 36 (1): 125–42.

Gu, Yao. 2005. "Review of China's PVC Market." *China Chemical Reporter*, April 6.

———. 2007. "Review of China's PVC Market." *China Chemical Reporter*, May 16.

Gu, Zongqin. 2004. "Woguo Huagong Yuanqu de Jianshe he Fazhan" [The Construction and Development of China's Chemical Parks]. *Guoji Shiyou Jingji* [International Petrochemical Economics] 12 (6): 52–55.

Guan, Shitai, and Xinli Song. 2003. "Guanzhu Huagong Yuanqu Wushui Chuli de Jinkou" [Pay Attention to the Imports into Chemical Industrial Park Wastewater Treatment Plants]. *Zhongguo Huagong Bao* [China Chemical News], October 23.

Gunningham, Neil, Robert A. Kagan, and Dorothy Thornton. 2003. *Shades of Green: Business, Regulation, and Environment*. Stanford, CA: Stanford Law and Politics.

Guo, Peiyuan. 2005. "Corporate Environmental Reporting and Disclosure in China." *CSR Asia*, June.

Halkos, George E., and Evangelinos I. Konstantinos. 2002. "Determinants of Environmental Management Standards Implementation: Evidence from Greek Industry." *Business Strategy and the Environment* 11 (November/December): 360–75.

Hall, Derek. 2002. "Environmental Change, Protest, and Havens of Environmental Degradation: Evidence from Asia." *Global Environmental Politics* 2 (2): 20–28.

Hall, Jane V., Duane L. Chapman, William Barron, and Clement A. Tisdell. 1994. "Environmental Problems of Pacific Rim Development." *Contemporary Economic Policy* XII (October): 1–22.

Hall, Rodney, and Thomas J. Bierstecker. 2004. *The Emergence of Private Authority in Global Governance*. Cambridge: Cambridge University Press.

Harrison, Kathryn. 1999. "Racing to the Top or Bottom: Ecolabelling of Paper Products in Canada, Scandinavia, and Europe." *Environmental Politics* 8 (4): 110–36.

———. 2002. "Paper Trails: Environmental Regulation in a Global Economy." Paper presented at the American Political Science Association Annual Conference, Boston, August 29–September 1.

Hartman, Raymond S., Mainiul Huq, and David Wheeler. 1997. "Why Paper Mills Clean Up: Determinants of Pollution Abatement in Four Asian Countries." World Bank Policy Research Paper 1710. Available at Social Science Research Network: http://ssrn.com/abstract=604921.

Harvey, Alexandra. 2008. *The China Price: The True Cost of Chinese Competitive Advantage*. New York: Penguin Press.

He, Xiaoxia. 2003. "Lüse Chanpin Jiance de Fazhi Jianshe" [The Construction of a Legal System for Monitoring Green Products]. *Zhongguo Renkou Ziyuan Yu Huanjing* [China Population, Resources, and Environment] 13 (5): 98–101.

Head, Keith, and John Reis. 1996. "Inter-city Competition for Foreign Investment: Static and Dynamic Effects of China's Incentive Areas." *Journal of Urban Economics* 40:38–60.

Henderson, Vernon J. 1996. "Effects of Air Quality Regulation." *American Economic Review* 86 (4): 789–813.

Henry, Richmond S. 1992. "Saving Hong Kong's Environment." *China Business Review*, September/October, 39–43.

Hernandez, Zenaida. 2004. "Industrial Policy in East Asia: In Search for Lessons." Background paper prepared for World Bank's World Development Report 2005. http://siteresources.worldbank.org.

Hettige, M., Susmita Dasgupta, and David Wheeler. 2004. "What Improves Environmental Compliance? Evidence from Mexican Industry." *Journal of Environmental Economics and Management* 39 (1): 39–66.

Hildebrandt, Timothy, and Jennifer L. Turner. 2002. "Environmental Journalism in China: Event Summary." China Environment Forum, Woodrow Wilson International Center for Scholars. October 18. http://wilsoncenter.org/cef.

Hills, Peter, and William Barron. 1990. "Hong Kong: Can the Dragon Clean Its Nest?" *Environment* 32 (8): 17–20, 39–45.

Ho, Peter, and Eduard B. Vermeer. 2006. "China's Limits to Growth? The Difference Between Absolute, Relative, and Precautionary Limits." *Development and Change* 37 (1): 256–71.

Hoffman, Andrew J. 2000. *Competitive Environmental Strategy: A Guide to the Changing Business Landscape*. Washington, DC: Island Press.

———. 2001. *From Heresy to Dogma: An Institutional History of Corporate Environmentalism*. Stanford, CA: Stanford Business Books.

Hu, Tao, Dongmei Guo, Xiaoyue Shen, and Yuping Wu. 2005. *2005 WTO Yu Shengtai Biaozhi* [The WTO and Environmental Labels]. Beijing: Zhongguo Huanjing Kexue Chubanshe [China Environmental Sciences Press].

Hua, Youbing. 2003. "Zonglun Woguo Shiyou Huagong Hangye Fazhan Fanshi" [Discussion on the Developing Paradigm in the Petrochemical Industry in China]. *Dangdai Shiyou Huagong* [Modern Petrochemicals] 11 (2): 33–36.

Huang, Cun. 2003. "Rang Huagong Yuanqu Dabu Kuaru Shijie Chaoliu" [Let Chemical Industrial Parks Take a Big Step into the Global Wave]. *Zhongguo Huagong Bao* [China Chemical News], October 27.

Huang, Yasheng. 2003a. "One Country, Two Systems: Foreign-invested Enterprises and Domestic Firms in China." *China Economic Review* 14:404–16.

———. 2003b. *Selling China: Foreign Direct Investment During the Reform Era*. New York: Cambridge University Press.

Human Rights Watch. 2006. "A Great Danger for Lawyers: New Regulatory Curbs on Lawyers Representing Protesters." *Human Rights Watch Report*, December.

Hutson, Andrew M. 2004. "Diffusion of Environmental Practices Through Value Chain Relationships in the United States and Mexico." Paper prepared for the 26th Annual Research Conference of the Association for Public Policy and Management, Atlanta, GA, October 29.

Jaffe, Adam B., Steven R. Peterson, Paul R. Portney, and Robert N. Stavins. 1995. "Environmental Regulation and the Competitiveness of U.S. Manufacturing: What Does the Evidence Tell Us?" *Journal of Economic Literature* 33 (1): 132–63.

Jahiel, Abigail R. 1998. "The Organization of Environmental Protection in China." *China Quarterly* 156:757–86.

———. 2006. "China, the WTO, and Implications for the Environment." *Environmental Politics* 15 (2): 310–29.

Javorcik, Beata Smarzynska, and Shang-jin Wei. 2004. "Pollution Havens and Foreign Direct Investment: Dirty Secret or Popular Myth?" *Contributions to Economic Analysis & Policy* 3 (2): 1–32.

Jian, Cheng. 2002. "Jiekai Jiazhuang Jiancai 'Lüse Zhapian' de Miansha" [Remove the Veil of "Green Fraud" in the Home Building Materials Sector]. *Jingli Ribao* [Managers Daily], August 20.

Jiang, Jingjing, and Chuan Qin. 2005. "Paper Plant Starts Production amid Outcry." *China Daily*, March 28.

Jiang, Taiping. 2000. "Riben Huanjing Zhengce de Bianqian Ji Dui Zhong-Ri Maoyi de Yingxiang" [Changes in Japan's Environmental Policies and the Influence on Sino-Japanese Trade]. *Yatai Jingji* [Asia-Pacific Economics] 4:75–76.

Jiang, Tingsong, and Warwick J. McKibben. 2002. "Assessment of China's Pollution Levy System: An Equilibrium Pollution Approach." *Environment and Development Economics* 7:75–105.

Jiang, Wenran. 2006. "China's Booming Energy Relations with Africa." *Jamestown Foundation China Brief* 6 (13).

Jiangsu Statistical Bureau. 2004. *Jiangsu Tongji Nianjian* [Jiangsu Province Statistical Yearbook]. Beijing: Zhongguo Tongji Chubanshe [China Statistics Press].

Jing, Jun. 2000. "Environmental Protests in Rural China." In *Chinese Society: Change, Conflict, and Resistance*, ed. Elizabeth J. Perry and Mark Selden. London: Routledge.

Johnston, Alastair Iain. 1998. "China and International Environmental Institutions." In *Energizing China: Reconciling Environmental Protection and Economic Growth*, ed. Michael B. McElroy, Chris P. Nielsen, and Peter Lydon. Cambridge, MA: Harvard University Committee on Environment.

Kamieniecki, Sheldon. 2006. *Corporate America and Environmental Policy: How Often Does Business Get Its Way?* Stanford, CA: Stanford University Press.

Kellher, Macabe. 2002. "Exporting a Problem." *Far Eastern Economic Review*, December 12.

Kennedy, Scott. 2007. "Transnational Political Alliances: An Exploration with Evidence from China." *Business & Society* 46 (2): 174–200.

Kennelly, James J., and Eric E. Lewis. 2005. "Degree of Internationalization and Corporate Environmental Performance." *International Journal of Management* 19 (3): 478–89.

Kim, Sunhyuk. 2000. "Democratization and Environmentalism: South Korea and Taiwan in Comparative Perspective." *Journal of Asian and African Studies (JAAS)* 35 (3): 287–303.

King, Gary, Micahel Tomz, and Jason Wittenberg. 2000. "Making the Most of Statistical Analysis: Improving Interpretation and Presentation." *American Journal of Political Science* 44:347–61.

Kirk, Brandon. 2007. "China's Environment: From Compliance to Best Practice." *China Law & Practice*, April.

Klee, Julia Epley, and Felicity C. Thomas. 1997. "An Evolving Environmental Framework." *China Business Review*, January/February, 34–40.

Klevorick, Alvin. 1996. "The Race to the Bottom in a Federal System: Lessons from the World of Trade Policy." Symposium issue, *Yale Law and Policy Review/Yale Journal on Regulation*, 14 (2): 177–86.

Konisky, David M. 2006. "Do States Race to the Bottom? Perceptions of State Environmental Regulators." Paper presented at the Midwest Political Science Conference, Annual Meeting, Chicago.

———. 2007. "Regulatory Competition and Environmental Enforcement: Is There a Race to the Bottom?" *American Journal of Political Science* 51 (4): 853–72.

Lague, David. 2001. "A Way Out of the Mire." *Far Eastern Economic Review*, May 3.

———. 2006. "Corruption Is Linked to Pollution in China." *New York Times*, August 24.

Lam, K. C. 1986. "Environmental Protection in the Shenzhen Special Economic Zone: Achievements, Problems, and Implications." In *China's Special Economic Zones: Policies, Problems, and Prospects*, ed. Y. C. Jao and C. K. Leung. Oxford: Oxford University Press.

Legal Studies Department of China's People's University. 1992–. *Zhongguo Shenpan Anli Yaolan* [Overview of Important Judgments and Cases in China]. Beijing: Zhongguo Renmin Daxue Chubanshe [Renmin University Press].

Lei, Peng, Baijin Long, and Pamlin Dennis. 2005. "Chinese Companies in the 21st Century." WWF's Trade and Investment Programme.

Leonard, H. Jeffrey. 1984. *Are Environmental Regulations Driving U.S. Industry Overseas?* Washington, DC: Conservation Foundation.

———. 1988. *Pollution and the Struggle for the World Product: Multinational Corporations, Environment, and International Comparative Advantage*. Cambridge: Cambridge University Press.

Levinson, Arik. 1996. "Environmental Regulations and Industry Location: International and Domestic Evidence." In *Fair Trade and Harmonization: Prerequisites for Free Trade*. Vol. 1, *Economic Analysis*, ed. Jagdish Bhagwati and Robert E. Hudic. Cambridge, MA: MIT Press.

Li, Fugui, Bing Xiong, and Bing Xu. 2008. "Improving Public Access to Environmental Information in China." *Journal of Environmental Management* 88:1649–56.

Li, Jing. 2008a. "Arming Up in the Battle for a Greener Future." *China Daily*, March 28.

———. 2008b. "Environment Ministry Adds 2 Departments." *China Daily*, July 11.

Li, Xiaopeng. 2005. "Qujiang Shenjia Huagong Yuanqu Huanjing Baohu Bu Hao Guanjian Shi Lingdao Mei Juexin" [The Key Reason for the Poor Environment in the Qu River Shenjia Chemical Park Is Leaders Lack Determination]. *Zhejiang Ribao* [Zhejiang Daily], June 15.

Li, Zhiping. 2000. "Jiaru WTO Hou Woguo Kongzhi Waiguo Wuran Zhuanyi Falü Duice de Tiaozheng Yu Wanshan" [The Adjustment and Perfection of Legal Countermeasures to Control the Transfer of Foreign Pollution After China's Entrance into the WTO]. *Fazhi Yu Guanli* [Law and Administration] 12:6–7.

———. 2005. "The Challenges of China's Discharge Permit System and Effective Solutions." *Temple Journal of Science, Technology, and Environmental Law* 24 (1): 375–95.

Lieberthal, Kenneth. 1995. *Governing China: From Revolution Through Reform*. New York: W. W. Norton.

Lin, Catherine K., Linan Yan, and Andrew N. Davis. 2002. "Globalization, Extended Producer Responsibility and the Problem of Discarded Computers in China: An Exploratory Proposal for Environmental Protection." *Georgetown International Environmental Law Review* 14:525.

Lin, Gu. 2005. "China Improves Enforcement of Environmental Laws." *Xinhua, China Features*, September 29. http://uk.chineseembassy.org.

Lin, Michael (president's office manager, Formosa Plastics). 2005. "Experience Sharing of RC Implementation." Presentation materials from China Responsible Care Conference, breakout session one, Beijing, June 14.

Lin, Shuwen Jolene. 2004. "Assessing the Dragon's Choice: The Use of Market-based Instruments in Chinese Environmental Policy." *Georgetown International Environmental Law Review* 617 (Summer).

Liu, Chailing, Bin Zhu, and Jun Liao. 2004. "Mangmu Jianshe Chengwei Yuanqu Fazhan de Yintong" [Blind Construction Has Become Industrial Park Development's Secret Anguish]. Xinhua, part of the series entitled "Huagong Yuanqu Shifo Hui Chongdao 'Jingkaiqu' Fuzhe?" [Are Chemical Parks Following the Disastrous Road of the "Economic Development Zones"?]. www.cq.xinhuanet.com.

Liu, Fangbin. 2003. "Tese—Huagong Yuanqu de Hexin Jingzhengli" [Distinguishing Features—the Core Competitive Strength of Chemical Parks]. *Zhongguo Huagong Bao* [China Chemical News], October 27.

Liu, Jiangqing. 2007. "At the Centre of China's Environmental Storm: Interview with 'Hurricane Pan.'" *Nanfang Zhoumo* [Southern Weekend], January 23. http://english.cbcsd.org.cn/news/news/5022.shtml.

Liu, Jinguo, and Guohua Sun. 2005. "Gao Hao Neng Chanye Xiang He Chu Qu?" [What Is the Direction for Energy-intensive Industries?]. *Guoji Shangbao* [International Commerce], March 31.

Liu, Shixin. 2005. "Yunnan Senlin Weiji Ji Bian Yunnan Sheng Cheng Fa Lin Zhe Duo Shi Dangdi Baixing" [The Fierce Argument on the Crisis in Yunnan's Forests: Yunnan Province States Those Felling the Trees Are Mostly Local Citizens]. *Zhongguo Qingnian Bao* [China Youth News], February 23.

Liu, Yingling. 2007. "China's Coastal Pollution Necessitates Rethinking Government Role." *Worldwatch Institute, China Watch*, November 8. www.worldwatch.org.

Liu, Yuqi. 1997. "Tigao Liyong Waizi Shuiping Jiakuai Huaxue Gongye Fazhan" [Improve the Level of Foreign Investment and Increase the Speed of Chemical Industry's Development]. *Zhongguo Touzi Yu Jianshe* [China Investment and Construction], September: 21–22.

Ljungwall, Christer, and Martin Linde-Rahr. 2005. "Environmental Policy and the Location of Foreign Direct Investment in China." East Asian Bureau of Economic

Research, China Center for Economic Research Working Paper E2005009. www .eaber.org.

Lo, Carlos Wing-Hung, Shui-yan Tang, and Shek-Kiu Chan. 1997. "The Political Economy of EIA in Guangzhou." *Environmental Impact Assessment Review* 17:371–82.

Lo, Carlos Wing-Hung, and Plato Kwong-To Yip. 1999. "Environmental Impact Assessment in Hong Kong and Shanghai: A Cross-city Analysis." *Journal of Environmental Planning and Management* 42 (3): 355–74.

Low, Patrick, and Alexander Yeats. 1992. "Do 'Dirty' Industries Migrate?" In *International Trade and the Environment*, ed. Patrick Low. Washington, DC: World Bank.

Lu, Yiyi. 2007. "Environmental Civil Society and Governance in China." *International Journal of Environmental Studies* 64 (1): 59–69.

Luken, Ralph A., and Casper van de Tak. 2002. "Industrial Environmental Management and the WTO Rules: The Case of China." In *China in the WTO: The Birth of a New Catching-up Strategy*, ed. Carlos A. Magariänos, Yongtu Long, and Francisco Colman Sercovich. Houndmills, UK: Palgrave Macmillan.

Lyons, David. 2005. "Environmental Protection in Taiwan: Is It Too Much Too Fast?" *Journal of Contemporary Asia* 35 (2): 183–94.

Ma, Changbo, and Nan Xu. 2006. "Kuaguo Gongsi Zai Hua Wuran Diaocha" [An Investigation of Multinational Corporations' Pollution in China]. *Nanfang Zhoumo* [Southern Weekend], October 26.

Ma, Xiaoying, and Leonard Ortolano. 2000. *Environmental Regulation in China: Institutions, Enforcement, and Compliance*. Lanham, MD: Rowman & Littlefield.

Mabey, Nick, Richard McNally, and Lyuba Zarsky. 2003. "Foreign Direct Investment and the Environment: From Pollution Havens to Sustainable Development." Surrey, UK: World Wide Fund for Nature, United Kingdom.

Man, Thomas Y., Yan Zeng, and Jing Jean Sun. 2008. "Foreign Investment Industry Catalogue: New Revisions & Alignment with National Development Strategy." *China Law & Practice*, December/January.

Mani, Muthukumara, S. Pargal, and M. Huq. 1997. "Does Environmental Regulation Matter: Determinants of the Location of New Manufacturing Plants in India in 1994." World Bank Working Paper 1718. Available at Social Science Research Network: http://ssrn.com/abstract=614970.

Mani, Muthukumara, and David Wheeler. 1997. "In Search of Pollution Havens: Dirty Industry in the World Economy, 1960–1995." *Journal of Environment & Development* 7 (3): 215–47.

Martens, Susan. 2006. "Public Participation with Chinese Characteristics: Citizen Consumers in China's Environmental Management." *Environmental Politics* 15 (2): 211–30.

Matthew, Ed. 2001. "Asia Pulp and Paper: Briefing." Friends of the Earth. June 22. www.foe.co.uk.

McElwee, Charles R. 2008. "Who's Cleaning Up This Mess?" *China Business Review*, January/February, 20–23, 45.

McGregor, Richard. 2006. "China Defends Its Expansion into Africa." *Financial Times*, October 26.

Mitamura, Hose, ed. 2008. *China's Environment 2008*. Hong Kong: China Economic Review Publishing.

Mock, Elizabeth. 1998. "Interstate Competition for Jobs and Industry Through Laxity of Environmental Regulations: Pennsylvania's Response and the Effects." *Dickinson Journal of Environmental Law and Policy* 7:263.

MOFTEC (Ministry of Foreign Trade and Economic Cooperation). 1991. *Guanyu Cong Yan Shenpi Liyong Waizi Juban Jinkou Feijiu Jinshu Jiagong Fuchukou Xiangmu de Tongzhi* [Notice Concerning the Strict Approval for the Reprocessing of Imported Waste Metals for Export]. October 5. www.chinalawinfo.com.

Moore, Allison, and Adrian Warren. 2006. "Legal Advocacy in Environmental Public Participation in China: Raising the Stakes and Strengthening the Stakeholder." *China Environment Forum* 8:3–25.

Morrison, Wayne M. 2006. "China's Economic Conditions." Congressional Research Service (CRS) Issue Brief for Congress. Order code IB98014. May 15.

Morton, Katherine. 2005. *International Aid and China's Environment: Taming the Yellow Dragon*. New York: Routledge.

Mosley, Layna, and Saika Uno. 2007. "Racing to the Bottom or Climbing to the Top? Economic Globalization and Collective Labor Rights." *Comparative Political Studies* 40 (8): 923–48.

Nagle, John Copeland. 1996. "The Missing Chinese Environmental Law Statutory Interpretation Cases." *New York University Environmental Law Journal* 5:517.

National Bureau of Statistics. 1994–2004. *Zhongguo Duiwai Jingji Tongi Nianjian* [China Foreign Economic Statistical Yearbook]. Beijing: Zhongguo Tongji Chubanshe [China Statistics Press].

Natural Resources Defense Council. 2006. "Submission to UNEP in Response to March 2006 Request for Information on Mercury Supply, Demand, and Trade." United Nations Environment Programme, Division of Technology, Industry, and Economics, Chemicals Branch. May 5. www.chem.unep.ch (under Mercury programme; Publications).

NEPA (National Environmental Protection Administration). 1988. *Guanyu Jianshe Xiangmu Huanjing Baohu Guanli Wenti De Ruogan Yijian* [Some Opinions Concerning the Environmental Management of Construction Projects]. March 21. http://law.baidu.com.

——. 1989. *Jianshe Xiangmu Huanjing Yingxiang Xiang Pingjia Zhengshu Guanli Banfa* [Administrative Measures for the Certification of Construction Project Environmental Impact Assessments]. September 2. http://law.baidu.com.

——. 1993. *Guanyu Jin Yi Bu Zuohao Jianshe Xiangmu Huanjing Baohu Guanli Gongzuo de Jidian Yijian* [A Few Opinions on Making Progress in the Work of Administering the Environmental Protection of Construction Enterprises]. January 11. www.chinalawinfo.com.

——. 1994. *Huaxue Pin Shouci Jinkou Ji You Du Huaxue Pin Jinchukou Huanjing*

Guanli Guiding [Regulations for Environmental Management on the First Import of Chemicals and the Import and Export of Toxic Chemicals]. Promulgated by Order No. 140 of the National Environmental Protection Agency, the General Administration of Customs, and the Ministry of Foreign Trade and Economic Cooperation. March 16. www.chinalawinfo.com.

———. 1995. *Huaxue Pin Shouci Jinkou Ji You Du Huaxue Pin Jinchukou Huanjing Guanli Dengji Shishi Xice* [Detailed Guidelines for the Registration of First Import Chemicals and Hazardous Chemical Imports and Exports]. February 16. www.chinalawinfo.com.

NEPA (National Environmental Protection Administration), and MOFERT (Ministry of Foreign Economic Relations and Trade). 1992. *Guanyu Jiaqiang Waishang Touzi Jianshe Xiangmu Huanjing Baohu Guanli de Tongzhi* [Notice on Strengthening the Environmental Management in Foreign Investment Construction Projects]. March 14. www.chinalawinfo.com.

Neumayer, Eric. 2001a. "Do Countries Fail to Raise Environmental Standards? An Evaluation of Policy Options Addressing 'Regulatory Chill.'" *International Journal of Sustainable Development* 4 (3): 231–44.

———. 2001b. *Greening Trade and Investment: Environmental Protection Without Protectionism.* London: Earthscan Publications.

———. 2001c. "Pollution Havens: An Analysis of Policy Options for Dealing with an Elusive Phenomenon." *Journal of Environment & Development* 10 (2): 147–77.

Niu, Hongyi, and Qunhe Wu. 2005. "Woguo Huanjing Yingxiang Pingjia Fazhan Xin Dongxiang" [New Directions in the Development of China's Environmental Impact Assessment System]. *Huanjing Kexue Dongtai* [Environmental Science Trends] (1): 48–50.

Niu, Xiaoqing. 2002. "Ruyuan Menkan Di, Huanbao Yishi Cha, Shenjia Huagong Yuanqu Huanjing Zhuangkuang Kanyou" [Park Admission Threshold Low, Environmental Awareness Low, Shenjia Chemical Park Environmental Situation Cause for Worry]. *Zhongguo Huagong Bao* [China Chemical News], July 5.

NPC (National People's Congress). 1979a. *Zhonghua Renmin Gongheguo Zhongwai Hezi Jingying Qiye Fa* [Law of the People's Republic of China on Chinese-Foreign Equity Joint Ventures]. Adopted at the Second Session of the Fifth National People's Congress. July 1. www.lawinfochina.com.

———. 1979b. *Zhonghua Renmin Gongheguo Huanjing Baohu Fa (Shixing)* [The People's Republic of China Environmental Protection Law (Trial)]. Approved in principle at the Eleventh Meeting of the Standing Committee of the Fifth National People's Congress, Standing Order No. 2. September 13. http://law.baidu.com.

———. 1986a. *Zhonghua Renmin Gongheguo Minfa Tongze* [General Principles of the Civil Law of the People's Republic of China]. Adopted at the Fourth Session of the Sixth National People's Congress and promulgated by Order No. 37 of the President of the People's Republic of China. April 12. www.lawinfochina.com.

———. 1986b. *Zhonghua Renmin Gongheguo Waizi Qiye Fa* [Law of the People's Republic of China on Foreign Capital Enterprises]. Adopted at the Fourth Session of the Sixth National People's Congress and promulgated by Order No. 39 of the President of the People's Republic of China. April 12. www.lawinfochina.com.

———. 1989. *Zhonghua Renmin Gongheguo Huanjing Baohu Fa* [Environmental Protection Law of the People's Republic of China]. Adopted at the Eleventh Meeting of the Standing Committee of the Seventh National People's Congress. December 26. http://english.mep.gov.cn.

———. 1997. *Zhonghua Renmin Gongheguo Xingfa* [Criminal Law of the People's Republic of China]. Adopted at the Second Session of the Fifth National People's Congress on July 1, 1979. Revised at the Fifth Session of the Eighth National People's Congress. March 14. www.lawinfochina.com.

———. 2002. *Zhonghua Renmin Gongheguo Huanjing Yingxiang Pingjia Fa* [Environmental Impact Assessment Law of the People's Republic of China]. Adopted at the Thirtieth Session of the Standing Committee of the Ninth National People's Congress and promulgated by Presidential Decree No. 77 of the People's Republic of China. October 28. www.sepa.gov.cn/law.

Oates, Wallace E. 2001. "A Reconsideration of Environmental Federalism." Discussion Paper 01-54, Resources for the Future. www.rff.org.

Oates, Wallace E., and Robert M. Schwab. 1988. "Economic Competition Among Jurisdictions: Efficiency-enhancing or Distortion-inducing?" *Journal of Public Economics* 35:333–54.

Palan, Ronen, Jason Abbott, and Phil Deans. 1996. *State Strategies in the Global Political Economy*. London: Pinter.

Palmer, Michael. 1998. "Environmental Regulation in the People's Republic of China: The Face of Domestic Law." *China Quarterly* 156:788–808.

Palmisano, Samuel J. 2006. "The Globally Integrated Enterprise." *Foreign Affairs* 85 (3): 127–36.

Pan, Derun, ed. 2004. *Zhongguo Huagong Yuanqu Gailan* [An Overview of China Chemical Industry Parks]. Beijing: China Petroleum and Chemical Industry Association.

Pan, Yigang. 1996. "Influences on Foreign Equity Ownership Levels in Joint Ventures in China." *Journal of International Business Studies* 27 (1): 1–26.

Panayotou, Theodore. 1998. "The Effectiveness and Efficiency of Environmental Policy in China." In *Energizing China: Reconciling Environmental Protection and Economic Growth*, ed. Michael B. McElroy, Chris P. Nielsen, and Peter Lydon. Cambridge, MA: Harvard University Committee on Environment.

———. 2000. "Globalization and Environment." Harvard Center for International Development Working Paper No. 53. www.hks.harvard.edu.

Paoletto, Glen, and Cindy Termorshuizen. 2003. "Chemical Governance in East Asia." In *East Asian Experience in Environmental Governance: Response in a Rapidly Developing Region*, ed. Zafar Adeel. Tokyo: UN Press.

Pasong, Suparb, and Louis Lebel. 2000. "Political Transformation and the Environment in Southeast Asia." *Environment* 42 (8): 8–19.

Pearson, Charles S. 1987. *Multinational Corporations, Environment, and the Third World*. Durham, NC: Duke University Press.

Pei, Minxin. 2007. "Corruption Threatens China's Future." Carnegie Endowment for International Peace Policy Brief No. 55. October: 1–8.

Pence, George. 2001. "Hook, Line, and Stinker." *Business Week*, July 23. www .businessweek.com.

Peng, Yanjun, and Zhihui Zhang. 2004. "Jingji Quanqiuhua Dui Woguo Gongye Wuran de Yingxiang" [The Influence of Economic Globalization on China's Industrial Pollution]. *Zhongguo Renkou Ziyuan Yu Huanjing* [China Population, Resources, and Environment] 15 (3): 43–49.

People's Daily. 2006. "Multinational Corporations in China Blacklisted for Pollution." November 1. http://english.peopledaily.com.cn.

Perkins, Richard. 2007. "Globalizing Corporate Environmentalism? Convergence and Heterogeneity in Indian Industry." *Studies in Comparative International Development* 42: 279–309.

Perlez, Jane. 2006. "Forests in Southeast Asia Fall to Prosperity's Ax." *New York Times*, April 29.

Porter, Gareth. 1999. "Trade Competition and Pollution Standards 'Race to the Bottom' or 'Stuck at the Bottom'?" *Journal of Environment & Development* 8 (2): 133–51.

Post, Diahnna. 2004. "Closing the Deception Gap: Accession to the European Union and Environmental Standards in Europe." In *Dynamics of Regulatory Change: How Globalization Affects National Regulatory Policies*, ed. David Vogel and Robert A. Kagan. Berkeley: University of California Press.

Pottinger, Matt, Steven Stecklow, and John J. Fialka. 2004. "China's Energy Appetite Poses a Pollution Threat with World-wide Scope." *Asian Wall Street Journal*, December 17.

Prakash, Aseem. 2000. *Greening the Firm: The Politics of Corporate Environmentalism*. Cambridge: Cambridge University Press.

Prakash, Aseem, and Matthew Potoski. 2006. "Racing to the Bottom? Trade, Environmental Governance, and ISO 14001." *American Journal of Political Science* 50 (3): 350–64.

Price, Lynn, Xuejun Wang, and Jiang Yun. 2009. In Press, Corrected Proof. "The Challenge of Reducing Energy Consumption of the Top-1000 Largest Industrial Enterprises in China." *Energy Policy*. www.sciencedirect.com.

Profaizer, Joseph R. 1993. "Economic Development and Environmental Law in China's Special Economic Zones." *Texas International Law Journal* 28: 319–355.

Pu, Guangzhu, Dinghui Liu, and Ma Pinyi. 2002. *Huanjing Fa Yu Huanjing Zhifa* [Environmental Law and Implementation]. Beijing: Zhongguo Huanjing Kexue Chubanshe [China Environmental Sciences Press].

Qiu, Zhao, Jiaquan Wang, and Ling Yi. 2005. "Zhongguo Zhengfu Gaodu Guanzhu Yinni Jinguang Jituan Yunnan Da Hui Lin Shijian [The Chinese Government Pays High-level Attention to Indonesia's APP Group and the Incident of Forest Destruction of Yunnan]." Xinhua, January 18.

Quzhou Municipal Government. 2005. "Shenjia Huagong Yuanqu Liangnian Nei

Huagong Qiye Quanbu Chechu" [All Chemical Enterprises in Shenjia Chemical Industrial Park Will Leave in Two Years]. December 28. www.qz.gov.cn.

Reardon-Anderson, James. 1992. *Pollution, Politics, and Foreign Investment in Taiwan: The Lukang Rebellion.* Armonk, NY: M. E. Sharpe.

Reuters, 1995. "China Sichuan to Invest 21 Bln Yuan in Chemicals."

———. 2005. "China Says Environmental Spending Falls Short." March 5.

———. 2006a. "China FDI Exceeds $60B in '05." January 13.

———. 2006b. "China Suffers Successive Spills." September 11.

———. 2007. "China to Fund Pollution Checks." March 4.

Revesz, Richard. 1992. "Rehabilitating Interstate Competition: Rethinking the 'Race to the Bottom' Rationale for Federal Environmental Regulation." *New York University Law Review* 67:1210.

———. 1997. "The 'Race to the Bottom' and Federal Environmental Regulation: A Response to Critics." *Minnesota Law Review* 82:535–64.

———. 2001. "Federalism and Environmental Regulation: A Public Choice Perspective." *Harvard Law Review* 115:555.

Richardson, Benjamin. 2004a. "Is East Asia Industrializing Too Quickly? Environmental Regulation in Its Special Economic Zones." *UCLA Pacific Basin Law Journal* 22 (Fall): 150–244.

———. 2004b. "Uneven Modernization: Environmental Regulation in China's Special Economic Areas." *Asia Pacific Law Review* 12 (2): 115–42.

Roberts, Dexter. 2003. "The Greening of China." *Business Week*, October 27.

Roberts, Michael. 1995. "Companies Begin Negotiations." *Chemical Week*, August 30.

Rock, Michael T. 2002. *Pollution Control in East Asia: Lessons from the Newly Industrializing Economies.* Washington, DC: Resources for the Future.

Rosen, Daniel H. 1999. *Behind the Open Door: Foreign Enterprises in the Chinese Marketplace.* Washington, DC: Institute for International Economics.

Rosenberg, Erika, and Vero Mischenko. 2002. "Conflicts over Transnational Oil and Gas Development off Sakhalin Island in the Russian Far East: A David and Goliath Story." In *Human Rights and the Environment: Conflicts and Norms in a Globalizing World*, ed. Lyuba Zarsky. London: Earthscan.

Ross, Lester. 1994. "The Next Wave of Environmental Legislation." *China Business Review*, July/August, 30–33.

———. 1998. "Patterns of Participation in Regimes and Compliance with International Norms." *China Quarterly* 156: 809–35.

Ross, Lester, Weixue Cheng, Mitchell A. Silk, and Yi Wang. 1990. "Cracking Down on Polluters." *China Business Review*, July/August, 38–43.

Ross, Lester, and Mitchell A. Silk. 1997. "Environmental Planning for Investment Projects in China." In *Doing Business in China*, ed. W. P. Streng and A. D. Wilcox. Huntington, NY: Juris Publishing.

Runnalls, David, Ruqiu Ye, Konrad von Moltke, and Wanhua Yang. 2002. *Trade and Sustainability: Challenges and Opportunities for China as a WTO Member.* Task Force on WTO and Environment, China Council for International Cooperation on Environment and Development. Winnipeg, Canada: International Institute for Sustainable Development. www.iisd.org.

Ruud, Audun. 2002. "Environmental Management of Transnational Corporations in India—Are TNCs Creating Islands of Excellence in a Sea of Dirt?" *Business Strategy and the Environment* 11 (2): 103–118.

Saich, Tony. 2001. *Governance and Politics of China*. Houndmills, UK: Palgrave.

Sanyal, Rajib N., and Turgut Guvenli. 2000. "Relations Between Multinational Firms and Host Governments: The Experience of American-owned Firms in China." *International Business Review* 9:119–34.

Savadove, Bill. 2005. "Villagers Seize Plant Accused of Poisoning." *South China Morning Post*, July 1.

Sax, David. 2004. "A Hungry Dragon." *Canadian Business* 78 (1): 27–28.

Schwartz, Jonathan. 2003. "The Impact of State Capacity on Enforcement of Environmental Policies: The Case of China." *Journal of Environment & Development* 12 (1): 50–81.

SEPA (State Environmental Protection Administration). 1998–2004. *Zhongguo Huanjing Tongji Nianbao* [China Environmental Statistical Yearbook]. Beijing: State Environmental Protection Administration.

———. 1999. *Jianshe Xiangmu Huanjing Yingxiang Xiang Pingjia Zhengshu Guanli Banfa* [Administrative Measures for the Certification of Construction Project Environmental Impact Assessments]. Approved by the SEPA Finance Bureau and promulgated by Order No. 2. March 17. www.chinalawinfo.com.

———. 2004a. *Huanjing Baohu Xingzheng Zhifa Shouce* [Enforcement Handbook of Environmental Protection Administration]. Ed. Guojia Huanjing Baohu Ju Zhengce Fagui Si [SEPA Department of Policies, Laws, and Regulations]. Beijing: Huaxue Gongye Chubanshe [Chemical Industry Press].

———. 2004b. *Huanjing Yingxiang Pingjia Biaozhun Huibian* [Compilation of Environmental Impact Assessment Standards]. Ed. Guojia Huanjing Baohu Ju Keji Biaozhun Si [SEPA Department of Technical Standards]. Beijing: Zhongguo Huanjing Kexue Chubanshe [China Environmental Sciences Press].

———. 2005. *Jianshe Xiangmu Huanjing Yingxiang Xiang Pingjia Zizhi Guanli Banfa* [Administrative Measures for the Certification of Construction Project Environmental Impact Assessments]. Approved by the SEPA Finance Bureau and promulgated by Order No. 26. July 21. www.chinalawinfo.com.

———. 2006. "Full Text of White Paper on Environmental Protection in China, 1996–2005." Xinhua, June 5.

———. 2007. *Huanjing Xinxi Gongkai Banfa (Shixing)* [Measures on Open Environmental Information (for Trial Implementation)]. February 8. www.zhb.gov.cn.

———. 2008. *Guanyu Jiaqiang Shangshi Gongsi Huanjing Baohu Jiandu Guanli Gongzuo De Zhidao Yijian* [Guiding Opinions on Strengthening the Supervision and Management of Environmental Protection of Listed Companies]. Promulgated by State Environment Protection Administration Decree No. 24. February 22. www.mep.gov.cn.

Seymour, Mike. 2004. "Partnerships to Support Sustainable Development and Conservation: The West-East Pipeline Project, China." *Conservation Biology* 18 (3): 613–15.

Seymour, Mike, Marilyn Beach, and Steve Laister. 2005. "The Challenge of Positive Influence: Managing Sustainable Development in the West-East Pipeline." *China Environment Series* 7:1–15.

SFA (State Forestry Administration). 2005. *Guojia Linyeju Guanyu Jinguang Zhiye (Zhongguo) Touzi Youxian Gongsi Zai Yunnan Sheng Zao Yuan Cailiao You Guan Wenti De Tongzhi* [State Forestry Adminstration's Notice Concerning Problems with the Creation of Raw Materials in Yunnan and APP China]. January 7. Originally posted to www.zjhotels.org; no longer available online.

Shapiro, Judith. 2001. *Mao's War Against Nature: Politics and the Environment in Revolutionary China*. Cambridge: Cambridge University Press.

Shi, Han, and Lei Zhang. 2006. "China's Environmental Governance of Rapid Industrialization." *Environmental Politics* 15 (2): 271–92.

Shi, Jiangtao. 2005a. "Claws Out as Watchdog Flexes Green Muscles." *South China Morning Post*, April 12.

———. 2005b. "Pollution in Cities and Seas the Toughest Clean-up Task." *South China Morning Post*, June 3.

Sitaraman, Srini. 2007. "Regulating the Belching Dragon: Rule of Law, Politics of Enforcement, and Pollution Prevention in Post-Mao Industrial China." *Colorado Journal of International Environmental Law and Policy* 18 (2): 267–335.

Smil, Vaclav. 1993. *China's Environmental Crisis: An Inquiry into the Limits of National Development*. Armonk, NY: M. E. Sharpe.

Smiley, Robert A., and Harold L. Jackson. 2002. *Chemistry and the Chemical Industry: A Practical Guide for Non-chemists*. Boca Raton, FL: CRC Press.

Song, Shutao. 2008. "South China Province Blacklists Heavy Polluters." Xinhua, February 23.

Spar, Debora L., and David B. Yoffie. 2000. "A Race to the Bottom or Governance from the Top?" In *Coping with Globalization*, ed. Aseem Prakash and Jeffrey A. Hart. London: Routledge.

Spencer, Richard. 2007. "China's Green Audit Put on Hold." *Telegraph*, July 23.

Stalley, Phillip. 2009. "Can Trade Green China?" *Journal of Contemporary China* 18 (61): 567–90.

State Council. 1982. *Zhengshou Paiwu Fei Zanxing Banfa* [Temporary Measures for the Pollution Levy Fees]. February 5. http://law.baidu.com.

———. 1983a. *Zhongwai Hezi Jingying Qiye Fa Shishi Tiaoli* [Implementing Regulations for the Chinese-Foreign Equity Joint Ventures Law]. September 20. www.chinalawinfo.com.

———. 1983b. *Guowuyuan Guanyu Jiaqiang Liyong Waizi Gongzuo De Zhishi* [State Council Directive on Work Related to Enhancing the Use of Foreign Capital]. September 3. http://law.baidu.com.

———.1986. *Duiwai Jingji Kaifang Diqu Huanjing Guanli Zanxing Guiding* [Temporary Regulations on Environmental Management in Economic Development Zones].

Approved by the State Council on March 4 and promulgated by the National Environmental Protection Administration on March 15. www.lawinfochina.com.

——. 1990. *Zhonghua Renmin Gongheguo Waizi Qiye Fa Shishi Xize* [Detailed Rules for the Implementation of the Law of the People's Republic of China on Wholly Foreign-owned Enterprises]. Approved by the State Council on October 28 and promulgated by the Ministry of Foreign Economic Relations and Trade on September 12. www.lawinfochina.com.

——. 1993. *Guanyu Jin Yi Bu Jianqiang Waishang Touzi Guanli Gongzuo Ruogan Wenti de Tongzhi* [Notice Concerning Some Problems in Making Strides Toward Enhancing the Management of Foreign Investment]. Promulgated by Decree No. 83. December 6. www.chinalawinfo.com.

——. 1995a. *Waishang Touzi Chanye Zhidao Mulu* [Catalogue for the Guidance of Foreign Investment Industries]. Approved by the State Council on June 7 and promulgated by Decree No. 5 of the State Planning Commission, the State Economic and Trade Commission, and the Ministry of Foreign Trade and Economic Cooperation on June 20. www.chinalawinfo.com.

——. 1995b. *Zhidao Waishang Touzi Fangxiang Guiding* [Provisions on Guiding the Orientation of Foreign Investment]. Approved by the State Council on June 7 and promulgated by Order No. 5 of the State Planning Commission, the State Economic and Trade Commission, and the Ministry of Foreign Trade and Economic Cooperation on June 20. www.chinalawinfo.com.

——. 1998. *Jianshe Xiangmu Huanjing Baohu Guanli Tiaoli* [Administrative Regulations for the Environmental Management of Construction Projects]. Approved at the Tenth Executive Meeting of the State Council and promulgated by Order No. 253. November 18. www.chinalawinfo.com.

——. 1999a. *Taotai Luohou Shengchan Nengli, Gongyi He Chanpin De Mulu (Di Yi Pi)* [Catalogue of Backward Production Capacities, Processes, and Products to Be Eliminated (First Batch)]. Promulgated by Order No. 6 of the State Economic and Trade Commission. January 22. http://law.baidu.com.

——. 1999b. *Taotai Luohou Shengchan Nengli, Gongyi He Chanpin De Mulu (Di Er Pi)* [Catalogue of Backward Production Capacities, Processes, and Products to Be Eliminated (Second Batch)]. Promulgated by Order No. 16 of the State Economic and Trade Commission. December 30. http://law.baidu.com.

——. 2002. *Taotai Luohou Shengchan Nengli, Gongyi He Chanpin De Mulu (Di San Pi)* [Catalogue of Backward Production Capacities, Processes, and Products to Be Eliminated (Third Batch)]. Promulgated by the State Economic and Trade Commission. June 6. http://law.baidu.com.

State Council Environmental Protection Committee, State Planning Commission, State Economic and Trade Commission. 1986. *Jianshe Xiangmu Huanjing Baohu Guanli Banfa* [Administrative Measures for Basic Construction Projects' Environmental Protection]. March 26. http://law.baidu.com.

State Economic and Trade Commission. 2001. "Huaxue Gongye 'Shi Wu' Guihua" [Tenth Five-year Plan for the Chemical Industry]. October 18.

State Planning Commission, State Economic Commission, and State Council Environmental Protection Leadership Small Group. 1981. *Jiben Jianshe Xiangmu Huanjing Baohu Guanli Banfa* [Administrative Measures for Basic Construction Projects' Environmental Protection]. May 11. www.chinalawinfo.com.

Strohm, Laura A. 2002. "Pollution Havens and the Transfer of Environmental Risk." *Global Environmental Politics* 2 (2): 29–36.

Sun, Xiaohua. 2007. "Foreign Firms Face Penalties." *China Daily*, September 18.

———. 2008a. "Environment Chief Vows to Add Muscle." *China Daily*, March 25.

———. 2008b. "Listed Firms Ordered to Submit Green Data." *China Daily*, February 26.

———. 2008c. "Pollution Emission Permits Delayed." *China Daily*, July 4.

———. 2008d. "SEPA Urges Multinationals to Clean Up Their Acts." *China Daily*, January 10.

———. 2008e. "Winds of Change for China's Environment Protection." *China Daily*, August 13.

Supreme Court of the PRC. 1997–. *Zhonghua Renmin Gongheguo Zuigao Renmin Fayuan Gongbao* [Gazette of the Supreme People's Court of the People's Republic of China]. Beijing: Zhongguo Renmin Daxue Chubanshe [Renmin University Press].

Swire, Peter P. 1996. "The Race to Laxity and the Race to Undesirability: Explaining Failures in Competition Among Jurisdictions in Environmental Law." *Yale Law and Policy Review* 14 (2): 67–110.

Tan, Zhuzhou. 2002. "Yi Yao Zuo Da Duo Qiang, Er Yao Jiaqiang Guanli" [First We Must All Make Effort, Second We Should Strengthen Administration]. *Huagong Guanli* [Chemical Management] 11:14–15.

———. 2003. "Huagong Yuanqu Bimian Di Shuiping Chongfu Jianshe" [Chemical Industrial Parks Must Avoid Low-level Redundant Construction]. *Zhongguo Jingji Shibao* [China Economic Times], October 31.

Tang, Shui-yan, and Ching-ping Tang. 1997. "Democratization and Environmental Politics in Taiwan." *Asian Survey* 37 (3): 281–94.

Tatlow, Didi Kirsten, and Kristine Kwok. 2005. "30,000 Clash with Police in Village Pollution Riot." *South China Morning Post*, April 12.

Taylor, Ian. 2006. "China's Oil Diplomacy in Africa." *International Affairs* 82 (5): 937–59.

Thompson, Peter, and Laura A. Strohm. 1996. "Trade and Environmental Quality: A Review of the Evidence." *Journal of Environment & Development* 5 (4): 363–88.

Tian, Gang, and Wei Xiao. 2003. "Xibu Feiyao Gao Daliang 'Yuanqu' Ma" [Does China's West Not Want to Produce a Large Amount of Industrial Parks?]. *Zhongguo Huagong Bao* [China Chemical News], October 16.

Tobey, J. A. 1990. "The Effects of Domestic Environmental Policies on Patterns of World Trade: An Empirical Test." *Kyklos* 43 (2): 191–209.

Tomz, Micahel, Jason Wittenberg, and Gary King. 2001. Clarify: Software for Interpreting and Presenting Statistical Results. Version 2.0. Cambridge, MA: Harvard University. gking.harvard.edu.

Trofimov, Yaroslav. 2007. "In Africa, China's Expansion Is Beginning to Stir Resentment." *Wall Street Journal*, February 2.

Tseng, Wanda, and Harm Zebreg. 2003. "Foreign Direct Investment in China: Some Lessons for Other Countries." In *China: Competing in the Global Economy*, ed. Wanda Tseng and Markus Rodlauer. Washington, DC: International Monetary Fund.

Turner, Jennifer L. 2003. "Cultivating Environmental-NGO Business Partnerships." *China Business Review*, November/December, 22–25.

UNCTAD (United Nations Conference on Trade and Development). 2004. "South-South Investment Agreements Proliferating," press release. United Nations symbol UNCTAD/PRESS/PR/2004/036. www.unctad.org.

UNCTAD. 2006. Foreign Direct Investment Database. www.unctad.org.

UNCTAD Secretariat. 2002. "Managing the Environment Across Borders." United Nations symbol UNCTAD/ITE/IPC/MISC.12. Geneva: United Nations Conference on Trade and Development.

US-China Business Council. 2006. "China Statistics and Analysis." www.uschina.org.

U.S. Department of State. 2005. *2005 Investment Climate Statement—China*. 2005 statement no longer available online; more recent statements available at www.state.gov.

U.S. Embassy, Beijing. 2002. "Environmental Protection in an Average Chinese Province—Controlling Water Pollution in Anhui." Originally posted to www.usembassy-china.org; no longer available online.

Van Beers, C., and J. C. J. M. Van den Bergh. 1997. "An Empirical Multi-country Analysis of the Impact of Environmental Regulations on Trade Flows." *Kyklos* 50 (1): 29–46.

van Rooij, Benjamin. 2006a. "Implementation of Environmental Law: Regular Enforcement and Political Campaigns." *Development and Change* 37 (1): 57–74.

———. 2006b. *Regulating Land and Pollution in China. Lawmaking, Compliance, and Enforcement; Theory and Cases.* Leiden: Leiden University Press.

Vogel, David. 1995. *Trading Up: Consumer and Environmental Regulation in a Global Economy.* Cambridge, MA: Harvard University Press.

———. 2000. "Environmental Regulation and Economic Integration." *Journal of International Economic Law* 3 (2): 265–79.

Vogel, David, and Robert A. Kagan. 2004. *Dynamics of Regulatory Change: How Globalization Affects National Regulatory Policies.* Berkeley: University of California Press.

Volden, Craig. 2002. "The Politics of Competitive Federalism: A Race to the Bottom in Welfare Benefits." *American Journal of Political Science* 46 (2): 352–63.

Walter, Ingo. 1982. "Environmentally Induced Industrial Relocation to Developing Countries." In *Environment and Trade*, ed. Seymour J. Rubin and Thomas R. Graham. Totowa, NJ: Allanheld & Osmun.

Wang, Alex. 2002. "The Downside of Growth: Law, Policy, and China's Environmental Crisis." *Perspectives* 2 (2): 1–8. www.oycf.org.

————. 2007. "One Billion Enforcers." *Environmental Forum*, March/April.

Wang, Hengjin. 2003. "Guoji Maoyi Zhong de Huanjing Bijiao Youshi" [Environmental Comparative Advantage in International Trade]. *Nantong Gongxueyuan Xuebao (Shehui Kexue Ban)* [Journal of Nantong Institute of Technology (Social Science Edition)] 1.

Wang, Hua, Jun Bi, David Wheeler, Jinnan Wang, Cao Dong, Genfa Lu, and Yuan Wang. 2004. "Environmental Performance Rating and Disclosure: China's Green Watch Program." *Journal of Environmental Management* 71 (2): 123–33.

Wang, Hua, and Wenhua Di. 2002. "The Determinants of Government Environmental Performance: An Empirical Analysis of Chinese Townships." World Bank Policy Research Working Paper No. 2937. Available at Social Science Research Network: http://ssrn.com/abstract=636298.

Wang, Hua, and Yanhong Jin. 2002. "Industrial Ownership and Environmental Performance: Evidence from China." *Environmental and Resource Economics* 36:255–73.

Wang, Hua, Nlandu Mamingi, Benoit Laplante, and Susmita Dasgupta. 2002. "Incomplete Enforcement of Pollution Regulation: Bargaining Power of Chinese Factories." World Bank Policy Research Working Paper No. 2756. Available at Social Science Research Network: http://ssrn.com/abstract=634469.

Wang, Hua, and David Wheeler. 2000. "Endogenous Enforcement and Effectiveness of China's Pollution Levy System." World Bank Working Paper 2336. http://econ.worldbank.org.

————. 2005. "Financial Incentives and Endogenous Enforcement in China's Pollution Levy System." *Journal of Environmental Economics and Management* 49: 174–96.

Wang, Jiye. 2004. "Huagongyuan Bixu Jujue Gao Wuran Xiangmu" [Chemical Industrial Parks Must Refuse Pollution-intensive Projects]. *Zhongguo Huanjing Bao* [China Environment News], May 19.

Wang, Liqun (business/technical development manager, Akzo Nobel). 2005. "Safe Today, Safe Tomorrow." Presentation materials from China Responsible Care Conference, breakout session 6, Beijing, June 14.

Wang, Mingyuan. 2008. "China's Pollution Discharge Permit System Evolves Behind Its Economic Expansion." *Villanova Environmental Law Journal* 19:95.

Wang, Qing-Jie. 2005. "Transparency in the Grey Box of China's Environmental Governance: A Case Study of Print Media Coverage of an Environmental Controversy from the Pearl River Delta Region." *Journal of Environment & Development* 14 (2): 278–312.

Wang, Wei. 2002. "Lüse, Bei Wujie He Lanyong de Secai" [Green Is Being Misunderstood and Misused]. *Guangdong Keji Bao* [Guangdong Science and Technology News], January 12.

Wang, Xiaolin, and Weidong Li. 2001. "Zhengshi 'Lüse Xiaofei' Wuqu" [Squarely Face "Green Consumer" Misperceptions]. *Renmin Ribao Haiwai Ban* [People's Daily Overseas Edition], April 21.

Wang, Xiaoyang. 2004. "Huagong Yuanqu Fazhan Ying Zhongshi Tiaozheng" [Necessary Adjustments n the Development of Chemical Industrial Parks]. *Zhongguo Huagong Bao* [China Chemical News], December 9.

Wang, Yan, Richard K. Morgan, and Mat Cashmore. 2003. "Environmental Impact Assessment of Projects in the People's Republic of China: New Law, Old Problems." *Environmental Impact Assessment Review* 23:543–79.

Wang, Yihui. 2003. "Wang Cheng 'Huanbao' Jiang Bei Diaocha" [Products Absurdly Called "Environmental Protection" Will Be Investigated]. *Zhongguo Huanjing Bao* [China Environment News], April 26.

Wang, Zhongyu. 2005. "APP Hui Lin An de Bei Hou" [Background of the Case of APP Destruction of Forest]. *Kexue Shibao* [Technology Daily], April 12.

Warwick, Mara. 2003. "Environmental Information Collection and Enforcement at Small-scale Enterprises in Shanghai: The Role of Bureaucracy, Legislatures, and Citizens." PhD thesis, Stanford University.

Warwick, Mara, and Leonard Ortolano. 2007. "Benefits and Costs of Shanghai's Environmental Citizen Complaints System." *China Information* 21 (2): 237–68.

Wedeman, Andrew. 2004. "The Intensification of Corruption in China." *China Quarterly* 180: 895–921.

Weidner, Helmut, and Martin Jänicke. 2002. "Summary: Environmental Capacity Building in a Converging World." In *Capacity Building in National Environmental Policy: A Comparative Study of 17 Countries*, ed. Helmut Weidner and Martin Janicke. New York: Springer.

Wheeler, David. 2001. "Racing to the Bottom? Foreign Investment and Air Pollution in Developing Countries." *Journal of Environment & Development* 10 (3): 225–45.

———. 2002. "Beyond Pollution Havens." *Global Environmental Politics* 2 (2): 1–10.

Woods, Neal D. 2006. "Interstate Competition and Environmental Regulation: A Test of the Race-to-the-bottom Thesis." *Social Science Quarterly* 87 (1): 174–89.

World Bank. 1997. "Can the Environment Wait? Priorities for East Asia." Washington, DC: World Bank.

———. 2004. "China's Environmental Issues: The Bigger Picture." World Bank News & Broadcast. www.worldbank.org.

———. 2006. "Forest Law Enforcement and Governance East Asia Pacific: An Introduction to Forest Law Enforcement and Governance East Asia Pacific (FLEG-EAP)." www.worldbank.org.

———. 2007. "Cost of Pollution in China: Economic Estimates of Physical Damages." Washington, DC: World Bank.

World Economic Forum. 2000–2007. *The Global Competitiveness Report*. New York: Palgrave.

Wu, Guowen, and Yuehai Pan. 2002. "Lüse Chanpin Mantian Fei Renzheng Jigou Bian Di Shi You Li Gui Yu Mu Hun Zhu Zhi Zhong Huan Huo Zhen Jia Shi." *Zhongguo Jianshe Bao* [China Construction News], August 15.

Wu, Kun. 2004. "Xinxing Gongye Yu Huagong Chanye Jiqun Fazhan de Tantao" [An Inquiry into the Development of Consolidation of New Industries and the Chemical Sector]. *Huagong Jishu Jingji* [Chemical Techno-Economics] 22 (5): 5–8.

Xiang, Ying. 2004. "Yazhou Zuida Zhijiang Gongsi Juandi Shiwei" [The Complete Story of the Encirclement of Land by Asia's Largest Pulp and Paper Company]. *Nanfang Zhoumo* [Southern Weekend], December 16.

Xiao, Nanzi. 2005. "Jinguang Jituan Yu Nongming: Daodi Shei Shi Zhenzheng de Hui Lin Zhe?" [APP and Farmers: In the End Who Is the Real Destroyer of Forests?]. *Renmin Wang* [People's Daily Online], February 28.

Xiao, Yunxiang. 2002. "Ruoda de Huagong Yuanqu Jingran Wei Zuo Huanping" [Huge Chemical Park Unexpectedly Fails to Conduct Environmental Impact Assessment]. *Zhongguo Huanjing Bao* [China Environment News], October 26.

Xin, Wen. 2002. "Huagong Yuanqu: Ni Ruhe Biguo 'Leiqu'?" [Chemical Industrial Parks: How Can You Avoid the "Minefield"?]. *Zhongguo Huagong Bao* [China Chemical News] , October 26.

Xinhua. 2004. "China's Overseas Investment Exceeds US $30 Billion." *China Daily*, May 27.

———. 2006a. "Full Text: Report on the Work of the Government." *China Daily*, March 14.

———. 2006b. "Ethiopian PM: China 'Not Looting' Africa." October 16. http://english .peopledaily.com.cn.

———. 2007. "Maximum Fine for Chemical Plant Pollution." January 26. www.china .org.cn.

———. 2008a. "China's Environmental Regulator Urges Crackdown on Three Gorges Polluters." Probe International. www.probeinternational.org.

———. 2008b. "China Targets Company Executives in the Fight Against Pollution." February 28. www.news.xinhuanet.com.

Xinjing Bao [Beijing News]. 2006. "Huanbao Zongju: Gongyuan Bufa Wuran Qiye Keneng Bei Chezhi" [SEPA: Officials Who Fail to Punish Polluting Enterprises May Be Removed from Office]. February 8.

Xu, Shiping, and Xing Zhao. 2004. "Wuran Miji Chanye Zhuanyi Yuanyin de Jingjixue Fenxi Ji Fangfan Cuoshi Jianyi" [Economic Analysis of the Causes of Pollution Transfer and Opinions for Preventative Measures]. *Jingji Luntan* [Economic Forum] 21:34–36.

Xu, Weixing. 2002. "Jianshe Huagong Yuanqu, Fazhan Woguo Shihua Gongye" [Construct Chemical Industrial Parks, Develop China's Petrochemical Industry]. *Zhongguo Gongcheng Zixun* [China Engineering Consulting] 10:45–46.

Yan, Jing. 1995. "Law Controls Trade in Toxic Chemicals." *China Daily*, March 14.

Yang, Guobin. 2005. "Environmental NGOs and Institutional Dynamics in China." *China Quarterly* 181:46–66.

Yi, Ling, and Jiaquan Wang. 2005. "Guojia Linye Ju: Zhongguo Zhengfu Jiang Chechao Jinguang Jituan Yunnan Hui Lin Xingwei" [State Forestry Bureau: The Chinese Government Will Thoroughly Investigate APP Groups Destruction of Yunnan Forests]. Xinhua, March 31.

Ying, Leu Siew. 2004. "Delta's Polluters Find a Welcome in the Green Hills of Qingyuan." *South China Morning Post*, June 19.

Yoon, Suh-kyong. 2001. "On a Greener Track." *Far Eastern Economic Review*, October 25.

Young, Alasdair R. 2003. "Political Transfer and 'Trading Up'?: Transatlantic Trade in Genetically Modified Food and U.S. Politics." *World Politics* 55:457–84.

Young, Ian. 1996. "China's Ambitious Specialties Strategy." *Chemical Week*, October 16.

———. 2003. "Investors Still Hungry for China." *Chemical Week*, October 8.

———. 2005. "New Laws Should Speed Project Approvals." *Chemical Week*, August 24.

Zarsky, Lyuba. 1999. "Havens, Halos, and Spaghetti: Untangling the Evidence About Foreign Direct Investment and the Environment." Paper presented at the OECD Conference on FDI and the Environment, The Hague, January 28–29.

Zarsky, Lyuba, and Kelly Sims Gallagher. 2003. "Searching for the Holy Grail? Making FDI Work for Sustainable Development." Gland, Switzerland: World Wide Fund for Nature.

Ze, Yang. 2004. "Jingti Tuliao Shichang Shang de 'Lüse' Xianjing" [Look Out for "Green" Pitfalls in the Paint Market]. *Zhongguo Jianshe Bao* [China Construction News], November 30.

Zeng, Ka, and Josh Easton. 2007. "International Economic Integration and Environmental Protection: The Case of China." *International Studies Quarterly* 51 (4): 971–95.

Zhang, Liuhao. 2006. "Blacklist Marks Foreign Offenders." *Shanghai Daily*, October 27.

Zhang, Wenge, and Liu Liu. 2003. "Yinni Jinguang Jituan Ju Touzi Wenshan Baiwan Mu Su Sheng Fengchan Lin Jiang Qidong" [The Huge Investment of the Indonesia APP Group in Wenshan for a Million Mu of Fast-growth High Yield Forest Is About to Commence]. *Yunnan Ribao* [Yunnan Daily], October 20.

Zhao, Jimin. 2005. "Implementing International Environmental Treaties in Developing Countries: China's Compliance with the Montreal Protocol." *Global Environmental Politics* 5 (1): 58–81.

Zhao, Shanxiong. 2003. "Mian Xiang Weilai de Lüse Xuanze" [Facing Future Green Choices]. *Zhongguo Zhiliang Bao* [China Quality News], December 19.

Zhao, Yuhong. 2007. "Trade and Environment: Challenges After China's WTO Accession." *Columbia Journal of International Law* 32 (1): 41–97.

Zhejiang Fandian Ye Xiehui [Zhejiang Hotel Association]. 2005. "Guanyu Dizhi Caigou APP Zhi Chanpin de Tongzhi" [Notice Concerning the Boycott of APP Paper Products]. www.zjhotels.org.

Zhong, Yang. 2003. *Local Government and Politics in China: Challenges from Below*. Armonk, NY: M. E. Sharpe.

Zhongguo Huagong Bao [China Chemical News]. 2003. "Hua Zai Yuanzhong Yue Qu Xiu Gong Ziqiang- Huagong Chanye de Fazhan Chulu Yu Yuanqu de Gaishan" [The Prospects for the Development of the Chemical Industry and Improvement of Industrial Parks]. October 27.

Zhongguo Huagong Wang [China Chemical Industry Network]. 2004. "Huagong Yuanqu—Yi Ba Shuangdao Jian" [Chemical Industrial Parks—A Double Edged Sword]. September 16. http://park.chemnet.com (under Yuanqu Fangtan [Chemical Park Discussion]).

Zhongguo Xinwen Zhoukan [China Newsweek]. 2004. "Yunnan Senlin Gaowei" [Crisis in Yunnan's Forest]. July 12.

Zhu, Mingshan. 2005. *Pohuai Huanjing Ziyuan Baohu Zui* [Environmental Protection Crimes of Environmental and Resource Destruction]. Beijing: Zhongguo Fazhi Chubanshe [China Legal Press].

Zweig, David. 2002. *Internationalizing China: Domestic Interests and Global Linkages.* Ithaca, NY: Cornell University Press.

Index

Page numbers in italic refer to figures or tables.

tic, 56–57, 73–75, 90, 140; compliance with Chinese standards, 5–6, 110–14; effect of country of origin, 157, 159–63, 167–69, 228–29nn6–7; effect of government ownership, 171; effect on domestic competitors, 5–6; follow-up activities, 130–31; gap between corporate and local standards, 114–16, 146–47; as "guinea pigs," 89–90; influence on domestic firms, 163–66; joint ventures, 119, 157–60, 167–68; lobbying of government by, 136–45; as minority partners, 119; overview, 7–9, 56–58, 149–50; pragmatism of, 137, 142; private authority of, 110, 117–28, 133, 136, 143–44, 148; reputation as motivator, 114, 117, 127, 129, 133, 164; research methods for study of, 110–11, 114; Shell Oil and West-East Pipeline Project, 119–24; using single set of standards, 5. *See also* EHS (environment, health, and safety) practices; green supply chain; training

MOFERT (Ministry of Foreign Economic Relations and Trade), 62, 214n7

MOFTEC (Ministry of Foreign Trade and Economic Cooperation), 65, 137, 214n7

Montreal Protocol, 53

MSDS (Material Safety Data Sheet), 131, 225n52

Nanhai, 143

Nanjing, 96, 152–53

National Development and Reform Commission (NDRC), 29, 183

National Energy Administration, 29

National Environmental Protection Model City status, 199

national ministries rules (*bumen guizhang*), 23

National People's Congress (NPC), 28

natural gas, 119–24

Natural Resources Defense Council, 36

NDRC (National Development and Reform Commission), 29, 183

NEPA (National Environmental Protection Administration), 60, 62–63, 137. *See also* Ministry of Environmental Protection (MEP)

Nescafé, 11

Nestlé, 115

Neumayer, Eric, 21

NGOs/ENGOs (non-governmental organizations), 11, 41–43, 51, 203–5, 212nn10

Nigeria, 186

NIMBY (not-in-my-backyard) politics, 173

"Notice on Strengthening the Environmental Management in Foreign Investment Construction Projects" (1992), 62, 213n1

notices (*tongzhi*), 56

Nu River dams, 42, 51

Oates, Wallace E., 194

OECD (Organization for Economic Cooperation and Development), 159–60, 169

oil/oil refining, 10, 186

Old Summer Palace lake-lining project, 50

Olympics, green, 2

opinions (*yijian*), 56

ore-dressing, 36

Ortolano, Leonard, 32, 51–52

outdated/backwards technology, 27, 57, 62, 68, 85. *See also* "Catalogue of the Backward Production . . . to Be Eliminated"

ownership structure, 118, 167–68, 171, 207n5